RELUCTANT ENTREPRENEURS

RELUCTANT ENTREPRENEURS

The Extent, Achievements and Significance
of Worker Takeovers in Europe

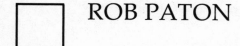

ROB PATON

With the assistance of Rainer Duhm, Silvia Gherardi,
Jean-Louis Laville, Carlos Otero-Hidalgo, Roger Spear and
Ann Westenholz

OPEN UNIVERSITY PRESS

MILTON KEYNES · PHILADELPHIA

Open University Press
12 Cofferidge Close
Stony Stratford
Milton Keynes MK11 1BY

and
1900 Frost Road, Suite 101
Bristol, PA 19007, USA

First Published 1989

Copyright © Rob Paton 1989

British Library Cataloguing in Publication Data

Paton, Rob
    Reluctant entrepreneurs: the extent, achievements
    and significance of worker-take-overs in Europe.
    1. Europe: workers' cooperatives
    I. Title
    334'.6'094

    ISBN 0-335-09233-0
    ISBN 0-335-09232-2 (paper)

Library of Congress Cataloging-in-Publication Data

Paton, Rob.
    Reluctant entrepreneurs : the extent, achievements, and
    significance of worker-take-overs in Europe / by Rob Paton ; with
    the assistance of Rainer Duhm . . . [et al.].
        p.   cm.
    Bibliography: p.
    Includes index.
    ISBN 0-335-09233-0 : £30.00. — ISBN 0-335-09232-2 (pbk.) : £12.50
        1. Employee ownership—Europe.   2. Corporate turnarounds—Europe—
    Management.   3. Corporate reorganizations—Europe—Management.
    4. Consolidation and merger of corporations—Europe—Management.
    5. Organizational change—Europe—Management. I. Title.
    HD5660.E9P38   1989
    338.6—dc20   89-34692
                                                                      CIP

Typeset by Inforum Typesetting, Portsmouth
Printed in Great Britain by the Alden Press, Oxford

To Rainer Schluter
and all his colleagues at CECOP

55

Contents

List of Boxes

Lists of Figures and Tables

Figures

Tables

Preface and Acknowledgements

This book has been written for both academic and professional readers. For academics (and students) it provides data, relevant contextual information, interpretation and analyses (that draw on a range of theoretical ideas), and linkages into the main areas of relevant literature. However, it does not pretend to offer a systematic exposition and critique of the different theoretical perspectives relevant to worker co-operatives and ownership, nor of the political debates surrounding them. Moreover, some of the more academic discussion is tucked away in notes. For professional readers – those with a more practical or policy interest in the field – the book is intended to provide a broad overview and a sustained analysis of some of the main issues, but in a way that is well-grounded in actual cases and which can orient and inform policy discussions. On the other hand, it is not intended as a 'how to do it' book. The difficulty has obviously been to meet the conflicting requirements of these two different audiences – without also irritating them too much in the process!

The backgrounds of the people involved – four academics with first-hand experience of worker takeovers (WTOs), two independent consultants who had supported WTOs, and one former civil servant who had helped develop policies for Local Employment Initiatives – help explain the scope and style of the book. It originated in work undertaken for the European Commission's Programme of Research and Action on the Development of the Labour Market – which has involved a number of studies into the problems and effectiveness of Local Employment Initiatives. This work enabled the seven of us most closely involved in the study to meet, and then to come together in a series of residential meetings. These meetings, as well as a number of bilateral visits, continued after the original policy study was completed.

This is definitely not one person's book – it makes extensive use of other people's contributions; nor is it an edited volume – it has aimed to be far more integrated, and consistent in style; but nor was it collectively authored – the barriers of time, language and distance ruled that out. Except for the first, second and last chapters, my colleagues provided drafts for me to work on, as follows:

Chapter 3 – Rainer Duhm
Chapter 4 – Silvia Gherardi and Carlos Otero-Hidalgo
Chapter 5 – Roger Spear
Chapter 6 – Ann Westenholz and Silvia Gherardi
Chapter 7 – Jean-Louis Laville and Roger Spear

However, this was not really a simple matter of co-authoring for two reasons. First, these drafts were themselves based on existing material to which we had all contributed (and likewise I drew on material by Ann Westenholz in Chapter 2). Second, I felt I had to take a fairly free hand in working up the drafts in order to demarcate the topics, to allocate cases between chapters, and to produce a consistent style (especially given the language problem). Inevitably, given also that I was preparing the first and last chapters, this must mean that my own interpretations and concerns have tended to dominate. Hence, I take responsibility for the form the book has finally taken, and I am grateful to my colleagues for allowing me this latitude – as well as for all the ideas, comments, support, good humour and companionship each has provided.

A number of other people have also made important contributions to the book. Isabel Mahiou and Danielle Demoustier assisted with the preparation of material on WTOs in France (the latter provided the information for the Manufrance and TCS cases), and Niels Mygind's advice on WTOs in Scandinavia was also hepful. Mark Holmstrom deserves a special thanks – not just for his assistance in the preparation of the Spanish case studies, but in his careful and challenging comments on the draft. As always, my colleagues in the Co-operatives Research Unit have been supportive and helpfully critical of successive drafts – as has John Skelton, my editor. June McGowan and then Jenny Cowan provided dependable and intelligent word-processing support which has been a real privilege.

I am grateful for the initial financial support from the European Commission (though it goes without saying that this book should in no way be taken as an expression of their views); for the subsequent support provided by the Open University; and for the willingness of the Angestelltenkammer, Bremen, to allow Rainer Duhm to work on the project. Finally, all of us involved are immensely grateful to numerous WTO activists, independent advisers, and officials in co-operative movement bodies and SAL federations, for providing information and for discussing the issues with us. Particular thanks go to Archadi Vilert of FCTAC who provided space for our meeting in Barcelona.

Rob Paton

1 | Introduction

This book is about people who became entrepreneurs, as one of them put it, 'not by choice but by necessity' – as a way of preserving their livelihoods and workplaces. It is about how, across Europe, many hundreds of companies, and many thousands of jobs, have been preserved by groups of workers who had the initiative and determination to take over failing and bankrupt enterprises, usually when no one else was prepared to. It is, more than anything, a book about change: how moribund organizations have been transformed and industrial capacity preserved and reconstructed; how new ways of working (and new roles for trade unionists) have developed; how established social and political ideas have been re-evaluated; how new networks and economic formations have emerged; and how men and women have surprised themselves by what they have become and have achieved.

The main purpose of the book is to describe and analyse the worker takeover phenomenon – to document what has been happening, where, why, and in what circumstances; to identify patterns of success and failure, and the conditions associated with them; to highlight barriers, pitfalls and dilemmas. A further purpose is to draw out the policy implications of the experience to date. Many of these arise from the comparisons made possible by an international study. The experience of worker takeovers (WTOs) in other countries quickly calls in question numerous features, for example, the commercial, legal, political, and trade-union practice, in our own country, that have hitherto appeared natural and inevitable. Finally, the book is also intended to highlight some questions raised by the phenomenon – for it offers rather more than simply some heart-warming tales of underdogs who, in varying degrees, succeed against the odds. The experience has now been sufficiently extensive to provide an interesting perspective on a range of other social and economic trends and issues – such as the changing role of trade unions and the scope for community-based economic development.

If such intentions seem surprising it is because the experience of WTOs in

Europe in the 1980s has generally been overlooked or dismissed. Indeed, according to conventional business ideas WTOs are a phenomenon that should not really occur at all – and any book on the subject could be expected to be nasty, brutish and short. Do we not know that where WTOs have been attempted, they fail? How could the workforce be expected to succeed where professional managers have had to admit defeat? Why raise the question of policy towards what are just 'lame ducks'? Such perspectives make any idea of support for WTOs – at the best – controversial.

Nor is a dismissal of the idea of WTOs confined to the business community. Many in the trade-union movement and on the political left have seen the attempt to create worker co-operatives or worker-owned firms out of failing businesses as doomed to failure, with the workforce having to accept an emasculated trade-union organization, pay cuts, intensified work, and financial losses, along the way.

The prevalence of such very negative views of WTOs means that in most countries there is a striking contrast between the actual achievements of WTOs and their publicly perceived weakness or failure. Before proceeding, therefore, it is important to explain how this mismatch has come about, and why, in general terms, the public image is no longer warranted – if it ever was.

Types of worker takeover and the reputation for failure

The well-known cases of WTOs in Europe – for example, the Scottish Daily News, KME and Meriden in the UK, Lip and Manuest in France, Clems in Italy – have several important features in common. To begin with, they generally concerned large plants whose closure would have led to hundreds of redundancies. The struggle by the trade unions to prevent closure was highly visible and political, and in the end fairly substantial amounts of public money were provided (even if, arguably, such funds often fell well short of what was required). The enterprises tended to be dominated by the trade unions whose leaders directed affairs through an attenuated management structure – an arrangement that often gave rise to struggles for control between those leaders and senior managers. Finally, with a few heroic exceptions (Manuest was one) the performance of these enterprises was disappointing: at best, slow decline; at worst, collapse. The case of Manufrance, summarized in Box 1.1, illustrates this pattern very clearly.

Box 1.1   The case of Manufrance

Manufrance, a large company created at the end of the nineteenth century and based in St Etienne in the Loire Department began to decline in the 1960s. As early as 1969 the managerial staff published a 'white paper' criticizing the low level of investment relative to the age of the machinery. Between 1977 (when it employed 4,000 workers) and 1978, several restructuring plans were attempted. These ended in a petition for bankruptcy being filed in 1979 and in the enterprise being bought out and transformed into the Nouvelle Société Manufrance (the New Manufrance Company) by an entrepreneur called Bernard Tapie in June 1979.

The refusal by the unions and the city council, which at that point was Communist controlled, to countenance what was considered a dismantling of the company (selling off shops with 350 staff, separating off the cycle-manufacture and mail-order divisions) led to a new petition for bankruptcy being filed a year later.

The enterprise was at that stage occupied by between six and eight hundred of the 1,800 workers. As the occupation was intended to last indefinitely if there was no solution, the idea of a co-operative was brought up by the communist union, the CGT. This scheme split the unions. The smaller union, the CFDT, which was reluctant to support such a course of action, was gradually left out of the proceedings. The rules governing the co-operative were lodged at the end of December 1980.

A campaign for support and financial contributions (mainly through the CGT, the Works Committees and the friendly societies under its control) brought in some 3,000 outside shareholders. The town of St Etienne showed its commitment to the co-operative by guaranteeing a loan of 16 million francs. The National Confederation of Co-operative Production Societies (CG SCOP), was hardly consulted at all and took no part in the launch. The survival of the co-operative, however, became a national and not just a local issue, the CGT wishing to make it an example, not only of the strength of the workers' struggle, but also of their ability to manage in the general interest. In March 1981, when the new, Mitterand, government came to power, the 500 worker co-operators set all the machines running as a symbolic gesture. The local legislative elections also marked a victory for the Socialist/Communist Left and the co-operative expected that financial help would be forthcoming from the new majority.

An agreement was signed with Bernard Tapie and, in May 1981, Manufrance was up and running, after a 225-day occupation. Its hope was, in the long term, to create 1,000 jobs. 170 million francs were needed to make the required new investment and provide working capital. The co-operators provided 20 million francs (9 million of which came from state allowances for job-creation). In April 1982, a finance and development plan was adopted: the state was to provide 80 million francs, half in subsidies, half in loans over a fifteen-year period; a group of banks and other organizations undertook long- and medium-term loans amounting to 70 million francs.

The good commercial prospects for 1983 (particularly the opening up of markets in Algeria) led the co-operative to increase the workforce to 800. When these did not materialize, the number was reduced again to 400 in 1984. Moreover, the age of the plant (and especially its location in the centre of St Etienne) necessitated rapid modernization. The local authority had to buy and renovate a factory on an industrial estate (20,000 sq. m; robots, computer-controlled machines; an investment of some 47 million francs). But because of long delays in financing and building, the new production unit only became operational at the point when the co-operative was forced to declare itself insolvent. At that point it had huge over-capacity: the new plant had been built to meet an annual production forecast of 70,000 guns; by then, only 25,000 had been ordered and 14,000 produced.

The short life of the co-operative was beset with numerous difficulties: it had productivity problems (the number of non-productive workers continued to grow until, in 1985, it was 240 out of 407); there were also conflicts between the different political parties (Socialists and Communists) and between the trade unions; the involvement of the workers also fell off and they refused, for example, to put their 'thirteenth' month's wages back into the business in 1982.

In spite of a total of 257 million francs of state aid, profitability problems simply continued to grow: 170 million francs were lost in three years, including 65 million in long-term debts

- in 1982, the trading deficit rose to 34 million francs;
- in 1983, it rose to 76 million francs (with a turnover of 60 million and a wage bill of 80 million);
- in 1984, the loss was 62 million (turnover: 40 million; wages: 60 million).

Support for the co-operative crumbled away: employees dismissed in 1983 wanted back the money they had invested; the new (Conservative) local council, elected in 1983, abandoned the co-operative; early in 1984, the Ministry of Social Security forced the company into liquidation over 4 million francs' worth of unpaid contributions; at the request of the owners of the factory buildings, the Commercial Court ordered Manufrance to pay 2.8 million francs in rent arrears.

Finally, early in 1985, the Government (through the Secretary of State for Social Economy, J. Gatel, and the Prime Minister, Laurent Fabius) refused any further financial involvement. On 10 April 1985, the co-operative was in liquidation and looking for someone to take it over.

Such highly *defensive* WTOs are not, in fact, at all common. By contrast, WTOs in the United States, though still arising in response to the threat of large plant closures, have generally been much less ideological. The right of capital to close down plants has not really been the focus of protest and opposition, so the workforce (and the local community) have directed their efforts towards the purchase of the operation and its reconstruction as a financially viable and self-contained unit (Stern and Hammer 1978). The trade union's role in this has been more limited, representing the workforce in efforts to arrange a multilateral financial package between the interested parties, and thereafter adopting a fairly traditional role within the enterprise. To be sure, moves towards more participative management within these enterprises are not unusual, but there has rarely been any question of workers' control or self-management. Indeed, it is quite common for the financial arrangements to circumscribe severely the control that employee shareholders can exercise over the appointment of the board and similar matters (Russell 1985). The performance of these worker-owned firms has varied – but generally it has been much better than those typified by Manufrance. This second pattern – of essentially *financial* WTOs – has also occurred in Europe, as the case of ELSA in Box 1.2 illustrates, though it has not been nearly so common there.

Box 1.2   The case of ELSA

ELSA is a large glass-making company which was taken over by its workforce in 1980. As in other traditional glass-making factories working conditions are intensely hot and very noisy. The factory was built in the early twentieth century in the town of Cornella in the Baix Llobregat district of Catalonia which became a suburb of Barcelona in the 1960s. In the 1960s and early 1970s the factory was grossly overmanned. In part this was as a result of Spanish labour protection legislation, but it also reflected the paternalistic management approach of the family owners. In the 1970s, shortly before Franco's death, ELSA was the arena for a nationally important strike (trade unions were still illegal at this time but clandestine unions were being organized, and the 'vertical syndicates' had been effectively infiltrated by communist and socialist activists). The strike lasted 54 days and there were many demonstrations and arrests and some other factories in the locality also became involved. After the strike ELSA gradually shed labour, reducing from, at one time, over a 1,000 workers to about 600 at the end of the 1970s. At this time competition was very fierce, particularly from a factory of Duran, the french glass-makers, which had been established in Spain to overcome the tariff barrier. By the end of the decade the company was in an acute commercial crisis.

It is unclear quite where the idea for a WTO came from but the leaders of the transition were mainly works council leaders with communist backgrounds who had played a part in the strike 4 or 5 years before. Formally, a board was created to manage the transition: 5 of its 11 members were appointed by the former owners, and 5 by the works council. The details of the transition are extremely complicated but, in essence, the firm was sold with its debts for 1 peseta. (Such an arrangement is not uncommon.) Trading was continued and the enterprise restructured through a substantial cash injection provided by the National Labour Protection Fund of the Ministry of Labour. Formally, this was provided as loans to the workforce to enable them to buy shares. This cash was provided in 2 stages over 3 years, and it was conditional on salary rises being kept below the cost of living. In addition, the Ministry agreed that the firm could allow its Social Security payments to fall into arrears (again, this is a common, if informal, arrangement).

The new firm employed just under 500 people, 100 having left with early retirement. This was not difficult to arrange since more than half of the workforce at the time of conversion were more than 50 years old. Some of the workers were reluctant to take on the loans and didn't buy shares in the new enterprise. As the chairman of the works council put it 'Those who didn't want to take shares weren't forced to, but later on many of them did.'

Some of the managers stayed on after the conversion to a worker-owned firm. The new general manager (or director general) is answerable to the board (the 'consell d'administració') which is elected by and represents the worker shareholders. The other representative body is the works council (the comité de empresa) which all companies are required by law to create. Although the board is mainly made up of people with a strong union past, some managers have also been elected to it and its membership is kept distinct from the works council. Hence, there is a deliberate effort to keep separate trade-union representation and the management of the company. As one militant put it regretfully: 'A small minority value self-management and freedom – most workers want to sell their labour for the best price'. Within this structure the union does have a fair amount of influence. For example, a new simplified pay structure in which there are only eleven different levels has recently been agreed. The management had doubts about this scheme but came round to accepting it after strong representation through the works council. Although the unions are eager to negotiate with management within this structure they do see ELSA as 'their' firm, and accept their situation is very different from that of other companies.

The restructuring of the business did not of itself make it more competitive. With entry into the EEC it became apparent that ELSA had no future if it was simply to continue struggling to produce cheap glasses in competition with foreign imports but using outmoded equipment. Hence the idea emerged that they should invest in producing a new, more expensive type of glass called Cristal. Market research indicated a rapid rise in sales in a number of countries.

Eventually it was decided to make this investment, which required very substantial sums of money, and the equipment was purchased in 1986. However, there were serious problems in producing the Cristal glass to a sufficiently high quality. For a time the new equipment had to be closed down; ELSA felt it could not risk jeopardizing its prospects in the new market by producing low quality products. As well as overcoming the technical and quality problems, success will depend on marketing the new product effectively.

  As of 1987 the firm had a workforce of 350, with up to a further 100 temporary workers depending on requirements. Overall, the position is that the company has been able to survive as a result of the restructuring but whether it has a future beyond a gradual run down and a marginal status depends on its substantial and risky investment paying off.

These two types of WTOs have been extensively described and discussed in books and articles.[1] This means that not only have such 'large plant' WTOs attracted extensive media attention, they have also dominated the more serious writing on the subject. The WTOs that are the main focus of this book are quite different. They are smaller; the workers themselves, rather than their trade-union leaders, have played the central role in setting them up; they have commonly experimented with more thorough-going forms of organizational democracy; they have been more successful and they have attracted far less attention. The contrasts between these three types of WTO are summarized in Table 1.1.

  Of course, this typology, like most of its ilk, is no more than a useful half-truth. Reality is never so tidy. Many WTOs do not correspond to any of these types and have instead a mixture of characteristics; others only approximate the pattern. Nevertheless, the typology does signal that WTOs are not all the same – they may differ considerably over a range of characteristics. Secondly, it provides a convenient way of indicating in general terms what is, and is not, the focus of this book. Finally, the typology also explains why it is that the reputation of WTOs is so out of line with their actual achievements: the type of WTO that attracts the most attention (because of the size of the enterprise, the economic impact of its closure and the political controversy it raises) is also the type that, on the evidence, seems least likely to succeed. Some of the reasons for the much better performance of participative WTOs compared to defensive WTOs will become apparent in the course of the book.

  In fact, the defensive WTOs have not just combined high visibility and low performance; in the countries where they have occurred, they have also tended to precede the participative WTOs in time, for each is expressive of a

Table 1.1   Types of worker takeover

	Defensive WTOs	Financial WTOs	Participative WTOs
Size	Large	Large	Small or medium-sized
Role of the workforce	Campaigning	Source of capital; shareholders	Planning, lobbying, source of finance, management
Role of the trade union	Guardian and controllers of the enterprise	Representing the workforce and brokers in the negotiations	Advisory assistance
Management structure	Attenuated, union dominated	Conventional, participative on occasions	Participative of self-managing
Outcome	Collapse or decline with success unusual	Varied; employee ownership often temporary	Varied, but overall quite good; comparable with other small firms
Visibility	National	Regional	Local

different social climate.[2] To some extent, therefore, the popular (and academic) image of WTOs was already established before the more recent and more successful WTOs began occurring in any numbers, and this has also contributed to the current mismatch between reputation and performance.

Before leaving this typology one important issue must be considered. So far it has been implied, in line with the popular perception, that the defensive WTOs were generally failures. In some cases, and Manufrance is surely one, such a judgement would be quite hard to dispute. But often this charge has been simplistic and contentious. The question turns, of course, on the criteria for success. One argument is that since the rationale for a WTO is the preservation of jobs in an area of high unemployment, many of these enterprises have been successful for quite long periods of time. Another is that, even when the enterprises have failed, many of those involved have seen the effort as immensely worthwhile – for a variety of reasons that generally concern the impact it has had on people's lives and the amount that they have learned. Such reactions are illustrated in Box 1.3 and are not confined to those who have been involved in defensive WTOs.

Box 1.3   The impact on individuals[3]

Nancy McGrath, leader of the Fakenham Women's co-operative that took over a branch factory and made clothes and leather goods from 1973 to 1978:

> The challenge of it, I think, was the main benefit, realizing that, yes, I wasn't wrong; I wasn't wrong about these people; that is what they want to do and we can do it together . . . . They were gaining in experience, belief in themselves, and that they were out for better things . . . . I noticed it in the way that a lot of them got more confident and people would say, 'Go on home, Nancy. You have done enough.' . . . I think I got an awful lot of happiness out of it, an awful lot of help myself, from people . . . . We miss it. We miss going down there in the morning and you didn't just come in and check on a machine 'one minute past eight,' you just walked in and hung your hat up and coat and whatever, and you did it because you wanted to do it and it was somewhere nice to do it . . . . I gained a lot of experience. To itemize a little thing, I can take books to balance point now, which is something I could never do before and I found, strangely enough – and I hated maths at school – but I found myself getting to like the whole thing more and more and more. I found, to sit down at a page with a debt and credit thing on it and even a day book to itemize the sales, and then try to balance it at the end of the month to see whether you have made a loss or a gain, it started to get a little bit fascinating. We did actually make a profit on one year and we allowed ourselves five pounds each in our wage packets as a Christmas bonus. But I gained a lot of practical experience . . . I think I am much more aware of people and the stresses they are involved in . . . I feel I drew so much from that, from that situation that it has made me a better person. It has made me more tolerant; it has made me more aware of people's problems. It has also made me aware that there is a better way of doing things if we can just find it.

John Burns was an active member of the Meriden Motorcycle Co-operative until shortly before its final closure. As a young skilled worker he could quite easily have found better paid jobs in other local factories. He finally left the co-operative when he believed it was bound to close:

> We started off with bingo and pop groups and discos and god knows what inside the factory. That was brill(iant). That was magic. It was ours now, you see. That was great . . . . The things we done there to keep that place going is unbelievable. You read about Leylands going out on strike for this, that and the other, and here's us working in no heat, no hot water – no water to make a cup of tea – stuff like that. Anywhere else they'd say, 'Christ! That's it, lads. Coats on and down the road!' That's when we used to say, 'Hey, you lot, you've got the electric fires on!' and all this.

It was good. I loved it, really.

. . . I took (my present) job really because I thought [Meriden's] closing; and then I thought, 'perhaps it might not, so I'll stick around.' [My wife] said, 'Oh no, we couldn't afford it.' Anyway we had this row and I was in the pub and I said 'all right I will have the job.'

. . . The first day when I came home and she said 'What's it like?' I nearly slung everything at her, you know what I mean. It was terrible. I thought I'd sold me soul. I really did.

Jean Webster was a designer with Exclusive Creations Limited which took over a factory in Brynmawr, Wales, and which traded for six months at which point it went into liquidation, but all debts and loans were repaid in full.

(To begin with) things went well, and there was a wonderful feeling of camaraderie in the factory. I was only brought in on an intermittent basis, being a designer. I have to create a range of bedspreads for the new company, and naturally I derived great joy from doing this. Our wide width boy designed an ingenious bedspread that actually had tufting on both sides of the spread. He was a wizard of a mechanic, and was never given his maximum scope with the old firm. The Co-operative members were wonderfully proud of this one range, which was their very own. I value those months with Exclusive Creations.

We had made a lovely profit from September to November, but from then on it was all downhill . . . . To try and yet to fail leaves one a lot nearer to success than if one had never even tried. Gone is the mouse whose stuffing was taken out of him by redundancy. I do not have a sense of failure, when I think about Exclusive Creations.

The obvious counter is to say that, although these arguments show that WTOs were not entirely without positive features, this hardly justifies the loss of substantial amounts of public money. Supporting such ventures is hardly a sound industrial policy. But this is precisely the point that Keith Bradley has challenged in a series of carefully argued publications.[4] He has argued that there is a strong case for supporting the larger WTOs that we have referred to as Defensive and Financial WTOs.

The pay-offs to government, mandated to reconcile a democratic political system with a substantial degree of free enterprise, are, succinctly:

(a) Political: the method deflects potentially embarrassing pressure groups at times of relative government vulnerability.
(b) Economic: the implicit incentive structure is reasonably appropriate to a market economy. This lowers the budgetary cost of

subsidization and minimizes long-term resource misallocation relative to other policies which might be induced by political pressures.

Therefore, both in the short and in the long term, the method of intervention possesses certain advantages. The most immediate advantage is its cushioning potential in employing labour, giving local labour markets time to 'unclog'. This holds even if the new employee-owned firm is unsuccessful and collapses.

(Bradley 1986: 64–5)

The last sentence is crucial. The point is that in the case of 'large plant' closures an important objective for governments is simply to manage the decline of the plant so as to minimize the adverse effects on the local economy and labour market. Bradley has presented detailed economic analyses to justify this view and to specify the conditions under which such support will be justified. This is not an argument in favour of intervention as such. It simply demonstrates that where some intervention is inevitable for social and political reasons, then support for a co-operative or other worker-owned enterprises will normally be the preferred instrument because it is 'self-limiting' and encourages (rather than discourages) efforts towards restructuring and greater efficiency.

Whether or not one accepts the political feasibility of Bradley's suggestions,[5] his arguments are very useful in demonstrating that the question of appropriate criteria for evaluating the success and failure of WTOs is not straightforward. Of course continuing commercial viability is desirable (not least to trade unionists concerned about 'self-exploitation') but the fact that a particular WTO enterprise does not match the popular image of a dynamic and profitable firm is not in itself a sign of failure. Clarity over the purposes of those directly and indirectly involved, and over the options realistically available to them, is essential, and a number of criteria will usually be required. These issues are considered in more detail in due course.

One other important point arises from this discussion: defensive and financial WTOs raise issues of industrial policy at a national level – indeed, Bradley's arguments explicitly take this as the policy context. This is much less relevant to participative WTOs whose significance is generally local. Hence, not only has the phenomenon of WTOs changed, so have the arenas in which support for them is being debated. The policy context now includes the areas of local employment initiatives and local economic strategy that have developed so rapidly in recent years. These developments provide an essential part of the background, not least because they help to explain why, and how, many of the recent WTO have taken place.

The local context of WTOs

The prolonged high levels of unemployment that began in the 1970s have induced a range of new initiatives by public authorities. Some of these have been introduced nationally – such as the changes in social security or unemployment benefit regulations aimed at encouraging and supporting enterprise creation efforts by the unemployed (e.g. the Enterprise Allowance Scheme in the UK; the provision for the capitalization of unemployment benefit in France). Indeed, the whole European Community, through the Council of Ministers, has now endorsed the shift away from 'paying people to do nothing' towards supporting them in enterprise creation.

At the same time local and regional governments have begun to intervene in the economy in order to support local industries and preserve employment. For example, the French government has removed restrictions on local government to enable this. And in the UK, economic development departments have been the only growth area in local government during a period when spending has been cut or restrained. Of course, the extent of these efforts have varied enormously depending on the seriousness of the economic crisis in the area and the range of powers available to the public authorities. But where the decline of traditional industries has produced something close to economic collapse, or where high concentrations of unemployment have emerged among disadvantaged groups, the public authorities, of whatever political persuasion, have taken steps to attract, stimulate and assist new enterprises.

Often these efforts have been undertaken in collaboration with the private sector, which has also felt obliged, by the scale of the economic and social problems that have appeared, to develop new responses. Thus, for example, when a large national or multinational firm closes a plant which is a major employer in the locality, a combined effort may be made to moderate the impact and find, attract or create new employment opportunities. Characteristically, this will involve the creation of funds to provide start-up grants and loans, retraining schemes, the provision of suitable small industrial premises and extensive business counselling. Often, too, these schemes will involve local community groups – in fact, such groups may well have initiated the schemes and then drawn in public and private support.

The variety of forms and approaches that have developed is considerable – some schemes are aimed at young people, some at starting co-operatives, some at promoting ethnic businesses, some are concerned with wider environmental improvement and community development, some have a strong labour orientation, and so on. As usual, countries and regions vary in the nature and extent of these developments – but it is undoubtedly a European-wide phenomenon and the scale of the activity now taking place is very considerable[6] especially in countries like Spain which have a tradition of municipal economic activity.

The significance of this for WTOs has been and remains considerable: it has meant that through the 1980s a diffuse infrastructure of agencies, special funds, policy instruments and advisory networks has been developing. These different elements have generally not been introduced to support WTOs (though as we shall see there are important exceptions); nevertheless, the infrastructure has been available, more or less, to groups of workers attempting to take over an enterprise threatened with closure. As later chapters will demonstrate, this has raised a wide range of problems and controversies. That said, the development of effective support networks has played an important part in the experience of WTOs to date – and it is one of the keys to further achievements in the future.

The wider relevance of WTOs

As was suggested earlier, the experience of WTOs is now sufficiently extensive to provide a useful contribution to the debates associated with a range of economic and political trends. A brief outline of these will therefore provide the wider context for the experience of WTOs detailed in subsequent chapters.

The rapid spread of employee ownership, and schemes to facilitate employee ownership, is one very relevant development. Within Europe, this trend has diverse origins. One factor has undoubtedly been the experience and example provided by the United States.[7] The crucial event there was the appointment of Russel Long as Chairman of the Senate Finance Committee, in 1972. A firm believer in employee share ownership, he was able to use his position to include provisions (mainly tax incentives) to stimulate Employee Stock Ownership Plans (ESOPs) in more than a dozen separate pieces of legislation over the following years. ESOPs have offered corporations cheap finance and flexibility regarding contributions to employee pension funds, and they have been widely adopted. Since the shares are generally held on the employees' behalf for many years, the question of employee influence seldom arises to any great extent. However, Employee Stock Purchase Plans – under which employees own the shares directly – have also been spreading rapidly. Taken together, these forms of employee share ownership have become very extensive indeed. It is estimated that by 1990, 30 per cent of the US workforce will be in companies that are more than

15 per cent owned by the workforce. By contrast, about 18 per cent of the US workforce are members of trade unions, and the proportion is falling.

This example has undoubtedly influenced both the British government (vide, the tax advantages for employee share ownership, and for profit-related pay schemes) and the French government (which introduced tax incentives for employee ownership in 1984). But in other countries the question reached the political agenda by quite different routes. For example, labour-owned companies were being created in Spain from the mid-1970s as a pragmatic response to the industrial and economic upheavals following the transition to democracy. And in Scandinavia employee ownership in the form of 'wage-earners funds' has been at the heart of controversies surrounding 'economic democracy'. The proposals for such funds have been based (essentially) on the view that the labour movement would be better able to pursue their objectives by sharing and exercising ownership rights – rather than by imposing further restrictions on those rights (as in the pursuit of industrial democracy).

The increasing interest in employee ownership has coincided with a resurgence of worker co-operative movements in Europe that is far broader than the well-known achievements of the Mondragon group.[8] This development has prompted a debate, variously conducted in terms of the 'social economy' (France and Spain), the 'third sector' (Italy) and the 'new social movements' (West Germany) – about the role of co-operation and decentralized forms of social ownership in a modern economy.

Another major development has been the gradual recognition by beleaguered labour and trade-union movements of the need to develop new strategies. Perhaps the shock to established strategies and assumptions has been greatest in the UK which has experienced not just high unemployment, but severe regional decline, a shift of employment away from large-scale manufacturing and extractive industries towards small and medium-sized units in service sectors, and a right-wing government committed to privatization and an 'enterprise culture', as well.

In this context it has become steadily less credible just to wait for 'normal service' to be resumed by the return of a Labour government. Albeit slowly and tentatively, new approaches have been tried and debated. For example the trade-union movement's banking initiative, Unity Trust, has begun promoting employee shareholding trusts; there has been a greater willingness to become involved in local employment initiatives and to support worker co-operatives – or, as in the case of the Wales TUC (1981), even to promote them; and quite fundamental policy questions (such as whether social ownership must necessarily mean public ownership) have been opened up. In different ways such initiatives and debates have been taking place in the labour and trade-union movements throughout Europe. These different trends are all interrelated – and so are the questions associated with them: What difference does employee ownership really make? What is the position of managers in such firms? Is employee ownership a form of worker capitalism or a new form of social ownership? – and what would be the difference? Are worker-owned firms likely to be viable in the long run? Are they capable of commercial innovation? Are they capable of organizational innovation (or are they doomed to degenerate)? Are trade unions only concerned with collective bargaining? Or do they have a role in promoting community recovery, or in promoting self-management?

These are all questions for which the recent WTO has particular relevance. For example, the debate about employee ownership covers a wide range of different forms depending on whether ownership is individual or collective, partial or complete – as the matrix of possibilities in Figure 1.1 illustrates.

The forms adopted by WTOs cover every point on the matrix – and they have occurred under a variety of conditions. Hence although WTOs cannot provide answers to all these questions they do have a relevance that extends far beyond their value as a tactic for preserving jobs.

The scope and structure of the book

Attempts at WTOs, and support for them, are one of a number of responses – including 'management buy-outs', 'community businesses' and other local economic initiatives – to company and plant closures under conditions

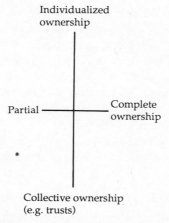

Figure 1.1   Forms of employee ownership

of rising unemployment and economic restructuring. There is no clear demarcation between some of these developments and some WTOs. For example, management buy-outs (that is, the purchase of an economic unit from its owners by a group of its managers) sometimes involve substantial and widespread employee shareholdings; and community businesses sometimes utilize the premises, and some of the equipment and employees, of failed enterprises. For the purpose of this study a WTO is defined as a case in which a business is continued, or created, on the basis of the assets of an endangered or bankrupt enterprise, by the workforce, or a part of it, within either a co-operative framework, or one satisfying the following conditions:

(i)   a substantial proportion of the voting shares are held by members of the workforce;
(ii) a substantial proportion of the members of the workforce own voting shares (or are members of a corporate body owning the shares);
(iii) the voting shares are fairly evenly distributed among those who own them, or in some other way it is ensured that ultimate control resides with the workforce.

Although many WTOs utilize co-operative legal frameworks to form workers' co-operatives, these conditions can be, and often are, satisfied by a wide range of structures using conventional company law. However, this definition does *not* include cases where an enterprise is purchased by a national trade union body and controlled by that body (as in Denmark).

Using this definition, WTOs may occur at any of three points in the decline of an enterprise or plant:

(i)   *Conversions* refer to WTO that are arranged before the commercial crisis becomes acute and before the unit ceases trading or goes into receivership. Such cases may occur where a company, or part of it, is still profitable, if marginally so, but where its underlying competitive position is weak. Often the WTO is a response to severe succession problems arising from the death or retirement of an owner-manager.
(ii) *Rescues* refer to WTOs that are arranged when the enterprise is in crisis, often under the control of the receiver, but generally with little or no loss of trading continuity.
(iii) *Phoenixes* refer to WTOs based on some of the residual assets of a liquidated enterprise after trading has ceased, sometimes several months later.

Although reference is also made to other countries where possible, the study is based on an analysis of the experience of WTOs in six countries: Denmark, France, Italy, Spain, the United Kingdom and West Germany.[9]

These countries include those with very extensive experience as well as some with very limited experience. Portugal, where some 1,500 WTOs took place in the 1970s, might appear to be an obvious omission. However, the circumstances surrounding these – in the period immediately after the overthrow of the dictatorship – mean they were quite different from those that have occurred since then elsewhere in Europe. (Only about 10 per cent of these 1,500 are thought to have survived and there have been very few WTOs in Portugal since then.)

Chapter 2 describes the scale of the WTO phenomenon through short overviews of the six countries. These also outline some key features of the social, economic, and institutional environment in each case. This leads to an analysis of the economic and cultural circumstances in which WTOs arise.

Chapter 3 analyses the WTO process starting from the moment closure is threatened. The organizational dynamics of what is often an intense collective learning experience are discussed in the context of devising a credible business strategy, of relations with the former owners, and of the need to obtain information and advice. The advantages and disadvantages of the 'rescue' and 'phoenix' routes to a WTO are compared, and the benefits and tensions associated with widespread workforce involvement in the takeover are analysed.

Chapter 4 discusses the financial problems facing WTOs and the attitudes of the commercial banks towards them. The different sorts of measures that have been used by local and national governments to finance WTOs are reviewed, with particular attention given to the comparatively extensive support provided in Italy and Spain.

Chapter 5 discusses the issues surrounding the choice of legal form for a WTO. It sets out the relevant underlying principles and the main forms that may be adopted. It then describes which forms are, in fact, more commonly used by WTOs in the different countries, and explains the factors which tend to restrict or influence a workforce's choice on this issue.

Chapter 6 reviews the performance of the enterprises created through WTOs and identifies a number of characteristic organizational and commercial dynamics. It discusses the ways in which WTOs reduce costs, strengthen their product-market position and develop new patterns of management and self-management. It highlights the importance of some continuing external advice and support in enabling WTO enterprises to go beyond a precarious survival and to consolidate as successful businesses.

Chapter 7 then considers the issues from the point of view of the support agencies and networks. It reviews the role of co-operative associations, trade unions and government bodies, and discusses a range of problems regarding support strategies and methods. A number of dilemmas inherent in efforts to support WTO are identified.

Finally, Chapter 8 considers the prospects for WTOs in terms of three different scenarios and in relation to the different reasons they may be supported. A number of policy implications are set out and some of the issues concerning the possibility of promoting 'economic pluralism' through support for WTOs are considered.

2 | Attempts at Worker Takeovers: Where, When and Why

Attempts by workers to take over and revive companies in crisis have been a recurring response to the threat of closure, particularly in times of economic recession. In Italy, WTOs have occurred periodically throughout this century and a majority of the worker co-operatives in Italy today originated in this way. In the United Kingdom, there are substantial and successful co-operatives that were formed through WTOs over 100 years ago, during the recession of the 1870s. In France, Acome, formed in 1932, through a WTO, is still referred to as one of the cornerstones of the worker co-operative movement. Likewise, the Mataró Glassworks, the oldest surviving producer co-operative in Spain, was the result of a WTO in 1920. So the current wave, beginning in the 1970s and manifest in varying degrees throughout Europe, conforms to a clear pattern.

Nevertheless, while rising unemployment and economic restructuring provide the general context, the incidence of WTO still varies enormously both within and between countries. So other factors must be considered in order to understand the phenomenon. The aim of this chapter is to indicate the variety of circumstances in which WTO have been attempted and to identify the underlying economic, institutional and cultural factors that seem to favour this response to the threat of enterprise closure rather than others. It offers a broad overview of the phenomenon starting with accounts of the incidence of WTOs and the circumstances surrounding them in the countries that are the main focus of the study.

Italy

For more than ten years worker takeovers of failing and bankrupt enterprises have been a comparatively common occurrence in Italy and many worker co-operatives have been formed in these circumstances. They have both received assistance from other co-operative organizations, and, in due course, contributed considerably to the size and strength of the co-operative movement.

Unfortunately, Italian statistics on co-operatives are unsatisfactory and inconsistent (Gherardi 1987; Earle 1986) and in any case there is no way of identifying those worker co-operatives that resulted from a WTO (nor has there ever been a survey of the phenomenon). That said what is known about the rapid increase in the number of worker co-operatives and in the size of this sector makes it unlikely that fewer than 1,000 WTOs occurred between the mid-1970s and the mid-1980s[1] with the majority occurring in the north of the country. In fact, so many worker co-operatives have been formed in this way that the phenomenon of a WTO is a 'normal' event and generally attracts no particular public interest. Despite the absence of statistics it is also clear that WTO co-operatives are concentrated in the more labour-intensive sectors. WTO have occurred frequently in the textiles, garments, graphic, newspaper, light mechanical, wood and transport sectors, and to some extent also in the service sector. They commonly employ between 30 and 100 people but some have been much larger.

The context in which this has happened is distinctive in a number of ways. First, the Italian economy is characterized by a substantial and very dynamic small-firm sector and by the common occurrence of collaborative commercial arrangements between small firms. Where both these features are most marked, as in Emilia-Romagna, the result is a rather distinctive economic formation (Brusco 1982) which appears to achieve many of the economies of scale while avoiding the diseconomies. The organization of the Italian Co-operative movement should be considered against this background of productive decentralization and inter-organizational collaboration.

Second, the strong and dynamic Italian Co-operative Movement, covering all the main forms of co-operation (consumer, housing, agriculture, etc.), has generally been able and willing to assist WTOs. Of course in particular instances this has proved difficult and expensive, and sometimes WTOs have been discouraged. Nevertheless, the movement's attitude has generally been positive and its elaborate networks of consortia and associations have been able to deliver extensive and continuing assistance.

Third, the main trade unions have, overall, been comparatively sympathetic towards WTOs – to the extent of reaching an agreement with the Co-operative Associations in 1985, over the nature and extent of the public support needed for the development of co-operatives and the joint action to be undertaken to ensure it was provided. Fourth, because the co-operative movement is linked through federations to the main political parties, the national and regional goventments have to some extent recognized its contribution and that of WTOs to the process of economic restructuring, and they have been willing to provide some resources to assist.

Spain

WTO in Spain are carried out in two different ways – by the formation of workers' co-operatives, and by the formation of Sociedades Anonimas Laborales ('Labour Companies' known by the acronym SAL). The latter, based on individual shareholdings, has been rather more commonly used, though both types are widespread. Both these forms of takeover have been, and continue to be, made possible by financial assistance obtained from public funds administered by loans through yearly programmes under the supervision of the Ministry of Labour.

Although the statistics for SALs have many deficiencies, they do refer almost entirely to instances of WTO, because very few 'new start' SALs were formed before the mid-1980s. On this basis one can say with some confidence that at least 1,300 WTOs have taken place involving a minimum of 50,000 workers (the true figure could well be 70,000 or 80,000). These WTOs have been very unevenly distributed across the country with the greatest concentrations occurring in the Basque country, Andalusia, Madrid and Catalonia. The figures also indicate a heavy concentration of SALs in such industries as metal-working, construction, timber, textiles and printing.[2] The same is likely to be true of WTOs using the co-operative form.

These developments must be understood against a background of political upheaval, economic crisis, rising unemployment and a poorly developed system of social security. The development of the economic crisis from 1976 coincided with a period of enormous political change. Spain was involved in a transition from a dictatorship to a democracy, and from a centralist state to one with 17 parliaments and 17 regional governments. This prolonged institutional upheaval has been accompanied by a highly politicized climate of opinion which has affected business organizations and the whole of Spanish life. Thus, for example, Spain had the highest rates of strikes and industrial disputes in Europe during the period 1977–82, which also saw intense inter-union conflict.

For much of this period, unemployment rates were the highest in Europe. Moreover the opportunities for emigration, which had been an important means of finding work during the years before the crisis, were decreasing.

There is no doubt that WTOs in Spain have experienced severe problems, that a significant number have failed, and that many are having to struggle to stay in existence – especially in the context of Spain's entry into the EEC (which means competing against firms with higher productivity than their domestic rivals). Nevertheless, there have also been a number of encouraging trends. First, several serious weaknesses in the original scheme used to provide loans to workers taking over a firm in crisis were removed in 1985 and 1986. So the funding is now provided on a much more realistic basis. Second, initial trade-union hostility to the very idea has changed to neutrality and, in some quarters, to clear support.

Likewise, they have increasing political support, especially on the left where there has been talk of SALs providing 'the socialism of the twenty-first century'. The SALs have now become organized into federations that are providing associated companies with assistance and greater negotiating leverage. Since entirely new enteprises that use the SAL framework are also now being created it looks increasingly likely that the SALs will become an established feature of the Spanish economy – just as the growing co-operative movement already is in the Basque country, Catalonia and, especially, Andalusia.

France

Until 1978 the co-operative sector was stable and homogenous (traditionally rooted in activities related to construction and printing). After 1978, it experienced an unprecedented expansion (rising from 571 worker co-operatives in 1978 to 1,269 in 1983) and also diversification: it expanded into various industrial sectors and achieved openings into material and intellectual service sectors. This expansion reflected, first, a relatively supportive attitude on the part of the national authorities – for example, the passing of a law relating to co-operatives that facilitated the conversion of enterprises into co-operatives and authorized local communities to give direct grants to co-operatives; and second, the wider development of local and national measures for enterprise promotion and support, in response to the economic crisis (for example since 1980 an unemployed person who wants to start an enterprise has been entitled to contribute up to six months' worth of unemployment benefit to the capital of the business).

A boom in WTOs played a large part in this expansion, often taking advantage of these measures, and contributing between 20 per cent and 40 per cent of the new co-operatives (and between 35 per cent and 60 per cent of the increase in employment in co-operatives) in the period 1978–83.[3] 1982 and 1983 were the peak years, with 109 and 95 WTOs respectively. This upsurge was associated with the arrival of the 'left' government, a change in policy by one of the major unions, and deliberate efforts by CG-SCOP, the centralized representative body of worker co-operatives, to support WTOs. Most WTOs occurred in the printing, textile and leather, furniture and mechanical engineering industries.

The boom was checked in 1984 in the context of changes in government and trade-union attitudes, and alarm within CG-SCOP over the problems of some of the newly created enterprises. Nevertheless WTOs continued with an average of well over 50 per annum in the following years. Although the size varied considerably, they were often quite small, with between 10 and 30 employees. The most successful results were achieved in the traditional sectors of co-operative activity. More recently the number of co-operatives formed in this way seems to have fallen quite sharply and it appears that more WTOs are now using the form of a conventional company. Part of the reason must certainly be the tax incentives for employee share ownership which were introduced in 1984.

The United Kingdom

WTOs have been much less common in the UK. Nevertheless, since the controversy surrounding the three large 'Benn' co-operatives has receded there has been a steady trickle of smaller 'rescue' and 'phoenix' WTOs. These have been less overtly political, they have received no national state funds (or support), and many have not received local funds, yet it is estimated that about 200 have taken place over the last ten years. These have occurred in a wide range of industries. Sectors well represented include engineering, clothing, newspapers, printing and services. On average the enterprises created have employed about 25 people.[4]

This quiet development of the WTO phenomenon has to be understood in relation to the broader political and economic context. The UK small firm sector has been the smallest in Europe. The economic recession in the early 1980s was particularly severe with the collapse of manufacturing activity and traditional industries most apparent in the North, the Midlands and on Merseyside. Regional policy has been widely seen as ineffectual. Industrial training and retraining efforts have increased but still lag behind many other European countries and they can only have a limited impact given the major obstacles to labour mobility presented by the housing market (a reducing stock of public housing; massive price differences between the North and the South).

In this general context local authorities, especially in the north and in major urban areas, have taken up the challenge of high unemployment by developing a range of local economic initiatives including enterprise boards and agencies, thereby creating a more supportive environment for WTOs. These developments have been one factor in the growth of the co-operative movement. In 1970 there were only about 30 worker co-ops, mainly long established businesses formed at the turn of the century. By 1980 there were about 300 and by the end of 1988 the number had risen to about 1,400 – though most were very small and vulnerable 'new start' enterprises (Hobbs

1989). This rapid development was greatly facilitated by the creation of numerous *local* co-operative support organizations (Cornforth *et al*. 1988). While most of the effort of co-operative support organizations has been directed towards 'new start' co-ops, it is clear that they have also played a significant role in relation to many WTOs, particularly the more established agencies.

In addition, during this period a fitful re-appraisal of the co-operative option within the trade-union movement was taking place – both a cause and an effect of local TU involvement in WTO and other co-ops. But, in general, the trade unions have remained very reluctant to support WTOs – which is in marked contrast to their attitude towards management buy-outs whose large numbers and success have been a feature of the 1980s (Wright and Coyne 1985). This 'last resort' attitude has been a major obstacle to WTOs: first outside buyers, then management, are given the option to purchase, and only thereafter might the workers get a chance. This considerably reduced the prospects of organizing sufficiently fast for continuous trading without losing suppliers, customers, and the more skilled workers. And, of course, it increased the likelihood that WTOs have occurred in the most dire circumstances.

West Germany

Workforce initiatives to take over their employer's firm to prevent closure have been rare in the Federal Republic. There have been 13 WTOs in the last two decades, but well over 30 attempts, most occurring in the 1980s. Many of these have occurred where quite large plants have closed in depressed regions. These efforts have had to overcome a combination of obstacles: the unfamiliarity of the idea among workers, restrictive procedures for receivership, the economic difficulties of turning a plant into a company, the absence of appropriate sources of finance, and, not least, the highly centralized and formalized traditions of industrial relations in Germany, which has meant a sceptical or disinterested attitude on the part of most trade union leaders (though the metal workers union is becoming more sympathetic). In addition the traditional co-operative movement has been politically and culturally remote from these efforts, with support being provided instead through informal networks that have drawn on assistance from the very vigorous alternative and ecological movement. Perhaps partly as a result of this several German WTOs, and attempted WTOs, have explored the scope for converting to socially useful and ecologically sound products. In general, the interest in and capacity to support WTOs has increased quite rapidly in the last few years

– particularly around Bremen – but starting from a very limited base, so that the obstacles remain considerable.

Denmark

Even less WTO activity has occurred in Denmark. Fourteen WTOs have succeeded (involving 500 employees) and there have been only four reported cases where unsuccessful attempts have been made (Westenholz 1987). The great majority of these have been commercially successful so the interesting questions are why there have not been more attempts and why there is not an increasing trend.

The answer seems to lie in a combination of factors. First, the generous unemployment provisions of the Danish welfare state mean that for an unskilled worker benefit will be 80 per cent to 90 per cent of the previous wage for 2½ years (thereafter the conditions for benefit become more complicated but it will usually be several more years before the benefit is reduced, in stages, to 50 per cent of previous wage). Second, the labour and trade-union movements have strongly centralized traditions and strategies – for example, the trade unions actually own a number of enterprises (employing about 7,500 employees) that arose from industrial struggles earlier in the century. Likewise, the labour movement's proposals for economic democracy have been based on the idea of a central fund. Third, there is a strong individualist tradition of entrepreneurial activity in the substantial sector of small and medium-sized enterprises. The owner-managers have a quite different lifestyle, and they expect to keep control to themselves. Such people would be very sceptical of selling their firm to employees – or of buying a firm with other employees.

The variety of closure threats

From the preceding broad overview it is clear that attempts at WTO are more common in labour-intensive industries – such as metal-working, wood-working and textiles – that are in decline, or being restructured, whether as a result of cyclical downturns, technological change, changes in tariff regulations or as part of wider changes in the international division of labour. In such cases, resisting closure of a plant or firm may be impossible because the owners see no scope for a return to profitable operations and no buyer is available. Unless the workers take it over, the plant will close and remain closed. If unemployment is already high or rising this may provide incentive enough to consider the WTO option – especially if the workforce possesses industry-specific skills. If, in addition the threatened enterprise employs more than, say, 100 people, the local authorities, suppliers, other business interests, community groups and trade unions may support or even promote the idea.

Hence most attempts at WTO arise (i) under very adverse economic conditions and (ii) where the need for job preservation is great. However, these two conditions do not always occur. In the first place WTOs have also been undertaken where the labour market for the skills concerned was comparatively buoyant and most employees were unlikely to face more than a brief period of unemployment. The significance of this will be considered presently.

Second, many attempts at WTOs arise in the context of viable or potentially viable enterprises and plants. It is simply not the case that WTO are only attempted in cases where there is little or no prospect of viability. If the owners and/or managers of an economic unit are unable or unwilling to arrange its profitable operation this does not necessarily mean the unit cannot be made viable; new owners/managers may succeed – as the considerable literature on business 'turn-arounds' testifies (e.g. Slatter 1984). Of course, if other purchasers for the business are not forthcoming it is commonly assumed that *therefore* the business has little if any prospect of profitability. But such an assmption may well be unjustified.

The general reason for questioning this assumption is that the market in firms, like other markets, has its imperfections. The *transaction* costs (Williamson 1975) associated with the purchase of a plant or enterprise are very high. Considerable uncertainty usually exists regarding the status of human and capital assets and market trends – an uncertainty likely to be accentuated by doubts about the competence and motivations of those selling the unit. Such uncertainties may be accentuated by time pressures. In addition, the management of acquisitions is notoriously difficult, especially where the acquisition involves unfamiliar (if related) processes and is geographically distant. The difficulties, costs and uncertainties associated with reducing staffing levels (especially where the plant is strongly unionized or where, as in Spain, employment protection legislation significantly reduces freedom of action) may be a particular disincentive. In addition, government industrial policy may make the alternative of developing a 'green field' site more attractive. Moreover, the number of possible purchasers may be very restricted for reasons that have nothing to do with the status of the threatened plant. For example, in regions with limited industrial activity (e.g. Andalusia) there may be very few entrepreneurs with the necessary resources or experience. Or the location of the plant in a region affected by political instability may deter purchasers from outside the region.

Clearly, the greater the transaction costs and perceived risks, the higher the return prospective purchasers will require to justify the investment. Hence, a unit that is making modest profits, quite apart from one that is losing money but is potentially profitable, may not attract purchasers. Such circumstances can arise in a variety of ways.

First, there are cases where a group of companies has failed but (for whatever reasons) it contains profitable (or potentially profitable) units within it. Possible purchasers may fail to appreciate the business opportunity available because they lack the inside information – the cases of SWA in Box 3.2 and Aire Habitat in Box 7.3 provide examples. Such circumstances have also provided the occasion for successful management buy-outs (Wright and Coyne 1985).

Second, there are the cases of 'obvious mismanagement' – where it is quite clear to at least some of the workforce that the company's difficulties were avoidable and the underlying business prospects are sound. Often such failures arise from financial mismanagement during a period of rapid growth. But the mismanagement can take other forms as well. Northwest Pre-Cast in Boxes 4.1 and 6.1 provides a clear example.

Third, there are cases of corporate divestment (usually of smaller units) that fail to find buyers. Such divestments may arise because a unit is *insufficiently* profitable, or may follow from changes in business strategy, or may be the result of conglomerate mismanagement and under-investment leading to poor results. The Lake School of English in Box 2.1 provides one example. Other are Red Dragon Stores (Thomas and Thornley 1989), Publications Elysée in Paris, and several others among the cases presented in later chapters. Stern and Hammer (1978) provide North American examples. Again, many management buy-outs have arisen in similar circumstances. Such divestments have also occurred as part of strategies of productive decentralization; that is, particular production activities are closed down and contracted out to a smaller firm. In Italy the workers concerned have sometimes taken over the necessary equipment and formed a co-operative based initially on sub-contracting to their former employer – see Box 3.1. This has also occurred in Denmark where employers in the newspaper industry have wished to avoid being directly involved in managing industrial relations in a period of technological restructuring.

Fourth, there are the cases (again usually smaller units) where an older owner-manager dies or wishes to retire. If, despite being profitable, the competitive position of the firm is weak, it may be hard to interest prospective purchasers. Where management-worker relations have been harmonious, all concerned may consider a WTO the obvious solution, and it

Box 2.1   Lake School of English[5]

Lake School of English is based in Oxford where they teach English as a Foreign Language (EFL). They employ seven full-time teachers and a full-time administrator, and work from smart new offices that they had specially converted to serve the needs of the school. The co-operative originated from the closure of the EFL department of a large tutorial college. There appear to have been two reasons for the closure: first, the college considered the department was not making enough money and wished to use the separate building in which the EFL teaching took place for other more lucrative activities. Second, relationships between EFL staff and the college were strained – the staff had even refused to teach one course because they believed the college had made misleading claims about its facilities to prospective students.

Led by the head of department, five of the staff (about half of the department) decided to set up a co-operative (they had heard this was a quick and cheap way of registering a business – there was no strong ideological commitment to co-operation at that point). They started in 1978 and the first years were very hard.

They ran the business from a small office in the town centre, and put on their courses in an old church hall on the outskirts of town. Then in 1981 they acquired new premises and British Council recognition, which was very important in marketing terms.

In the early years the job of administrator had been rotated on a yearly basis between the members of the co-op who were all teachers. Administration at Lake is a big job (it involves arranging accommodation and a social programme, as well as attracting students), and eventually the members decided that it would be better and more efficient if they employed someone full-time to do the administration. This improved efficiency. However, the teaching staff all spend some time in the office – and this has had to increase as the business has grown.

Regular meetings of the co-op take place on Friday afternoons. This is where the information is exchanged and decisions are made. It is also something of a social event as they wind down at the end of the week. Decisions are nearly all made by consensus. Over the years the members of Lake have developed a strong commitment to co-operative working.

may be fairly straightforward to arrange. A French case is described in Job Ownership Ltd. (1986).

Fifth, where a company is in some difficulty (because of e.g. high labour costs, obsolescent plant or products, financial mismanagement etc.) its efforts to resolve the problems may be resisted by the unions, which can lead in due course to threats of closure and escalating conflict. As a result, possible purchasers of the enterprise, and private and public sources of finance, may be put off from investing by strikes, occupations and poor industrial relations – even though the underlying commercial problems are not particularly severe. Such situations have been quite common in Italy and the CLG case in Box 2.2 has many of these features (they were also an element in the Lake case – see Box 2.1). The usual pattern is for a prolonged period of uncertainty, and conflict during which production is suspended and demonstrations and negotiations with a range of interested parties take place in pursuit of a solution that will preserve the enterprise. In due course (perhaps after some of the workforce have drifted away and thus solved the redundancy problem) a WTO with the support of a Co-operative Association may be arranged. That such an outcome should result from the original difficulties is certainly not planned or intended – and sections of the workforce may at first be strongly opposed to a WTO.

Box 2.2   The case of CLG – Part I

CLG was born out of the Salgraf Company of Verona, which was engaged in photolithographic work, mainly for Mondadori (a colossus in the sector). The firm had a good volume of work, was well-equipped and in 1975 had 80 employees. Salgraf owned two other firms as well and had become involved in a number of complex large-scale deals and operations. However, in 1974 it found itself faced with a liquidity crisis and it tried to cope with this by dismantling the group and winding up one of the three firms. The trade unions resisted this move and management undertook to restructure the company's finances in other ways instead. However, a year later in 1975, and with no prior warning and no negotiation with the trade union, the owners placed the entire workforce in Cassa Integrazione Guadagni. This is an instrument providing guaranteed wages in situations of temporary company crisis and is paid by the Instituto Nazionale di Previdenza Sociale to the order of 80 per cent of the worker's last wage and for the temporary period during which it is assumed that the company will recover and be able to take all or some of its workers back on again. The company made this move despite the fact that the firm had a full order book and was having to resort to overtime. The workers reacted with determination against what seemed to them to be a non-existent crisis deliberately created in order to shift capital towards more profitable undertakings. A strike was called to force the owners to negotiate. However, production did not start up again and the conflict escalated: the workers occupied the factory and took their case to the courts, where an order was issued for the confiscation of the factory and the owner's house in order to provide a guarantee for wages owed to his employees.

After three months, about half the workforce, worn down by uncertainty, intimidation and false promises, left the factory for employment elsewhere, and the owner applied to the courts for the introduction of Aministrazione Controllata' of the firm (a system whereby debt repayment is temporarily suspended in order to enable the entrepreneur to overcome his economic problems). However, his application was rejected on the grounds that absolutely no plan for overcoming the crisis had been forthcoming. Thus two more months passed until the remaining workers applied to the courts to have the firm declared bankrupt. And, in fact, five months later, Salgraf was declared bankrupt.

The employees of Salgraf were mainly young people with good school education and professional training. They were also more unionized in comparison with small firms in the sector. During the months of factory occupation, the idea had begun to grow of forming a co-operative in order to save their jobs, and a heated debate ensued between the two main trade unions (CISL and CGL) over the relationship between self-management and trade unionism. However, although two trade unionists came into the factory to join the co-operative's administration while it was being set up, the unions were usually conspicuous by their absence.

On the other hand, local political forces had been involved right from the start, by the workers' council, which orchestrated the complex Italian ritual for the rescue of firms in crisis: public meetings and the involvement of the press and political, cultural and social associations. The search for a purchaser for the company was conducted half-heartedly, since it was thought that the particular situation of Salgraf was not one that would attract a suitable entrepreneur. In the permanent assembly the workers began to discuss the idea of self-management, but with serious misgivings: how could a workers' co-operative be set up in a sector with such special characteristics as the graphics sector, without financing, with the market lost, the firm's image ruined in the eyes of its customers and so many workers with irreplaceable skills lost? Nevertheless, at the end of February 1976 the assembly decided on self-management. At the begining of March the co-operative was legally constituted and applied to the courts for the factory premises to be leased to them. This raised a number of legal questions, since bankruptcy law is either oriented towards the dismantling of failed firms to pay off their creditors or, in exceptional and limited circumstances, towards temporary management by the official receiver while warehouse stocks, perishable goods etc. are cleared. The workers' council rallied public support and organized sufficient pressure to 'persuade' the court to grant them the lease of the premises. At the end of March the contract was drawn up, and at the beginning of April the co-operative started up with 25 member-workers.

(*The case is continued in Box 6.2*)

The underlying logic of such cases is clear: where industrial relations are a major factor in the enterprise's problems, then the strategy of a WTO and the formation of a co-operative is likely to have a competitive advantage over other possible solutions, and to be viable where others would not be – because it provides a different foundation to worker-management relations. This seems particularly to be the case in labour-intensive industries where performance is strongly affected by the cost and quality of labour. (Of course, the suggestion that the co-operative option will possess a competitive advantage in such circumstances does not mean that all industrial relations problems disappear in a co-operative.)

Sixth, there are cases where the only prospective purchasers are unacceptable to the parties involved. L. H. Reklame in Box 2.3 is an example. This may also occur when the purchasing company has a reputation for 'asset-stripping', or is openly proposing to run down the plant for short-term financial gains. In such cases, local political interests may join with the workforce in pressing the existing owners to reject the offer, and in preparing a counter-offer based on the maintenance of productive activities in the locality. (The case of MOSTA in Box 6.4 is another example.)

Box 2.3   L. H. Reklame

L. H. Reklame is situated in a Danish provincial town called Kolding. It is an advertising agency producing a large variety of advertisements. It was established by an entrepreneur who died suddenly in 1980. This was a great shock for the six employees, all women. The firm was doing well, and the employees had harmonious relationships, and very good and independent jobs. The day after the death of the owner the employees heard that two or three local competitors each planned to take over the firm. The employees could not accept any of these potential buyers as they would not continue to be employed under the management of any of them.

They had the alternatives of either finding jobs elsewhere or taking over the firm themselves. The job opportunities were uncertain, and they decided to try the second alternative. The two heirs of the deceased founder approved of the idea of a workers' takeover and agreed that the capital be divided into eight equal shares, thus creating a co-operative society with pro rata liability for the six female employees and the two heirs.

They had no problems in raising the money – each of them was liable for an amount of 40,000 K.Dr. (about £3,300). The greatest support in the phase of establishment came from the customers. They encouraged the six women to continue on their own and placed many orders with them, so in the first year of the takeover the six owners had a full order book and little spare time. They also received strong support from their families. But still, the first years were difficult, and they had to work very hard. First of all they had no experience in running a firm. The financial administration in particular was a great problem. During the early years this was placed in the hands of an accountant who, however, did not take sufficient care of the finances. Today, five years later, they are able to handle the financial administration themselves.

They also needed legal expertise but succeeded in finding a good lawyer. The trade union, of which they were all members, took a negative attitude, expelling them from the union as they were now looked upon as employers, not as wage earners. This was not legal, but the women did not know that until later. So they joined the unemployment insurance fund of owner-managers instead. As a further complication it turned out that three of the women were pregnant and one was ill. After five years of financial instability they are now in a safe position. They have employed four new people, who are not owners. This question has not been discussed, and until now it does not seem to have any effect on the way in which the firm is managed. Everybody – owners and non-owners – have an informal discussion each day of problems and co-ordination questions. The financial administration is being taken care of by one of the new employees. The climate of the firm is characterized by a great flexibility and a readiness to help one another; in particular there is a great consideration for the care of the children. Nine of the workers are young women, and they think that it would be difficult for a 'traditional' man to fit into this type of flexibility. They earn equal pay in accordance with collective agreements.

In all such cases, an offer by the workforce to purchase and run the unit prevents a failure in the market for enterprises and the closure of a profitable or potentially profitable unit. The fact that other purchasers are not available cannot therefore be taken as demonstrating that a WTO will not be viable. A worker's 'turn-around' may be perfectly possible. The impression generated by well-publicized cases, that WTO only occur in the most adverse economic circumstances, does not fit the facts and is seriously misleading.

The institutional and cultural dimensions

Given that WTOs can be and are attempted in a variety of closure situations, it is, nevertheless, quite clear that the threat of closure and unemployment does not automatically lead to a WTO being considered. The WTO option is frequently ignored or overlooked. And there are enormous variations between countries. Why is this?

One obvious explanation is that in countries that have a well-developed welfare state the costs of unemployment for individuals are much less severe than in countries where security provisions are far more limited. It would be surprising if this fact did not contribute to the frequency and intensity of attempts at WTO. Thus Demark, where generous earnings-related unemployment benefit is virtually guaranteed for many years, has had very few WTOs. By contrast, Italy and Spain, where unemployment benefit is more limited, have seen many.

However, the Swedish experience of WTOs suggests that this explanation is far too simple. Like Denmark, Sweden provides generous unemployment benefit – but a much larger number of WTOs have taken place there. During the 1980s more than 80 WTOs have occurred. This is nothing like Spain or Italy – but it indicates a higher rate of WTOs than the UK, which has poorer unemployment benefit and a population more than six times larger.

Clearly, therefore, other factors are at work. One likely explanation for the differing experience of Sweden and Denmark is the existence of a rudimentary support structure for WTOs in Sweden (associated with local employment initiatives), and the virtual absence of such a structure in Denmark. This highlights a point of general significance: attempts at a WTO are not only, or always, a purely spontaneous initiative by the workforce. An attempt is much more likely where the idea of a WTO is available to the workforce and has credibility. It is a response to the threat of closure which has variously been promoted or discouraged – either explicitly or tacitly.

In this respect the roles adopted by local and national governments, by trade unions and co-operative movement bodies, and by networks of sympathetic professionals, are very important, as the country overviews have already indicated. However, the attitudes and measures of these various bodies do not develop in isolation. They affect each other, and reinforce each other. Success can breed success.

A successful WTO tends to stimulate others to consider the WTO option, just as the failure of a WTO, or the absence of any recent or local WTO, makes it more likely the option will be overlooked or discarded. At the same time, successful WTOs tend to legitimize support by the co-operative movement, trade unions and governments and their agencies (and failure undermines such support). In addition, as later chapters demonstrate, the more extensive and experienced the support for WTO attempts, the more likely they are to succeed, and the more likely the enterprises created are to survive and to consolidate. Thus, in due course, the enterprises created from WTO can strengthen the worker co-operative and worker-owned sectors – which are then better able to support other WTOs in the future.[6]

Needless to say, these self-reinforcing tendencies either in favour of or against the WTO phenomenon do not operate invariably and automatically. There are numerous cases of isolated WTOs. Nevertheless, the distribution of WTOs and attempted WTOs in the last ten years does not simply reflect the distribution of industries undergoing restructuring or the rate of unemployment. Marked concentrations appear in particular regions and localities. Northern Italy and parts of Spain have already been mentioned. Perhaps even more strikingly, about one-third of the WTOs in the Federal Republic of Germany in the last five years have occurred in the small city-state of Bremen, where an effective support network linking the 'alternative' groupings, labour movement organizations, and government agencies, has developed. Similar networks and concentrations of WTO activity seem to be developing within the UK in Scotland, Yorkshire and London.

The presence, or near absence, of WTO activity seems also to reflect broader institutional and cultural traditions.

For example, it is noticeable that the concentrations of WTO are high in Andalusia, Catalonia and Emilia-Romagna, regions that have strong cultural traditions of mutual aid and self-reliance (apparent in their strong anarchist movements earlier this century). From this perspective, the contrasting socio-economic structures of Denmark and Italy can be seen as different 'historic solutions' to the labour movement's search for greater economic security. Such differences both express and reinforce significant cultural differences – for example, the strong tradition of a well-developed welfare state and of individualist entrepreneurs in Denmark, compared to the more collective entrepreneurialism of Italy, in which labour solidarity can be achieved through the market, not only in opposition to it.

This cultural dimension appears in another way. When the WTO in different countries are considered as an expression of the national character of those countries, it becomes clear that although, as participative WTOs, they have a great deal in common, they are not all the same sort of event. In Italy they are a classic Italian compromise – in this case, between the principles of the market and of solidarity. In Spain they represent a pragmatic exploration of a populist socialism. By contrast, in Britain they are a (dubious) 'last resort' and in West Germany a form of industrial deviance. Finally, in Denmark they have appeared as social inventions, while in France in the early 1980s they had the character of an ideological deduction (Gherardi 1988).

Such variations suggest there are different sorts of WTO prompted by rather different motivations.

'Job-saving' and 'firm-saving' WTO

It was noted earlier that some WTOs take place in circumstances where, if closure went ahead, those involved were unlikely to be unemployed for any significant length of time (Sweden, for example, has largely avoided the high rates of unemployment experienced elsewhere in Europe). In such cases the WTO cannot be driven by the usual 'job-saving' concerns; those involved must have other reasons for going to the considerable trouble of taking over the enterprise in which they work. The case of IKP in Box 2.4 is a particularly clear example.

Box 2.4 IKP (The Institut for Kommunal Planning)

In 1959 a consulting firm providing shopping-centre-planning was established in Copenhagen by two very big chain-stores. In the 1960s and in the early 1970s the firm increased its staff to about forty employees developing new complex planning services for local authorities. At the same time the structure of the firm developed towards collective leadership, and the influence of the board was drastically reduced. In 1974, however, the firm experienced a drop in orders which reactivated the members of the board. The situation turned into a matter of principle concerning the future of the firm. The board wanted to return to the original services and a hierarchic structure. A minority of the employees accepted this, whereas the majority resisted, as it would imply going back to more boring tasks, or looking for new jobs elsewhere (which would have been very easy at that time). However, they felt that it was worth while saving their firm, as they assumed that the market would require their type of complex services in the future, and for such tasks a collective leadership was considered more suitable than a hierarchical structure. They also preferred the democratic structure for ideological reasons, and it would be hard to find that elsewhere.

After many hard negotiations (lasting nine months) among the employees themselves, and between the majority and the board, it was decided to divide the firm into two separate firms, and in 1974 IKP was established as a collectively owned and managed independent institution. This was done in a way that meant new members did not have to contribute capital to the firms, and that members who left could not withdraw capital from the firm. The employees transferred the complex tasks to the new firm, and such capital as was needed was provided without problems by overdraft facilities.

The following eight years were financially successful. The net capital of the firm increased, the number of employees grew to twenty-one, who received reasonably good salaries. They developed and provided services that earned a high reputation, and new technology was introduced. During this period they developed the collective leadership structure so that, among many other things, nobody could be elected to a management committee for a period longer than four years.

In 1982 there was a shortage of new contracts, and the problem was aggravated by very strong cuts in public spending, which sapped the market. This was the beginning of an economic crisis which led to the closure of the firm in 1984. At first they tried to solve the problems by reducing working hours and wages and salaries for all employees. At the same time they tried hard to switch over to new services, but they did not succeed.

Until the very last months it remained uncertain whether they would be able to survive with a reduced staff. They did not – not just because they had no money left for wages and salaries, but also because they had chosen not to keep the firm alive on the basis of the type of services which were required by the market at that moment. They could have done that, but it would have meant jobs for very few – and jobs with very little challenge. Instead they applied for jobs elsewhere either in more traditional firms or in public institutions. IKP had succeeded in surviving for a longer period than traditionally owned consulting firms, producing the same services, and competing with it.

The term 'firm-saving' WTO will be used to designate such cases since the primary concern is no longer that of preserving employment, but of ensuring *a particular kind* of employment. Often, this reflects a concern to preserve harmonious working relationships or otherwise distinctive and rewarding working practices. However, it may also arise from an identification with the product, or from seeing a WTO as an opportunity to promote particular concerns or ideals – and hence the term 'firm-saving' is not wholly satisfactory.

Two points must be emphasized, regarding the job-saving/firm-saving distinction. First, it is clearly a continuum. Pure firm-saving cases like IKP are not common; but cases that combine job-saving and firm-saving motivations do occur more often. L. H. Reklame in Box 2.3 and AN in Box 3.3 are examples. Second, the distinction concerns the *initial* motivation for the WTO – because it is quite common for those who start off undertaking a WTO on the basis that it is a necessity which no one really wants, to develop quite quickly thereafter other more complex motivations.[7]

Using this distinction a more comprehensive explanation for the varying nature and incidence of WTO in Europe can be suggested. First, attempts at WTO are more common where the probability and cost of prolonged unemployment is greater – that is regions with high unemployment and a poorly developed welfare state. Secondly, attempts at WTOs are also more common where the environment is favourable (e.g. accessible financial and advisory assistance; examples of successful WTO enterprises; sympathetic trade-union attitudes, etc.). Thirdly, to the extent that WTOs do occur in a country or region, the job-saving type will predominate in areas where unemployment constitutes a serious problem, and firm-saving WTOs will be more common in areas where unemployment is not such a serious problem.[8]

3 | The Worker Takeover Process

To be successful an attempt at a WTO must resolve a number of interrelated and complex issues concerning legal, financial, marketing, production and organizational questions. These questions will be unfamiliar to the workforce and its leadership, and tackling them commonly requires access to external advice as well as political support, especially regarding negotiations with third parties. These difficulties involve conflicting economic and social imperatives, and may be compounded by severe time pressure. Moreover, for a number of very practical reasons it is important that as far as possible these issues are addressed by the workforce as a whole – and not just by leaders or advisors on behalf of the workforce. Each takeover is an intense learning process for the workforce as an organization,[1] as well as for individuals – there is a change of social roles, new attitudes are required, and, sometimes, the WTO-situation is taken as an opportunity towards realizing new ideas of a self-managed and more socially responsible production. The aim of this chapter is to highlight the problems that characteristically arise in this complex and very uncertain process. In doing so attention will also be drawn to some ways in which these problems are greatly accentuated in the context of large plants, compared to the situation in the smaller units that have provided the more successful WTO experience.

It is not possible to provide figures on the proportion of WTO attempts that succeed, or to provide any kind of quantitative analysis. Those involved with the support of WTOs find it difficult even to make estimates since a WTO may be considered but discarded without a serious attempt being mounted (often for very good reasons, of course). Hence there is a problem over what constitutes an 'attempt'. It also seems that the proportion of unsuccessful attempts varies considerably between countries. Thus, in Denmark there seem to have been very few unsuccessful attempts – but this almost certainly reflects the fact that the idea is so uncommon that it only arises and is seriously pursued in quite favourable circumstances. Where the idea is better known but the support for WTOs is still limited and lacking experience, then there are far more unsuccessful attempts – an estimate for the UK, for example, was that only one WTO is achieved for every five occasions when the option is quite seriously explored. This is comparable with the one-in-four success rate in the FRG over the last five years. Finally, there are countries like Italy (and to a lesser extent France and Spain) where there is much more experience of WTOs. In such cases the proportion of successful attempts seems, once again, to be much higher – partly because WTOs are more accepted and there is effective support for them; but probably also because the support agencies are more ready to discourage the idea in contexts that they recognize as having poor prospects.

Before proceeding it is worth emphasizing that the initiative for a WTO does not always come from the manual workforce – although this is most common. Especially in countries where the idea of a WTO is well established, it may be stimulated and encouraged by other parties. For example, the initiative for transforming an enterprise into a co-operative or SAL may come from the existing entrepreneur: he or she suggests to the employees that they should form a co-operative, either to share the risks or to avoid conflict and its consequent cost. The initiative is usually supported by a paternalist culture, either with artisan origin or deriving from a culture originating in advanced industrial relations. Alternatively, the entrepreneur may propose to employees that they take over part of the production cycle as a co-operative, guaranteeing their continued links with the company through work orders and various administrative services. In this situation, co-operation and dependence are interwoven.

Another possibility is that the idea of a WTO is promoted by trade-union officials, local-government departments, co-operative movement bodies, or some combination of these. This is more common with larger WTOs where the impact of a closure on the local economy would be more significant. Examples of both these types of WTO are provided in Box 3.1. Such external promotion of a WTO can have a considerable influence on the subsequent life of the enterprise, both socially and commercially.

Box 3.1   Externally promoted WTOs in Italy

Cierre was converted into a co-operative on the joint initiative of the entrepreneur and a small group of young people and an agency for the co-ordination of co-operatives in Verona. By means of a major programme of innovative investment Cierre tried to acquire new markets. However, it was not able to identify areas of the market suited to its new machinery. It was forced to operate in conditions of plant under-utilization and after a short time had to embark on a recovery programme.

Cabel was born on the initiative of the ex-owner, who put forward the idea to his employees (all very young) to set up a co-operative, since the firm's sole customer for its assembled television sets was beginning to show signs of crisis. It seemed, therefore, more sensible to look for new markets and new products. The entrepreneur wanted to share the risks involved and to avoid the costs of industrial conflict. The workforce was sceptical, and it was only by the efforts of a trade-union leader that the conversion was made possible. Production changed over to videos, video games and monitors, with great success, and the entrepreneur took on the responsibility of training the young technicians himself.

Didial arose out of the bankruptcy of a clothes factory operating in an unprofitable sector of the market (low-quality garments). The firm was too large for its market, at a time when the entire garments sector was in the process of restructuring. The firm's bankruptcy had been preceded by a period of major trade-union effort aimed at saving jobs and recovering productivity: this led to the formation of an 'organizing group' of workers. During the ten months of official receivership, a purchaser was sought in vain. The receiver pronounced himself against the winding-up of the firm and proposed the idea of a co-operative to the workers. A permanent assembly was set up with the task of analysing the production cycle, costs and work organization, and of drawing up a detailed plan for the rescue of the firm and its transformation into a co-operative.

Pellicciai Riuniti arose from a large firm in the furs sector with 520 employees in 1976 and a sales volume of 20 billion lire. Its situation became critical and in 1980 its staff had dwindled to 138. During this period the trade union was severely hampered by conflicts among the workers. While the union contemplated self-management, a group of office workers set up a co-operative. The shopfloor workers, however, remained sceptical and were unable to decide whether to commit themselves to the co-operative. In time, though, the workers were forced to make up their minds: they joined the co-operative, and negotiations started over the assignation of the firm. The owner leased the trademark and the buildings, the management assisted in the setting up of the new administration, and a recently formed company (in which the ex-owner had interests) made a large order. Pellicciai Riuniti was unable to meet the costs of purchasing raw materials (mink) and of maintaining an autonomous marketing network. Consequently, it moved into the subcontracting market, providing a high-quality service. As profitability increased, it started up the manufacture and marketing on its own account of reversible sheepskin suede coats (where the cost of skins is lower).

The closure announcement and the role of receivers

The announcement – whether official or unofficial – that an enterprise is going to close provokes strong emotional reactions among the workforce – shock, disbelief, anger, depression. If the closure is not to take effect immediately there is time for talks and negotiations, time to consider various possible solutions and come to terms with the stark choices, time for collective activities and decisions, such as preparing alternative proposals and seeking external support, and more time for individual decision-making: if it comes to it, who favours individual solutions such as looking for a new job elsewhere, enrolling in a long-term training scheme, going on the dole, applying for early retirement; and who would be prepared to help in takeover activities.

Various factors shape the agenda during this period – such as the industrial relations climate within the enterprise, the extent to which the workers have read the signs of impending crisis and anticipated such an announcement, and the attitude of local union officials. Sometimes the provisions governing such matters as redundancy payments, outstanding wages and salaries due, and social-security entitlements become the targets of most concern. However, as long as many in the workforce believe the enterprise can be made viable the main effort goes into trying to reverse the decision. Of particular importance in this context is the regulatory frame-work governing company closure and receivership. This varies considerably, and in very important ways, between different countries.

In France and particularly in Italy there is more state involvement in reorganization and rescue attempts prior to, as well as in, conditions of insolvency or bankruptcy. Both countries have developed measures and institutions to assist companies in difficulties: Comités de Restructuration in France; Casa Integrazione Guadagni and Aministrazione Controllata in Italy – see the case of CLG (Box 2.2). The explicit intention in France (at least since the new bankruptcy law came into effect in 1986), and certainly the effect in Italy, has been to make the preservation of the company in crisis a major concern in its own right, as far as the commercial courts are concerned. Of course, the commercial courts may still be reluctant to co-operate with an attempt at a WTO for a variety of reasons. Nevertheless, these measures create a context for insolvent or bankrupt enterprises that contrasts starkly with that in countries like Germany and the UK whose rather inflexible procedures for receivership and liquidation are framed entirely in terms of the interests of creditors, and take no account of the interests of other affected parties (Holand *et al.* 1986). In these countries little credibility attaches to the idea of rescuing failed enterprises – which makes WTOs, as rather controversial attempts, look even more quixotic.

In consequence, attempts by workers to take over companies controlled by receivers face additional obstacles in these countries. For example, the workforce may lose its right to information in Germany[2] and it will almost always face acute time pressure. To be sure, receivers do have some discretion over how they exercise their duties and they certainly prefer to sell off an enterprise as a going concern. But if no likely purchasers can be identified the receiver must act quickly in order to prevent additional losses: if the workforce has not already been dismissed, it will be at this stage. Of course, in principle, a proposal from the workforce to buy the firm on a 'going concern' basis should appeal to the receiver – and also to the less well secured creditors who stand to lose most from liquidation. However, the receiver would have to be persuaded that there was a good chance this could be arranged and the major secured creditors who will usually have put the company into receivership would have to be persuaded to wait while the finance was raised.

In practice, there is usually a wide social distance between a receiver and the workforce. The general feeling among those who have assisted WTOs is that they tend to be unsympathetic towards workers rescue initiatives – out of a combination of rank scepticism and a desire to avoid unfamiliar complications. As one such advisor in the UK put it, 'They want an easy life; worker buy-outs are a hassle.'

Nevertheless, in Germany and the UK a WTO of a firm under the control of a receiver may still be possible – much depends on the individual receiver appointed.[3] The case of SWA in Box 3.2 provides an extraordinary illustration of this (though it is, clearly, a financial WTO). Moreover, even if a WTO at this stage is unsuccessful it may still be possible to secure essential assets from the liquidation of the company as the basis for a new enterprise. This means pursuing, in effect, a 'phoenix' (rather than a 'rescue') strategy. Considering the relative merits and appropriate contexts for these two strategies provides a convenient way of analysing the main dilemmas in the preparation of business plans for WTOs of failed enterprises.

Box 3.2   The case of SWA (Spinnerei und Weberei Augsburg GmbH)

The company (Mechanische Baumwollspinnerei und Weberei Augsburg AG/ SWA) was part of the Glöggler concern. This group was privately owned by Hans Glöggler who, between 1969 and 1975, bought numerous companies, thus pushing his concern into a leading position in West German textile manufacturing. By 1975, it was a multinational empire, co-operating with 38 inland and foreign banks, with the trade-union bank BfG as one of the main creditors. It was a total surprise to the employees, as well as to the public, when this concern went bankrupt in December 1975. While some parts of the concern could be saved without great difficulties, SWA had to file a petition in bankruptcy; management, state government (Conservative/CSU) and BfG among others, did not see a realistic rescue chance.

The receiver, taking over a company with 1,050 employees and with 60 million DM in debts, dismisses 300. Clever negotiations with suppliers and customers enable him to continue production with the remaining workforce. He succeeds in consolidating the business, though there is no chance of reducing the burden of debts. An extraordinary thing has begun: production, by a company under receivership, is continued until the rescue company is registered, finally, in February 1984 – eight years later, having produced profits for the last three years.

The rescue proposal was presented in mid-1983. The new firm was to be supplied with 10.6 million DM of equity – 89 per cent of which was to be provided by the employees (c.6 million DM from compensation payments and c.3 million DM was a type of labour administration grant) the remaining 11 per cent by suppliers and customers. The scheme was worked out by the receiver, in co-operation with the local authorities, the regional trade-union organization (Gew.Textil-Bekleidung) and the works council.

Once again, it was the BfG which almost caused a sudden end to this hopeful undertaking, this time indirectly. In order to reduce the extent of their funds at risk, they sold the freehold to the site which they held as security, thus giving away a very important element with which they could have supported a rescue quite decisively. The buyer, the owner of a building company, used the acquired rights for speculation and asked, instead of the 8 million DM which he had had to pay, for 16 million DM to sell it back to the new company – which would have made them bankrupt before they started. After long and delicate negotiations, a solution was found: a group of banks (BfG, the communal Augsburger Sparkasse, and a state development bank/Landesanstalt fur Weideraufbau) gave credits to SWA, including 15 million DM to the speculator. The local (Social Democratic) government underwrote the loans, which was quite unusual.

The company's 500 employees, including 45 apprentices, are represented in the limited company by a senior official of their union who acts as trustee. Once a year he has to report to them on the economic situation of the company. Apart from that he makes his own decisions. On the board the workers hold three out of nine seats, but there is no more workforce influence or workforce protection than in any conventional enterprise in West Germany. (In early 1989 it was reported that SWA was again in difficulties and under the control of a receiver.)

Rescue and phoenix strategies compared

The essence of a business plan is a cash-flow forecast which indicates the outgoings and income anticipated in the early months and years. Such forecasts must be based on credible proposals for who the customers will be and how they will be reached; the quantity, quality and price of the goods or services to be provided; the facilities, equipment and labour of different categories that will be needed and that are available; the borrowings, repayments and interest charges required to finance these activities; how the effective monitoring and co-ordination of operations will be achieved – and so on. Clearly, to develop these proposals in any detail may require a considerable amount of time. Of course every question cannot be answered, not all the aspirations will be proved realistic, and everyone will not agree on everything – in a WTO as in any other business plan. But the more definite the proposals, the clearer the grounds on which they are based and the greater the consensus on priorities, then the greater the confidence and unity of the workforce, and the more credible the plan will be with external bodies. Once a firm is in a commercial crisis, such a recovery plan will essentially be based on one of two broad strategies.

The more common 'rescue' strategy, is directed towards reaching agreement with the owners or receiver for a transfer of the business assets and activities to the workforce in such a way that there is little or no break in production and trading. Where it is possible, this strategy has the advantages of providing continuity of employment and of protecting the existing customer base. It also avoids a number of problems that may arise when the plant is allowed to close without a definite plan for it to reopen – such as the loss of key workers, and the difficulty of maintaining the organization of the workforce after the closure. Moreover, a workforce whose planning for a WTO is sufficiently well advanced to arrange a 'rescue' may be well placed to negotiate the transfer of equipment and stocks on good terms as part of a redundancy settlement.

On the other hand, the 'rescue' strategy also has some severe disadvantages. First, there will often be insufficient time for a thorough appraisal of business prospects or for the workforce to come to terms with the implications of commercial self-reliance. This may lead to the new enterprise losing money and having to make further reductions in labour in its early months. Second, in several countries the continuity of employment may compromise employees entitlement to redundancy benefit (even though this may be needed to finance the new venture). Third, the workforce may have to pay a high price for the assets – because they are valued as a 'going concern', or because they are transferred in total whereas not all are required for the new enterprise; or because many of the liabilities of the old business (e.g. to suppliers) must also be accepted – as in the case of MOSTA (Box 6.4).

The 'phoenix' strategy is marked by a clear break in production and trading. It is adopted when a takeover of the existing business without interruption is either impossible or undesirable. Characteristically, a group of former employees tries to purchase a selection of the residual assets from a receiver or liquidator to provide the basis for a new, and generally much smaller, enterprise. Hence, following a 'phoenix' strategy to form a workers' co-operative or worker-owned enterprise will be much more like starting up a new enterprise 'from scratch' – except that those involved will already know each other, having worked together in the old business; they may be able to obtain equipment and stocks cheaply; and they may already have a range of personal contacts among potential customers. The cases of Aire Habitat (Box 7.3) and Duncans of Edinburgh (Box 3.4) are examples.

This approach has a number of advantages: because there is usually more time, it is easier to plan the business on a realistic basis (for instance, by obtaining more suitable premises). The problem of job losses becomes rather more tractable. Everyone has already lost their jobs – so the question is no longer 'Who will be made redundant?', but instead 'Who are suitable and willing to join the project?' As a result, selection and a self-selection seem to ensure a more committed workforce, an effect often enhanced by the delay which allows time for attitudes to change and for additional training to be undertaken (see Duncans of Edinburgh in Box 3.4). For these reasons the phoenix approach is preferred by some agencies (for example, the Scottish Cooperative Development Committee – see Box 7.1). On the other hand, the proportion of jobs saved in a 'phoenix' is usually much smaller; and too much uncertainty and delay may undermine commitment and lead to workers with vital skills drifting and seeking employment elsewhere. Experts at CG-SCOP believe that if the closure lasts for more than three months the enterprise will tend to fail.

Each of the strategies will be more appropriate in particular circumstances. A 'rescue' is more likely to be attempted where the workforce has advance warning of closure, where the existing owners are not obstructing the WTO, where trading continuity is important, and where the new enterprise will provide a similar, or somewhat reduced range of goods or services. A 'phoenix' strategy will be more appropriate where the activity of the business must be more radically reduced or redirected, where trading continuity is less important, and where a smaller (and more coherent) group of workers is involved.

In practice, of course, a workforce may set out to achieve a 'rescue', but in the end only a 'phoenix' may be realized. And very often what happens will fall somewhere between the two strategies – so much depends on the particular circumstances and the reasons for the company's crisis (e.g. insolvency arising from financial mismanagement; a long-term failure to modernize equipment; a problem of management succession; etc.). Nevertheless, the distinction is useful because it highlights the different commercial logics on which a WTO may be based. Moreover, the collective dynamic and organizational problems and processes associated with these strategies are usually very different. Finally, the distinction throws some light on the particular problems of 'large plant' closures. These are often marked by conditions that make it difficult to prepare a credible business plan especially in the time available. In many cases key workers will have been transferred elsewhere, and the plant and equipment is obsolete, so the prospects for an enterprise of any size being salvaged will be extremely poor. However, it is not uncommon for plants with many skilled workers and containing quite modern equipment to be shut down. When this has happened it has been reasonable to consider whether a new range of products could be developed or introduced to provide the commercial basis for a WTO, thereby protecting the local community from the full impact of the closure.

The problem, however, is that the identification, development and introduction of new products requires time, facilities, and resources. Hence, this can only be undertaken, if at all, by first achieving a WTO on the basis of some existing products (a 'rescue'), or on the basis of some niche in other markets, such as subcontracting (a 'phoenix'), thereby providing a financial, technical and organizational basis for the development of new products. But in practice this approach is precisely what is so difficult. A rescue, for example, will often be impossible because of, for example, parent company control of existing markets, the fact that the plant is solely a production unit lacking other management functions, over-capacity in the sector, etc. And where rescues of large plants have been achieved by the workforce it has for a variety of reasons proved very difficult to undertake product development thereafter.[4] A 'phoenix' strategy, on the other hand, may well generate one or more viable businesses, but generally these will only involve a fraction of the workforce and will be too small to sustain the facilities and costs of product development.

Conflicting economic and social imperatives

All WTOs experience a fundamental tension between their conflicting economic and social goals. The need to ensure continuing economic viability confronts both the broader social concerns of a firm-saving WTO and the desperate concern to preserve employment, in a job-saving WTO. It could be argued in the latter case that the conflict is more apparent than real: economic viability must take precedence or all the jobs are endangered. In practice it is seldom so straightforward – it is a matter of judgement and risk assessment.

Moreover, a WTO that remains unanimously and single-mindedly a job-saving affair is actually quite rare. Much more complicated attachments to the undertaking usually emerge, especially among those who commit considerable time and energy to making it happen. If they are to be sustained such efforts require rather more by way of inspiration than the hope that it will be a short sentence, that one can get rid of it all before too long to a new owner and turn the clock back. In general, people resist change that is not, for them, goal-directed; but if they have to change they will soon devise some personally relevant goals to pursue through the change. Perhaps this is just a matter of giving some meaning to what would otherwise be experienced as simply an imposition. But in any event, people usually try to make the best of things – in a WTO that means they start investing the project with a range of other aspirations.[5]

In consequence it is not unusual for a WTO to be seen as, in some measure, an opportunity to 'do things differently', for example:

- to change working methods and the organization of production by e.g. reducing the degree of division of labour, allocating more decision-making and responsibility to shop-floor level, by abolishing highly competitive or otherwise demeaning structures and procedures;
- to develop management forms which support and stabilize co-operative elements in the new employee-owned firm, and to ensure those who have taken the risks are kept informed and their concerns given full consideration;
- to reduce or abolish wage differentials or to change methods of payments;
- to set up social and environmental criteria for production decisions and new products to be developed.

The case of AN in Box 3.3 provides a very clear illustration of this.

Box 3.3   The case of AN (AM Maschinenbau-und Umweltschutzanlagen GmbH/Bremen)

AN was rescued from the Bremen plant of J M Voith GmbH, a South German company with a good name in mechanical engineering. The Bremen plant was established in 1941 as part of war industry, with civil production after 1945. In the 1970s employment peaked at 320. Closure of the plant was announced in October 1982, to take place in 1983. After negotiations, the date of closure was postponed to 31 March 1984. When closure was first announced, employment was down to 170. Preceding the announcement, the mother company had invested huge sums in new technology (thus avoiding taxes on much of their profits). The central production capacities created thereby had to be used, so orders were shifted from Bremen to South Germany, piecemeal, even though the Bremen plant was still an effective production unit.

However, the works council had become aware of these early signs of plant closure, and its chairman, supported by some other workers, was well prepared. A few weeks before the closure was announced they had set up a 'new products' working group, knowing that if the company should withdraw from Bremen they needed to have some product ideas as a precondition for saving the firm. Nevertheless, negotiations after closure was announced failed. Instead of becoming unemployed the workers decided to take over the firm. The first step was to set up an 'economy (and legal questions) commission' and to transform the new product working group into a 'technology commission', serving as basic managerial organs of the rescue initiative and as basis for the co-operation of worker activists and external advisers and experts. Plenary meetings every two weeks, open to staff and supporters, completed the basic structure and was co-ordinated by the works council chairman.

The worker takeover initiative successfully negotiated support from the state government which, in the end, rented the premises, using part of it for a youth training centre and subletting the rest to AN. The state also bought the machinery and let it to the workers' initiative. The company was moved to provide some minor support which helped to make it possible to continue with the old business and to prepare the new company at the same time. This necessary bit of co-operation was, last not least, secured by the workforce of the company's main plant when they threatened to take industrial action unless the company showed a supportive attitude towards the takeover initiative in the Bremen plant. It was made clear, however, that the workers' company would not be allowed to continue with the old production.

The new company, AN, officially started trading in April 1984, one day after the Voith plant had been closed. It used the legal structure of GmbH (limited company). Fifty of the employees had formed an association, open to supporters, which is the collective shareholder (with contributions by the employees of 1,000 DM each); some sympathy capital had multiplied the available sum of money a few times. However, the new enterprise was severely under-capitalized. The workers decided not to seek bank loans. Instead, initial wage costs were heavily reduced by unemployment benefits and other labour administration payments, as well as by employing few members at the start – only five full-time. By September, 1986 employment was up to forty-three. The first larger sum of outside money came in in 1985 when the federal government, complemented by a regional government grant, reacted positively to an AN application for research and development money for a new product (an-aerobic fermenting facilities) totalling 1.5 million DM.

The company still relies on contract work – which is quite different from what the workforce had intended when they decided to produce new products which had to be 'socially useful, ecologically sound and not related to any military production'. They have achieved the first step towards economic consolidation, but there is still a long way to go to realize the central ideas in their plan.

This is also true for their ideas of a co-operative self-management. Unprofessional management, lack of discipline, of social awareness and responsibility, among other things, have led to a partial (and temporary?) retreat from ideas like equal pay, individual autonomy within collectively agreed frameworks of work organization, and other 'grass roots reforms'. At present, there is a tendency by the majority of the workforce to go back to more traditional ways of managing the company and organizing production and labour processes.

Regardless of whether and how widely such broadly social aspirations have emerged, the first occasion when economic and social priorities come in conflict is usually over the question of job losses. This is also the occasion when the workforce must start embracing the implications of their own responsibility for achieving viability. This is the case even if the workforce is not directly involved in preparing the plan – because otherwise they may reject a well-considered plan prepared by others. In smaller units with good management–worker and worker–worker relations this appreciation of commercial realities may develop quickly. Needless to say, in some larger units, especially in Britain, France and Italy, the situation is very different. In these cases a very fundamental reorientation on the part of the workforce is required. Indeed, this reorientation may not be achieved so that the pursuit of a WTO, and external support for it, is in reality another means to preserve the existing enterprise, rather than a means of transforming it.

The clearest indication of the extent to which this reorientation is occurring is provided by the attitude of the workforce towards staffing levels. Since the rationale for the attempt is the preservation of jobs, and given the pre-eminence of solidarity as a trade union value, the reluctance to countenance substantial reductions in the numbers employed is utterly understandable. Nevertheless, substantial reductions will often be required. In strictly commercial terms, most WTO are typical cases of the business 'turnaround' situation – and, in varying degrees depending on circumstances, the usual 'turnaround' strategies will be required (Slatter 1984). Indeed, one of the reasons for the crisis may have been a reluctance to cut back the business to a profitable core, soon enough. At the extreme, a large economic unit may contain only the basis for one or two quite small businesses, based on particular skills, assets, or local markets. More normally, a substantial part of the enterprise may have prospects for viability, based on cost reductions and a reorientation towards more specific market segments.

It is not surprising, therefore, that insofar as figures are available *substantially fewer workers are employed after a WTO than in the same enterprise before the WTO.* Moreover, a reluctance to grapple with this issue may prevent the attempt succeeding (quite apart from prejudicing its longer term success). For example, a refusal by the workers' leadership to contemplate the job losses required for any chance of viability contributed to the collapse of discussions on a WTO before the closure of a large factory in Clydebank, Scotland. Nor can it be assumed that in such cases the leaders are really hoping to maintain employment but have miscalculated the prospects for external support: more likely their decisions represent an informed choice reflecting both the view that closure is better than an abandonment of deeply held principles and a pragmatic assessment of the financial risks and complications in respect of redundancy payments etc. Which is another way of saying that, in the event, a WTO is not an option that everyone will choose, however dire the circumstances.

On the other hand it often happens that steps are taken, more or less deliberately, by the workforce or by external parties, to accommodate the conflicting economic and social imperatives. That is, involuntary job losses are minimized in ways that are compatible with the workforce's acceptance of the need for enterprise viability. This can occur in one or a combination of the following ways:

First, some of the older workers, appreciating the need for job losses, may volunteer for redundancy to assist the WTO. Government early retirement schemes, where they exist, have certainly made this easier.

Second, the issue is not strictly one of job losses, but of cost reduction. Although not popular with trade unions, short-time and part-time work are options that have been chosen, usually as temporary devices. The Public Labour Administration in the Federal Republic of Germany has on occasions collaborated in such arrangements and paid unemployment benefit to those working less than a certain number of hours. It should also be noted that where jobs are lost, this may only be temporary. There are cases where some or all of those who lost their jobs have been offered the chance of re-employment later, when the business improved.

Third, where the enterprise in crisis has ceased trading but the WTO attempt is subject to delay and uncertainty, workers may drift away – for example, to take other jobs, or because they do not believe the project will succeed.

Fourth, the need to plan a viable operation does not necessarily mean the attempt is completely determined by existing market forces. As experience in the Federal Republic demonstrates, public funding may be available for specific services – such as industrial training, the production of particular non-market goods or the development of socially useful products – even though such schemes may be difficult to arrange. Likewise, the purchasing arrangements of local government can be used to assist a WTO. The point is simply that anticipated outgoings must not exceed the anticipated income – wherever it comes from.

Fifth, the extreme difficulty of the 'jobs issue' is more easily tackled in the context of an established co-operative movement – as in Italy, where other co-operatives may assist the rescue either by taking on some of the redundant workers, or by placing orders with the new enterprise. As yet there are limits to the scope for such assistance. But numerous instances exist, and they suggest that the labour and co-operative movements may create conditions in which they can pursue solidarity more effectively among enterprises rather than simply within them. Arguably, such a model, midway between plan and market, deserves far wider consideration.[6]

The importance of searching for ways of reconciling the conflicting social and economic principles is worth stressing. It will often be possible to impose on a group attempting a WTO an expert solution concerning the best level of employment. When this happens a crucial learning opportunity is cut short and the psychological ownership of the project is undermined. In addition, the experts, sympathetic or otherwise, do sometimes get it wrong: in one case in the German printing industry, the workforce's insistence on saving all the job forced the external advisory group to reconsider its initial analysis of the commercial situation of the company. In doing so they became convinced that it was basically a sound business that had suffered an insolvency crisis; and that cutting back the business and reducing the workforce might endanger the recovery altogether.

Obtaining information and advice

A credible business plan is based on information – in particular, information on markets and costs. In this respect the attitude of the existing owners and management, or of the receiver, is likely to be critical. Where there is a positive attitude, the necessary business information is readily provided – indeed, contracts may be offered to the new enterprise and the transfer of fixed assets, stocks etc., may be negotiated on reasonable terms (in some cases, as part of a redundancy settlement). Such assistance may be prompted by sympathy, a desire to maintain good public relations, a concern to manage the closure smoothly, or out of a commercial interest in seeing an independent business survive, at least for a time. The case of Duncans of Edinburgh in Box 3.4 illustrates the enormous difference such assistance can make (see also the rich combination of motives in the case of Northwest Pre-Cast in Box 4.1).

Box 3.4   The case of Duncans of Edinburgh

Duncans were a well established Edinburgh confectioners who, at their own suggestion, were taken over by Rowntrees in 1927. Rowntrees were, and remain, one of the country's leading chocolate manufacturers and they have a reputation as a progressive employer (for the better part of a century the name has been associated with philanthropic activity and social reform – through the work of Joseph Rowntree and the Trusts he established). For many years the Duncans range was continued and sold under its own name, enjoying great popularity, especially in Scotland. However, in 1967 Rowntrees phased it out – at that time demand for speciality sweets was weak; the market was interested in well-known varieties. Nevertheless, the main Duncans factory continued in operation and an extension to the factory was added in the mid-1970s. Ten years later the picture had changed: technological developments meant that larger volumes of chocolates could be produced in far smaller spaces – the old Duncans factory, which still employed about 800 workers (about 600 full-time and 200 part-time), was no longer needed and plans for closure were announced in December 1984.

For six months the trade unions explored the possibility of maintaining a chocolate manufacturing presence in Edinburgh that would employ several hundred people. This came to nothing, but Bob Baxter the maintenance manager believed a smaller scheme might be viable. He brought together a group of fourteen workers – mainly skilled production personnel like himself – to plan a new firm and they soon developed the idea of re-establishing the Duncans name (at one point members of the group stood on busy street corners with questionnaires to find out how well the name was remembered). Initially, Rowntrees were distinctly unenthusiastic about the initiative: they had taken enough stick in the press already about the impending closure and did not want to make matters worse by being associated with what they felt was a commercially misconceived venture. Nevertheless, they were concerned over the effects of the closure on the local community, so in collaboration with the Scottish Development Agency (SDA) they provided some funds for a feasibility study. The consultants reported favourably: people were tiring of volume-selling products, they were more restrained and discerning, there was an opportunity for a speciality Scottish manufacturer – and the Duncans name was still well enough remembered, by those aged 35 and above, to be an important asset.

Rowntrees remained sceptical: where was the management team, the business plan? Bob Baxter remained determined: he and his group began working with the Leith Enterprise Trust (Rowntrees has established links with three local enterprise agencies as part of the employment counselling prior to closure) and also with Jim Marshall, a successful Scottish businessman, who became an advisor to the project (and subsequently a non-executive chairman of the board) and who provided much needed commercial experience. In early 1986 Bob himself took a six-month, part-time, small-business management course and at about the same time he was able to recruit Mike Dunning, one of the senior Rowntrees salesman for Scotland, to join the proposed company – although not based at the Duncans factory he was well known to Bob and the others from many years' experience with Rowntrees in Scotland. Like several others in the group he had been offered another job elsewhere with Rowntrees but was reluctant to move. He brought with him vital sales and marketing experience and numerous personal contacts in the trade. In due course they went back to Rowntrees and the SDA with a detailed business plan.

Faced with this and a well-rounded management team Rowntrees were persuaded that the project could work – and from then on did a great deal to make sure it would work. They provided, free, all the plant and machinery the new firm needed and could use; they gave them use of all the original Duncan copyrights and brand names; they sold the new factory annex to the company for what the new owners considered a very fair price indeed; they provided an interest free loan; and they provided advice (on a continuing basis as it has turned out) on a range of matters from the requirements of the labelling regulations to the price of hazelnuts. Perhaps one impulse behind all this assistance was a concern to make good the Rowntree image locally; but Rowntrees never publicized the extent of their assistance. More likely, the project had galvanized the company's philanthropic tradition.

In any event, with this help – and increasingly the support of major customers and suppliers – the promoters were able to put together a financial package based on share capital totalling nearly £125,000 (mainly redundancy payments, but topped up by personal savings including some from friends and family), the Rowntrees loan, a loan from a high street bank on commercial terms, and smaller loans, but on favourable terms from the SDA and British Coal Enterprise (Edinburgh was one of their 'assistance areas').

With Bob Baxter as managing director, Duncans of Edinburgh started trading in March 1988, some nine months after the Rowntrees factory closed and six months after the last workers were laid off. The response of Scottish sweet eaters – and the Scots are notorious sweet eaters – was immediate and enthusiastic. As demand rose to four times what had been anticipated the business plan was quickly left behind, and Duncans were taking on more staff and struggling with how to finance their own expansion. Within a year they were employing over forty people full time – and in the run up to Christmas when additional part-time and temporary staff were taken on, there had been seventy employees on the books. After the euphoria of these early months Duncans is now entering a phase of more steady growth and consolidation in which it aims to extend its product range and secure 'shelf space' on a permanent basis in an even wider range of outlets.

The organization of the company has changed enormously. For example, there are no longer any job demarcations and the wage structure has been reduced to three bands only – for process workers, for supervisory and maintenance staff, and for the management group. Most importantly, there is now a quite different atmosphere on the shop floor with far more commitment being shown, far fewer of what Bob Baxter calls the 'unnecessary squabbles', and a greater sharing of information about the progress of the business. Partly this arises from the sense of ownership among shareholders – but even the non-shareholders feel the difference and admit to having a different attitude to the new firm.

The project was not conceived in any sense as a co-operative. The founding group do not have all equal shareholdings and there are a minority of outside shareholders. Nevertheless, the shares are not freely transferable – they must be offered first to other shareholders. Originally, the investment seems to have been, for most of those involved, simply a way of buying a job. With the firm's success, feelings about the employee shareholdings have become more complex: it offers protection against a takeover but those holding the shares cannot ignore the potential capital gain they would realize if they decided to sell up – and already one or two discreet enquiries have been made by large firms. However, at this stage the firm is still establishing itself and the need to raise additional capital will provide a chance for more employees to buy in. In the longer term Bob Baxter's personal feeling is that he would like to keep majority control within the workforce. One possibility is that Duncans will adapt another Rowntrees idea and create a shareholding trust that would gradually buy out the original shareholders, thus rewarding their effort and sacrifice while providing a more permanent arrangement for substantial employee ownership.

By contrast, a negative attitude can result in even the most basic information being withheld, obstruction regarding the purchase of assets, or unrealistic valuations being placed on them. The extent of such obstruction, and the reasons for it, vary considerably – from having an ideological or personal hostility to the attempt and its leadership, to the fear of having the new company as a competitor. Whatever the reasons, such negativity often prevents WTOs from proceeding, and it is often one reason why external political support is so important: it can be used to put pressure on the owners to provide information to the workforce.

In cases where the existing owner is not co-operating with the WTO the problems of obtaining the necessary information – be it formally or informally – are accentuated when:

- the members of the workforce attempting the takeover do not include any managerial or senior office staff;
- the plant is purely a production unit, with marketing design and finance functions located elsewhere;
- the WTO cannot be based on the existing product or service, so information about these will be less relevant;
- the WTO has to develop a new customer base;
- the imminent closure of the plant, or auctioning of assets, creates acute time pressure;
- part of the company information held by some members of the workforce is deemed 'strictly confidential', and they could in principle face prosecution for sharing it (this has been a real problem in Germany where labour law has soaked into all the cracks and chinks of industrial relations).

The more of these conditions hold – as, for instance, in the case of many large plant closures – the more difficult it will be to prepare a credible plan.

Moreover, the problem is not simply one of obtaining information – a great deal of essential knowledge and experience, especially in the field of production know-how, is already held by the workforce. Yet it requires organizational skill and leadership to ensure the workers make their knowledge available to the planning process. In addition the very concept of business plan is likely to be unfamiliar to those involved in the WTO, who will also have to make difficult decisions on a legal and organizational framework for the venture. Hence the workforce will require quite extensive support and advice in grappling with these issues.[7] In practice, however, for a whole variety of reasons many WTO attempts have difficulty in obtaining the sort of competent, sympathetic and sustained advice that they require.

In the first place the leaders of the workforce will not be aware of all that they need to know – and they may even be reluctant to acknowledge their need for assistance. Hence they may fail to seek out, or to accept, offers of assistance from those with relevant expertise. Instead, they may rely on the efforts of union or co-operative association officials who may have time, but still lack vital experience.

Second, conventional business advice agencies are generally quite unsuitable. They are unfamiliar with co-operative or self-managed legal frameworks and organizational forms. They usually do not identify socially or politically with a WTO project. Above all, their conception of the consultant–client relationship is too restrictive: it does not include promoting managerial understanding and skills among the workforce.

Third, advice from more appropriate sources may be unavailable because no support agencies or networks exist in the locality; they lack relevant experience or expertise; or they lack the time and resources (they may even be working voluntarily) to support an uncertain venture over a prolonged period.

Fourth, there may be cultural or other differences between those who might provide the support and trade-union-based attempts at WTO. For example, in Germany and the UK, the established co-operative movements have sometimes been unsympathetic to attempts at WTO; and the marked cultural differences between the alternative or new co-operative movements on the one hand, and industrial workers on the other, have proved an obstacle (though not insoluble) in some cases.

Fifth, a wide range of expertise will often be required, including industry-specific knowledge of market trends or production technology, expertise in business planning and financial appraisal, familiarity with company law and procedure regarding receivership and bankruptcy, negotiating experience and expertise, and familiarity with the numerous questions concerning legal frameworks. In addition, such potential advisors must have the credibility and 'consulting skills' to work effectively with the workforce and its leadership during an intense, even traumatic, period – as well as with state officials, bankers, suppliers and customers.

Some of these reasons also help to explain the difficulties that have sometimes arisen in the relationship between the workforce and the advisors. The advisors may become impatient with the reluctance of the workforce to accept the realities of the situation or to follow their advice. The workforce may dump their frustrations on the advisor, who will often be the bearer of bad tidings. The leadership of the workforce may feel their position is being undermined by the suggestion of new ways of involving the workforce. Or they may feel that the aims of the WTO (and their position) are being subverted by managerial approaches. Or it may be that different advisors are involved in respect of different issues, but their approaches and suggestions are incompatible, thereby leading to splits between the 'political' and the 'technical' leaders and their associated advisors.

Getting organized

The planning activities we have been considering require the creation of an organization. Who is included in the project and on what terms? Who is entitled to negotiate with other parties? How are the contents of the plan decided? What legal entity will take over the assets? Hence the planning process is simultaneously an organizing process. Moreover, the forms and style of organization that emerge will have enormous implications for the success, or otherwise, of the WTO. In the first place, the extent to which the organization is initiated and steered by the workforce itself affects their understanding of and commitment to the project. In addition, the emerging organization will be expressed in a choice of legal framework, and in a constitution and structure that will constrain many future developments. Finally, the planning, negotiation and preparation for the takeover are a formative experience for the enterprise that emerges – its precedents, unwritten rules and myths are being created, its character and identity are taking shape. This process continues into the period after the takeover, but even if they have to be reassessed later, these initial assumptions, practices and norms will profoundly affect the development of the enterprise.

It is this organizing process – the urgent creation of a business organization of, by and for the workforce – that gives a WTO its special character (and distinguishes it from conventional 'turnarounds', management buyouts, 'new start' co-operatives, and other employment initiatives). Hence an appreciation of the distinctive organizational dimensions is essential in understanding WTO as a social phenomenon. It is also an absolute precondition for any consideration of measures and strategies to support WTOs.

As we have seen, WTOs have on occasions been stimulated and guided by external parties – trade unions, co-operative associations, or agents of the local government; and they may also be initiated, directed and executed by a comparatively small group of established leaders (shop stewards, technical or administrative staff) on behalf of the workforce and with their acquiescence. In such cases the WTO itself may be achieved in a very orderly fashion. More commonly, however, a WTO is a somewhat desperate collective undertaking in which a substantial proportion of the workforce is, for varying periods, actively involved. In these cases it is not uncommon for the process to be marked by confusion, uncertainty and conflict. Which, then, of these types of WTO tends to be more successful in the longer run – the orderly, directed and 'well-organized'; or the disorderly, improvised and self-organized?

Allowing that the question is simplistic – most WTOs have elements of both patterns and fall between the pure cases – it could certainly be argued, on the basis of available case material, that those WTOs achieved through a 'disorderly' process perform at least as well if not better than their 'orderly' counterparts. A more cautious answer, in the absence of anything like adequate data, is that both patterns may succeed or fail depending on circumstances.

Thus, it is clear, especially from the French experience, that directed WTOs often run into commercial difficulties – they fail to achieve the necessary improvements in performance. On the other hand, where, for example, a recapitalizing of the enterprise is the main requirement for viability without a need for far-reaching changes in production activities and organization; or where the workforce does not wish to take on management responsibility as well as ownership; then the 'orderly' WTO process can provide an appropriate foundation for the new enterprise. They are, in effect, small-scale versions of financial WTOs. In a comparable way, it is clear, especially from the Italian experience (e.g. the case of CLG in Boxes 2.2 and 6.2), that a 'disorderly' process need not be debilitating and doomed to failure – though these certainly can be the effects. It seems that a good measure of disorder can often be creative and lead to more effective forms of organization. Because a WTO is often a moment of rapid organizational change it is not surprising if it often appears passionate, untidy, and incoherent. In such circumstances, static and conventional conceptions of 'proper organization' are quite inappropriate. In particular, the widespread and active involvement of the workforce in the organization of the WTO is often essential for several reasons.

First, the sheer range of tasks to be undertaken in order to formulate a credible scheme requires the time and effort of a wide number of 'activists'. Such tasks may include enlisting community and political support as well as working on business, organizational and legal issues.

Second, the workforce will usually need to make a financial contribution in one way or another through individual loans or shares, or the negotiation of redundancy terms that partly substitute collective compensation in the form of assets for individual payments. Again, this is only likely – and, indeed, proper – if the workforce has debated the problems and possibilities in sufficient depth to appreciate the risks involved.

Third, substantial cost reductions in the production area are usually required and may involve reduced wages, reduced staffing levels, new working practices and a changed approach to supervision. Attempting to impose such changes on the workforce achieves, at best, far less than is possible when the workforce themselves identify the problems and formulate their own solutions. In addition, of course, the workforce may wish to change the production organization and payments system for other reasons.

Finally, a significant proportion of the workforce will *expect* to be closely involved in mounting the attempt at a WTO. Especially when the failing enterprise has a history of poor industrial relations, a WTO is likely to become a vehicle for aspirations towards worker's management and democratic control. For a minority, such views are an expression of an explicit political ideology and commitment; more commonly these aspirations are less specific and reflect a populist ethos of collective self-reliance. The extent of the greater influence desired, and its significance for individuals, usually varies greatly. Many will not be interested; and others because of their personal economic prospects will consider it entirely secondary to the primary concern of saving jobs. Such differences in orientation may be hard to reconcile and they have on occasion contributed to severe conflicts between political and technical leaders. Hence, occasions that enable a widespread involvement in preparing the WTO are needed not just to satisfy the expectations of some workers, but also because it is important to generate a shared understanding of the philosophy of the project – this will usually be needed for the constitution of the enterprise as a legal entity, quite apart from other reasons.

In short, it is through their involvement in the takeover process that the workforce take on the *psychological* ownership of the project and evolve a shared appreciation of its meaning and priorities. It is from this psychological ownership and common understanding that the determination and willingness to change established patterns of work arises. Nevertheless, the difficulties in achieving and sustaining such involvement are formidable.

In the first place, the complexity, uncertainty and unfamiliarity of the issues involved in preparing a WTO may be intimidating and overwhelming for many of the workforce. Passivity, fatalism and a sense of powerlessness are understandable reactions. Hence, even if workers attend meetings they remain spectators. This is partly a problem of understanding – arising from the difficulty of grappling with unfamiliar issues and ideas (legal questions, cash flow, market trends etc.). More fundamentally, however, the social process of the WTO is actually rather threatening: a WTO undermines established occupational roles – for example, clerk, supervisor, trade unionist. But these are a large element in our social and personal identities. Especially for those who have over many years become accustomed to restricted roles, the demands of a WTO are often unsettling: it offers the anxiety of autonomy in place of the security of dependence. For example, at the end of a long conference to plan a WTO one shopfloor worker expressed outright fury at the proceedings: he had come to hear what he as an ordinary machinist would have to produce, and he had heard nothing concrete all week – only vague talk about problems and possibilities that he considered were nothing to do with him. Because he had expressed his frustration, it could be discussed and the underlying assumptions about his role in the WTO explored. The person concerned went on to play a leading part in the rescue and enterprise created.

In short, involvement in a WTO often changes people's lives. Partly for this reason it may be very stressful, and many of the workforce may be very reluctant to become involved because of the demands it makes on them. They may also come under strong family pressure not to participate (through strong family support also occurs). A reluctance to become in-volved may coexist with the diffuse expectations of greater influence and control mentioned above, and hence the attitudes of the workforce will often be varied and complex. Some will be determined to be closely involved; some will refuse to become involved, insisting that the leadership should be trusted and widespread participation is unnecessary and dangerous; many will be ambivalent, uncertain, and on occasions inconsistent. How many of the workforce respond in these different ways obviously varies greatly, but in general it seems that the older and less skilled the employees, the more hesitant or reluctant they are likely to be about becoming actively involved in the WTO.

A second obstacle to widespread active involvement may be provided by the social divisions among the workforce. For example, traditional tensions between different occupational groups (skilled and unskilled; manual and non-manual) may generate distrust, tension and defensiveness. (The case of Pellicciai Riuniti in Box 3.1 provides an example.) Or existing authority relations may be carried over into the organization of the WTO so that participation is inhibited. Or the presence of different trade unions with rival strategies and philosophies may generate conflicts which deter some workers from becoming involved and restrict the accepted contribution of others. By contrast, it is noticeable that when only a fairly homogenous group of the manual workers remains to attempt the WTO, it is usually far more cohesive and effective – though obviously the absence of other types of worker creates other problems. Not surprisingly, therefore, it seems to be the case that more people become more effectively involved in a 'safe' social setting.[8] Such an atmosphere is more difficult to achieve where the social divisions run deep – which is, of course, more common in larger enterprises.

A third obstacle is often provided, paradoxically, by the very trade-union organization through which most WTO attempts arise and are pursued. Often, the structure of a trade-union branch is strongly hierarchical and unitary, and decision-making and consent is usually achieved through representatives, mass meetings and a heavy emphasis on the norm of solidarity. These can provide acceptable mechanisms for democracy in the adversary contexts of industrial relations, where decisions will be reduced to simple binary choices (e.g. accept the offer or not; take industrial action or not).

However, the organizational training this provides (on top of the socialization of the day-to-day work experience) can be a serious handicap. In planning a WTO the business and organizational issues involved cannot be sensibly handled as if they are binary choices. This is because by the time the issues have been structured and simplified to this point, most of the key decisions will already have been resolved. In reality, the decision-making process in preparing a WTO involves a multiplicity of options, great uncertainty and considerable ambiguity. As the discussions proceed, as the external situation changes, as more information becomes available, as attitudes change, the issues are continually reformulated. At particular points, important strategic choices sometimes become, or appear evident. But the process is iterative, as much concerned with redefining options as with choosing between them. Hence those who are not involved in this process and the learning associated with it are often unable to appreciate the options that result from it.

Different ways of organizing participation are therefore necessary in order to facilitate involvement and promote cohesion – mass meetings, single representative channels and appeals for solidarity, are insufficient. Such problems are accentuated where the initiative for a WTO arises externally from union or co-operative association officials adopting a 'top-down' approach (France, Italy). They are also accentuated where there is conflict between unions or groups of workers: in such situations wider participation may be seen as a threat to unity and the leadership's control.

The inadequacies of conventional trade-union organization as a vehicle for a WTO and self-management are shown most clearly in cases of 'trade-union management' – where the leaders attempt to combine their trade-union position with that of senior day-to-day management. This pattern has occurred quite often in both France and the UK and it is usually disastrous – both commercially and in terms of worker participation and influence (the cases of Unicorn (Thomas and Thornley 1989) and TCS in Box 6.3 are examples). However, there is nothing at all inevitable about such developments and trade unionists have on occasions abandoned their traditional practices and experimented with much more open and flexible forms (the cases of AN in Box 3.3 and CLG in Box 2.2 are relevant).

Fourth, external pressures commonly provide a further obstacle to widespread participation. The shortage of time – sometimes a very few days – may mean that the WTO has to be arranged by a small group of leaders and external advisors, even if their own preferences are for wider involvement and self-management (this was certainly the case at Barnsley Metal Finishers, described in Barnsley Metropolitan Borough Council (undated)). Likewise, the need for continuity of personnel in negotiations with external parties tends to concentrate information, decision-making and authority in a few hands.

In summary, despite its importance, the widespread participation of the workforce in mounting a WTO will often be hard to achieve and maintain. This is likely to be true even if the workforce, its leaders and its advisors are committed in principle to workforce involvement and self-management – because the obstacles are structural, cultural and contextual. As such, the problems of developing effective self-management of the WTO attempt anticipate many of the problems of self-management that arise after a WTO has been achieved. Hence, the importance of the process of organizing the WTO as a formative experience and a learning process for the enterprise that is created.

The problems and possibilities of self-management

Given these obstacles, it is not surprising that the workforce sometimes allows a takeover to be managed on their behalf, or that the numbers who become involved and the extent of their participation are both fairly limited. On the other hand, the threat that the workforce faces, and the simple desire to do something to protect themselves, can generate a powerful collective dynamic towards action and involvement. Hence, despite the obstacles, it is not unusual for substantial numbers of workers to become fully involved in the discussions and preparations leading up to the takeover. In such cases the same factors that tended to restrict involvement become reasons why the organizational process is often conflict-ridden and disorderly.

Thus the complexity and uncertainty of the issues can lead to confusion and rumours and sharply fluctuating attendance at meetings. The social divisions in the workforce can give rise to distrust and power struggles as different groups try to exercise control or protect their positions. Trade-union structures may reflect and polarize these divisions, or become a base for the political leadership in conflict with the technical/managerial leadership and its advisors. The centralization of authority required by urgent and vital external negotiations makes it difficult for the workforce to feel it can influence the process, and may undermine trust – or alternatively, the preparation of the WTO becomes unco-ordinated and inconsistent because many of those involved feel entitled to act and speak on behalf of the project.

Such problems can be severe and raise questions about the wisdom and feasibility of widespread workforce involvement. Thus some of those who have tried to advise WTOs or who have otherwise had dealings with them, consider such 'politicization' and 'radicalization' of the process to be an unfortunate and damaging perversion of the real purpose of the project – the preservation of employment in a credible commercial undertaking. In these terms, the excitement, rhetoric, controversy and confusion are at best an understandable consequence of the tension and anxiety the workforce is experiencing; and at worst the seeds of conflict and disillusion for the future when, after the WTO has succeeded, the commercial requirements for 'proper management' must reassert itself. These views generally appreciate that there are real commercial advantages in improved worker–management relations and a more committed workforce. What they criticize is the undermining of management and the underestimation of its importance which they see as the consequences of attempts to develop participative forms of self-management.

It is obviously true that participation in WTO, as in other contexts, can have costs as well as benefits and doubtless there have been occasions when WTOs have been fatally weakened or discredited by indecisive, inconsistent or incompetent decisions. Nevertheless, as a general comment on the organization of WTOs such views are unduly negative towards ideals of self-management and co-operation. Often, these criticisims seem to be based on a narrow conception of the way management functions and roles must be allocated and organized, and the sorts of people who can undertake them.[9] Alternatively, the criticism fails to appreciate the learning process that is taking place. For example, a temporary phase of opposition to practically any organization of managerial functions and a mistrust of anyone advocating managerial roles occurs quite often in WTOs and is often a comment on the workforce's previous experience of management. Such views and their underlying resentment and mistrust cannot be overcome by trying to dissuade the workforce from pursuing self-management and trying to persuade them they need 'proper' management. Rather, in such situations self-management is probably the quickest route to a realistic appreciation of competent management. In other words populist or radical aspirations towards worker self-management can provide an important bridge between a pre-existing workforce culture of opposition to management on the one hand, and a responsible attitude towards self-management, on the other. They can be functional in facilitating a change of attitudes by helping maintain self-respect and consistent identifications when long-standing assumptions and roles are being transformed.[10]

There is a further reason why these criticisms seem misconceived: self-management may be a necessity because a managerial vacuum exists that cannot realistically be filled by recruitment. It is quite clear that many attempts at WTOs fail or are abandoned because no one is available or willing to take on management roles. To the extent that a commitment to self-management encourages individuals to take on new roles and respon-sibilities – and thereby discover and develop new abilities – it makes a crucial contribution to the success of WTOs.

This issue, perhaps more than any other, is one where the size of the undertaking is crucial. The larger the enterprise the greater the danger that the pursuit of self-management will lead not just to a disorderly, though on balance fruitful, learning process, but to prolonged conflict, demoralization and factionalism. But other factors are important, too, as will be clear in Chapter 6 where the topic is considered further in the light of what happens after the takeover.

4 | The Financing of Worker Takeovers

No amount of careful planning and organizing will achieve a takeover if the workforce is not also able to secure the support of a number of external parties. Suppliers must be persuaded to supply materials – and preferably on normal credit terms, or better. Customers must be found – and preferably ones who will give undertakings or sign contracts that will demonstrate to others that a market exists. Premises may have to be arranged and equipment purchased or leased – again, on the most favourable terms possible. The receiver and major creditors may have to be persuaded to allow more time while preparations for the WTO are completed. But above all, a bank must be persuaded to provide loans – either for working capital, or additionally, to assist in purchasing the fixed assets. This is usually the main obstacle and the problems WTOs face in relation to normal financial institutions explain why, often, a measure of public support is also required. This chapter analyses these problems and reviews the range of measures that have been used to provide an element of public funding for WTOs.

The workforce will not, usually, be able to provide more than a small proportion of the capital required to finance the new enterprise. Redundancy payments (UK and Germany) and the capitalization of unemployment benefit (France and Spain) may mean that some resources are available to them – without concentrating their risks unreasonably by committing savings or using homes as security for loans (though this, too, has happened). Although management buy-outs may also have some difficulties in this respect, the very limited availability of 'own capital' is a distinctive problem in the financing of WTOs – and often of other worker co-operatives and other worker-owned firms.[1] The workforce may be able to reduce the extent of the problem by attracting some 'sympathy capital' (Bradley and Gelb 1983a) – funds provided by friends, relatives, members of the local community or other sympathizers on a non-commercial basis, as in the case of AN (Box 3.3) and also Duncans of Edinburgh (Box 3.4), though in the latter case the share purchases have probably turned into an excellent investment. Once it has exhausted the possibilities of 'own capital' and 'sympathy capital' a WTO has basically three possible sources of funds to approach: the banks, or others prepared to lend on commercial terms; specialist 'soft' loan funds for worker co-operative or similar enterprises;[2] and the government (whether local or national). Although in practice, the specialist institutions and government funds are normally approached first (in order to reduce the amount required from a commercial bank to a more plausible proportion of the total) it will be helpful to start by considering the attitude of the bank towards WTO. In this way some general problems which concern the financing of co-operatives and worker-owned firms and which are relevant to the operation of the speicalist funds and the question of public support, can be outlined.

WTOs and the banks

Not all attempted WTOs have the potential to develop as viable businesses. But those that do are still likely to have trouble in obtaining the finance they require from commercial banks (this includes the large banks associated with the established co-operative movements in the UK and Denmark, or, as in Germany, the trade-union movement; any differences in their lending criteria are not visible to the naked eye – see, for example, the case of SWA in Box 3.2). The reasons for this concern the capital structure of WTO enterprises; the problems of assessing the commercial prospects of a WTO; and the fact that financial institutions are unfamiliar with WTOs. These points are dealt with in turn.

Capital structure: WTOs, like other businesses of a similar size, normally seek to obtain loans to meet their financial requirements. This is immediately problematic, however, because of the need to provide security. As we have seen, the workforce will often be unable to provide anything like sufficient collateral for the loans. Even if a third party (e.g. the local government) is prepared to guarantee the loans or provide some unsecured loans itself, this may still result in a weak financial structure with a very high ratio of debt to equity. Loans are an expensive form of finance, especially for new enterprises. Hence a WTO that relies heavily on loans will be burdened with disproportionately high interest payments and this may raise doubts about the viability of the project.[3]

One solution is to seek to attract equity capital instead of loans – thereby reducing the cost of capital in the early years. However, equity usually carries the right to participate in the control of the enterprise and to enjoy a much greater return if it is successful and grows. As discussed further in the next chapter, this means that external equity participation is problematic and controversial for co-operatives and may not even be an option. Moreover, whether or not a co-operative framework is being used, the workforce may well wish to retain ultimate control, or at least a very substantial degree of influence – which can easily discourage others from investing in the venture.[4] Nor can it be assumed that a merchant bank or venture capital fund would be interested in the first place, as they are generally involved in much larger projects.

Assessing the commercial prospects: When financial institutions assess a business proposal they basically consider two aspects – the idea, and the people. Assessment of the idea concerns the 'hard' business aspects – costs, prices, the extent of the market and so on. Such estimates will usually be subject to considerable uncertainty, and this is the case for many WTOs as well. Some proposals are obviously sound and others are obviously unsound. But most are not obviously one or the other. For example, how does one judge the prospects of an enterprise that has been offered considerable subcontracting work from one or a few major companies? – a common situation for WTOs. Such work may be profitable in the short-term, while leaving the enterprise dependent and vulnerable in the medium and longer-term. Nevertheless, in principle, assessing the basic business ideas of a WTO is no more (and no less) difficult than assessing the business idea of other more conventional enterprises.

Assessment of the people in the project is, however, quite a different matter in the context of a WTO. Normally, banks make judgements about the competence and experience of the person or persons in charge of the project – because without effective management even good ideas will fail, while with effective management even uninspired ideas may be made to work. In the context of a WTO, however, this otherwise reasonable approach is problematic. This is not because the management of the project (in a broad sense) is any less important, but because control of the project is likely to be more fluid and dispersed; and because those playing leading roles are likely to be very different from the usual small business owner-managers.

Of course judgements about the capacity of those involved to run the enterprise effectively must still be made – commitment and determination are not in themselves sufficient. Table 4.1 lists the sorts of factors that could be relevant in forming such judgements, and which those who have been closely involved in supporting WTOs would normally take into account. Clearly, it is hardly surprising if a banker used to assessing conventional small businessmen finds it difficult to assess these factors instead – even if he or she were to recognize their importance.

Table 4.1   Assessing the management capacity of a WTO

Internal

1 *The capacity of the workers leadership*

- Ability and willingness to involve the workforce (e.g. frequency and type of meetings; attention given to informing them etc.).
- Ability to respect the commercial as well as the social concerns of the project (e.g. attitude to job losses).
- Attitude to management (e.g. recognition of importance of managerial functions even if former structure is rejected).

2 *The workforce*

- Adaptability (e.g. age; skill; division of labour; willingness to undertake additional responsibility or training).
- Solidarity and commitment (e.g. homogeneity; shared priorities; attendance at meetings; financial contributions).
- Appreciation of commercial requirements (e.g. willingness to modify working practices).

3 *The management*

- Commercial abilities (e.g. role in failure of source company; skills and experience etc.).
- Suitability for and commitment to the WTO (e.g. management style, willingness to make a financial contribution).

External

4 *Advisory support*

- Suitable advisors available on a continuing basis.
- Relationship with the workforce and its leaders.

5 *Trade-union support*

- Attitude and experience of local officials regarding WTO.

6 *Co-operative movement (or equivalent) support*

- Technical or managerial expertise (consultants, contacts with managers in a similar line of business).
- Cultural support for management and workers (e.g. training; transfer of relevant experience).
- Possibility for commercial support (e.g. contracts, collaborative ventures with other enterprises etc.).

The unfamiliarity of WTOs: A WTO is usually an unconventional proposition which is likely to challenge numerous widely held preconceptions about the capacities of workers to direct their own enterprise. While this may result in an outright ideological rejection of the very possibility, a more common problem is simply excessive caution. As was pointed out above, the 'facts' of any business proposal are usually ambiguous and uncertain and different consultants or experts may produce quite different judgements about the same situation. The 'mental set' of the persons making the appraisal (which is likely to be sceptical with regard to WTO) is therefore an inescapable element in the social definition of 'commercial prospects'. Such considerations do not rest easily with the banking profession's claim to expertise and objectivity. Nevertheless, they are taken for granted in many commercial circles, to the extent that they are the basis for much professional practice in the area of public relations.

These observations about the frailty of human judgement are not offered as an argument for the view that the matter of commercial prospects should simply be treated as a game or ritual. But they do mean that WTOs face peculiar difficulties in securing the support from banks. Even if, in principle, the evaluation of the business idea is no more difficult in the case of WTOs, in practice there is little doubt that the unconventional nature of the undertaking evokes more cautious and critical judgements than would normally be expected.

These three problems – of capital structure, of assessing viability (particularly regarding the people involved and their capacities) and of the attitude of banks towards WTOs – have been explained separately. In practice they are very closely intertwined and it is very difficult to judge their relative importance. For example, the lack of familiarity with WTOs adversely affects the assessment of the management capacity; and it often exaggerates the problem of capital structure (for example, in many contexts members loans are far more sensibly considered as part of the equity base – during the critical years of the enterprise neither they nor the interest they earn can really be withdrawn, and guarantees to this effect can be easily arranged). Likewise, the perceived risks associated with an untried and unfamiliar form of management will increase the concern that any loans are well secured . . . and the fact that an enterprise is being proposed with such high financial gearing will confirm the reservations about the competence of those running it, and the wisdom of the whole idea.

Hence, *taken together*, these three factors mean that WTOs face peculiarly difficult problems in obtaining adequate finance – regardless of the actual commercial prospects. Moreover, since the amount of finance available to an enterprise and the terms on which it is provided are important in affecting its viability, the whole question can easily become circular and judgements about 'poor commercial prospects' can be self-fulfilling prophecies.

This combination of problems is clearly illustrated in the case of Northwest Pre-cast in Box 4.1.

Box 4.1   The case of Northwest Pre-Cast – Part I

Northwest Pre-cast is located in the Lancashire village of Pilling, a small community near the coast. About thirty years ago a family firm started making pre-cast concrete building materials on the present site, trading under the name of Pilling Pre-cast. It was successful and the business grew until the death of the founder. The son who took over the firm was much less successful and in due course the company went into liquidation. It was bought from the liquidator by two businessmen and began trading as Tayban Pre-cast Ltd. Once again the firm prospered. It even opened a small additional factory in Chorley which concentrated on making standard items such as paving slabs and household inspection chambers. The specialist (and very skilled) work continued at Pilling and by the start of the 1980s nearly seventy people were employed there. At this stage, however, the general manager retired and one of the owners died. Once again, the son who came in to take over the management proved far less successful and the firm began to lose money. By 1984 Tayban Pre-cast was in a severe crisis. The solution adopted by Mr Banks the manager was to prepare to relocate the firm to the town of Horwich, near Bolton, and very close to the motorway. This would bring both sites under one roof, allow them to take advantage of the attractive grants and incentives offered by the local authority, and mean that they were well placed to enter the market for much larger items like concrete bridge spans and lintels. The difficulty was that they could not take their workforce with them (since the grants were dependent on creating local employment), and it would take time to build up a skilled workforce in Bolton. The plan, therefore, was for a run-down of the Chorley and Pilling sites while the Bolton site built up. To implement this plan, Bill Neill, then works manager, was given the job of picking the best dozen or so shopfloor employees to continue a skeleton operation at Pilling while the others were made redundant. The hope was that this small team would be able to complete outstanding contracts and maintain Tayban's presence in the specialist market while their capacity was being developed at Bolton. In due course, if there was sufficient work the Pilling operation could continue, but otherwise it would be closed down.

This was not a scheme which held great appeal for the workforce involved. In particular, Jim Stamper who had been estimating and costing for Tayban, considered the prospects to be extremely bleak. As the discussions progressed during the autumn of 1984 he began to put forward an alternative proposal –

that Tayban should transfer the site to a workers co-operative to continue the production. To begin with the rest of the workforce were not interested and Jim did not know who to contact for advice.

But Mr Banks himself was prepared to help. Evidently, he felt some concern about the local impact of his relocation decision and the forty redundancies that were in hand; but it is also clear that the scheme seemed to offer him several advantages – including the chance of a continuing rent from a site that would otherwise have been extremely difficult to let. Obviously, too, he did not see the co-operative as a serious competitor: the restructured Tayban would probably be concentrating on a different type of work. Besides, what prospects could there be for a firm with no real managers, no salesmen, no accountants. . . .

So it was Mr Banks who phoned around and was referred to the newly formed Lancashire Co-operative Development Agency. As a result, Mike Hynes drove up to Pilling on a cold grey day for a meeting in the canteen. It was a dismal occasion. There were no clear proposals – only vague ideas. Those present were prepared to pursue the idea of a co-operative because 'it was a straw they could grasp'. But at least it was a start. A series of meetings to explore the possibilities followed.

By the end of November Northwest Pre-cast was registered as a co-operative and some of the main elements of the plan were clear. The co-operative would lease the site and some remaining fixtures and equipment from Tayban Ltd. They would also be given the raw materials on site to allow them to complete the outstanding orders for which they would receive a percentage of the price from Tayban. By this time too Jim had persuaded twelve other people that the co-operative could be viable. He had argued that if they did not join the scheme they would have spent their redundancy money within a year, so even if the co-operative only lasted for that long they would do just as well as if they had been unemployed with their redundancy money.

Mike Hynes had the problem of putting together a financial package to make the WTO possible. He was optimistic: to be sure, the small management team was unproven and the co-operative could offer very little collateral for a loan as all the physical assets were to be leased from Tayban. But the business plan looked very good indeed – a pay-back period of nine months seemed perfectly realistic. Moreover the key assets on which these prospects rested were very clear – much of the raw material, physically there in the yard; the undeniable skill of the workforce; and above all the customers – many being personal contacts of Jim and the other office staff, and whom Tayban would be unable or unwilling to service for many months.

However, when Mike Hynes started approaching the main banks, it quickly became clear that his formidable business plan carried little weight against considerations of security and 'proper' management. In consequence, the potentially lucrative scheme was repeatedly rejected as 'unsound'.

Eventually, however, one bank was prepared to discuss the possibility of a loan – having cleared it with head office that a worker's co-operative would be an acceptable entity with which to deal. The shape of a scheme began to emerge: the bank would match the loans put in by the workforce – whose redundancy money came to £17,500. The bank's loan would be secured against a floating charge on the debtors of the co-operative. However, the £35,000 raised in this way still fell far short of the cash required, so the bank's loan also depended on the co-operative receiving support from Lancashire Enterprises Limited (LEL), the investment company created by Lancashire County Council (who had also promoted the CDA). Although Mike Hynes had already been exploring this possiblity, such support could not be assumed. LEL had been set up on a 'non-party' basis and had to operate on commercial terms (and hence raised again the problem of security). By this stage, too, time was running out. In the end the package was secured on Christmas Eve: Mike Hynes spent the afternoon drafting the investment agreement and went straight out to the LEL Christmas Party where he was able to talk at length to both the managing director and the chair of the board. In the great traditions of business dealing, agreement in principle was reached over drinks. The promise of this loan, which did not in fact arrive until April, was enough to get the show on the road.

Tayban closed the works in January. They stayed closed for a week to generate the entitlement to redundancy benefit and thereafter Northwest Pre-cast took over the operations and started trading. Tayban's expectations from these arrangements were very quickly and thoroughly confounded: their hopes of establishing themselves in Bolton proved to be over-optimistic. By contrast, things were going very well at Pilling. Within six months the Workers Co-op that Mr Banks had expected to limp along for a year or two before giving out, had recruited three of the five Tayban employees who had moved with the company to Bolton. By the end of the first year Northwest Pre-cast had reached a turnover well in excess of £400,000, it had made a (pre-bonus) profit of about £90,000, it was employing twenty-four people and it had clearly achieved or exceeded the projections of the business plan. Meanwhile, over in Bolton, Tayban were in increasing difficulties and were attempting to put together a financial package to restructure the business. By Easter these attempts had failed and the firm was put into liquidation.

(*This case is continued in Box 6.1.*)

Government support for WTOs

Since they are unlikely to obtain the necessary funds from conventional banking sources, WTOs must look elsewhere. The obvious place to try is, of course, the worker co-operative movements' own loan funds. However these, where they exist, are unlikely to be able to shoulder the whole burden either. As the previous section demonstrated, co-operatives have peculiar problems in raising cpaital. In general, co-operative movements feel they are disadvantaged compared to other businesses, as regards access to capital. Hence, especially during a period of rapid growth when there are many hungry mouths to feed, the movement's own resources have been stretched very thin. This is true even in Italy with a very powerful movement – its very success has simply stimulated the demand for finance from large numbers to new co-operatives and WTOs. This means that very often a WTO must turn to government sources – at local, regional or national level – for support.

The different ways in which governments have provided financial assistance to WTOs are summarised in Table 4.2.

Table 4.2 Forms of government financial assistance to WTOs

---

1 *Support provided through general instruments*

- Industrial and regional policy grants
- Training subsidies
- National enterprise promotion schemes (capitalization of benefits)
- Local schemes for enterprise support (start-up loans and grants, assistance with premises etc.)
- Conventional tax relief schemes

2 *Support provided through measures to assist worker co-operatives*

- Block loan or grant to co-op financial institutions (France, Italy, UK)
- Tax advantages for co-operatives (Italy, France)

3 *Ad-hoc measures for specific WTOs*

- Loans and grants
- Loan guarantees and loan interest subsidies
- Provision of premises on favourable terms
- Purchase and lease of assets
- Cancelling of outstanding debts (e.g. social security contributions)
- Placing orders for services
- Making ear-marked payments (for consultants, training etc.)
- Allowing those working in a WTO enterprise to go on receiving unemployment benefit temporarily

4 *Measures specifically for WTOs*

- Funds to provide loans to individuals to enable purchase and restructuring of firms in crisis (Spain)
- Creation of special loan funds to support WTOs (Italy)

The first type of financial assistance – that provided through policy instruments that were devised for other purposes – tends to suffer from a number of defects. For example, often, because they are larger, the financial needs of WTO far exceed the sort of money available from funds set up to support local enterprise creation and other employment initiatives. In addition, there are often problems for WTO in taking advantage of provisions designed for conventional company forms or that are really designed for much larger enterprises (such as many conventional regional and industrial policy measures). That said, these schemes can be extremely important – those for the capitalization of unemployment benefit are a case in point. Since the capital provided in this way is based on the number employed (rather than the requirements of the enterprise) it might have led to over-employment. However, in France at any rate, such a dangerous trend seems not to have occurred, perhaps because cooperatives are formed in sectors of relatively low capital intensity and therefore the capital needed proves to be proportional to the number of employees.

Another example of WTOs taking advantage of general measures is provided by the following arrangements that WTOs in Germany have been able to agree with the Public Labour Administration:

- officials can considerably contribute to reduced wage costs by keeping the employees on the unemployment list and paying unemployment benefits – as long as their earnings do not exceed certain limits;
- the labour administration can organize and finance any necessary training of the employees involved in the WTO;
- officials can also help to realize a WTO by supporting proposals which include setting up, within the company's premises, both a productive company and a vocational training centre financed by labour administration money; this can significantly reduce fixed costs;
- officials can also subsidize the creation of jobs in the new enterprise (and each preserved workplace can be considered to be a newly created one).

In general, labour administration offices have proved to be fairly flexible and inclined to collaborate if a realistic takeover conception is being presented (Duhm 1987).

The second type of financial assistance – support provided through measures to assist worker co-operatives generally – has occurred in Britain and France (and also Italy, which is considered later). In Britain, the West Midlands County Council was the first to provide funds to Industrial Common Ownership Finance (the formally autonomous financial arm of

ICOM, the main membership organization for worker co-operatives in the UK), for it to administer in supporting co-operatives in the West Midlands. A few other councils have subsequently copied this practice. Such an arrangement seems preferable to the attempts by other local authorities to create and administer their own funds. These have been bedevilled by a lack of expertise and experience, and by the bureaucratic environment of local government which has resulted in wholly unacceptable delays in the handling of applications and the actual provision of funds that have been approved (Spear 1987).

In France, CG-SCOP, the representative body of worker co-operatives, is a much stronger and rather centralized organization which has had its own Expansion Fund (Fonds d'Expansion Confederal) since 1975. This was originally funded by one-third of the annual subscriptions paid by co-operatives to CG-SCOP, but it has since received tranches of central government funding, particularly during the Mauroy government (1981–3). These funds were partly aimed at the support of WTO, as evidenced by the agreement signed in 1985 ('contrat de plan') in which CG-SCOP undertook to create 50 per cent of the new jobs in co-operatives through WTO. One advantage of these arrangements is that WTOs are in a position to receive other assistance as well as finance. In 1981 CG-SCOP set up a Development and Support Office to provide services to its members, including the provision of 'relief managers'; and sectoral collaboration among co-operatives is also being encouraged. However, for a combination of reasons (discussed in Chapter 7) these efforts to support WTOs produced rather mixed results, at least during the early 1980s.

In passing it should also be noted that although the provision of government funds in this way has obvious attractions for both governments and co-operative movements, it also raises some difficult longer-term questions (e.g. about the basis on which the funds operate, about possible dependency, and the distortion of the movement's priorities).

The third category of financial support – that provided by ad-hoc measures for specific WTOs – is very varied, proving, if nothing else, that where WTOs are legitimate, or where there is a political will to support a WTO, or where particular officials are sympathetic, then the absence of specific policy measures is no great obstacle. A way can usually be found or created. The case of SCOOP (Box 4.2), a WTO in Spain that did not depend on funds from the National Labour Protection fund, is a case in point.

The remaining category of financial support – that provided through funds created specially for the assistance of WTOs – covers the much more extensive experience of Spain and Italy. These are dealt with in separate sections.

Box 4.2   The case of SCOOP

SCOOP makes electronic equipment and employs upwards of 120 people. SCOOP was originally part of an electronics group that ran into difficulties. These seem to have arisen from the commercial and the production ends of the business not working together, rather than from any more fundamental weaknesses. The group sold SCOOP to an entrepreneur who proved unable to resolve the difficulties, and the situation deteriorated. By 1983 there was an acute crisis.

It seems that the idea for a co-operative may have come from the former owner – which is not unusual in Catalonia. As the current general manager put it, 'If he was not the first one to say "co-operative", he was clever enough to get others to say it.' To start with, a committee of four representatives of the owner and four of the workers was set up to establish the feasibility of the project. As usual, the arrangements that were finally made were very complicated indeed. In essence, the owner gave the assets to the workforce and the Government cancelled the debts of the enterprise to Social Security. However, for two or three months the workforce were, officially, unemployed – when in fact they were still working for the enterprise and receiving some unemployment pay or wages. The transition was effected by the formation of an interim co-operative which had only nine members. This held on to the assets as the workforce was sacked, then the full co-operative was formed and the workers were re-employed. The managing director remained as the sole employee of the old co-operative. (He is still not officially a member of the co-operative but he gets a share of the profits like the other members – this is just in case any of the former debtors were to take action against him.) The 'new' business was financed by the workers capitalizing their unemployment benefit: they received the equiv-alent of eighteen months' worth of unemployment benefit but temporarily lost the rights to benefit should they subsequently have become unemployed (they have now worked for two years and hence have built up that right again).

Before he left, the former owner suggested that they would have to raise prices and reduce their extensive international sales network. Instead the workforce did the opposite: they went for a cheaper model and maintained their sales network. When they took the factory over it was divided into three lines, one producing electronic machines and two other mechanical lines. Only the electronic machines were making money. The co-operative closed down and then transformed one of the unprofitable lines to produce other products, and they made the other one profitable. Since then they have moved entirely towards electronic machines and equipment. The company's activities have been affected by the switch to electronics. The direct workforce has now been reduced from 70 per cent of the total to 40 per cent and the sales network remains very extensive.

They sell their machines internationally, many overseas. They have recently had to make a decision whether they would allow manufacturing under licence in a Latin American country. This was a difficult decision involving some real risks – for example concerning the stability of the currency, and whether they might have their know-how taken by the collaborating partner who could then compete against them in other Latin American markets. However, they decided to go ahead and one person has (reluctantly) volunteered to go for eighteen months to pass on their know-how and supervise the operation. Nowadays, anyone joining the co-operative would have to pay about £1,000 or more to become a member, such is the present value of the business.

The co-operative is directed by the Consejo Rector (otherwise known as the Junta Rectora). The Consejo is elected by the members, but there is no very clear line between management and the representatives of the members. Some managers are in fact elected to it, but other managers are frequently called in to meetings anyway to help with making decisions. The council meets weekly and effects many of the decisions. Overall, however, the style of SCOOP is very informal. It has evolved a culture and practices which seem to work well – ad hoc groups are formed to tackle particular issues, people are called into meetings as necessary and the atmosphere in meetings is very relaxed with people sometimes walking up and down as they discuss the issues.

Among members there are reduced wage differentials. There are some non-member technical managers who are paid the market rate, which is rather more than the members; on the other hand they would not share in the profits. Although trade unionists played an important part in the transfer into a co-operative most are no longer trade unionists. Those members that are still in the trade union are members of the CNT (which has anarchist leanings); the president of the co-op is a former CNT member and still has anarchist sympathies.

The other important body is the general meeting which has to make decisions on all major matters. For example, the distribution of the surplus in 1987 was voted on and the general meeting by a quite narrow majority decided to distribute the entire surplus to the membership. This would be worth about £1,000 a head (200,000 pesetas). This decision was made after a long and passionate debate in which many members argued that they would have to plan for the future, and they had to think about the prospects for their children, whether there would be jobs for them. It appears in this case that both the young and the older workers were prepared to take a short-term view of this issue. On other occasions, however, the Junta has threatened to resign in order to get its way over the assembly, and it should be emphasized that the co-operative has been very successful indeed (it has had no trouble obtaining bank credits to extend and expand its operations). As another example of an assembly decision, the assembly agreed unanimously to keep working on polling day although it would be common practice in Spanish companies for a firm to close for half a day to enable people to go and vote.

According to the General Manager, 'In some ways a co-operative Manager has greater freedom to act.' In a private firm, as he sees it, there is pressure for short-term results and a distribution to shareholders. This makes it easy to close down, for example, one department or section of a company. This would be very hard in a co-operative, but on the other hand, in a co-operative it is much easier to invest or make big decisions – the workforce are much more likely to support you.

Note: SCOOP is not the co-operative's real name.

Spain and the development of the SAL system

In Spain WTOs have been made possible through the granting of loans by the Ministry of Labour through the Fondo Nacional de Protección al Trabajo (FNPT) – the National Labour Protection Fund, an agency that operated between 1960 and 1985 under a system that was supposed to be similar to that of a commercial bank (but it is uncertain to what extent these loans have actually been repaid to the FNPT).

The loans were of the following nature:

• They were personal loans made to individuals rather than the SAL or co-operative. For this reason, the workers had to provide individual guarantees in order to answer to the FNPT in case of default.
• They established a maximum amount per worker, which was adjusted annually by the Ministry of Labour.
• They offered advantageous conditions regarding interest and amortization periods (5–8 per cent and 8–10 years).

It is important to appreciate three features of this scheme.

First, the terms of this programme were modified on several occasions and in 1985–6 it was substantially redesigned. Assistance is now arranged through a newly created Directorate of Labour Co-operatives and SALs, within the Ministry of Labour. Loans are now granted to companies (rather than individuals) and on the basis of their financial needs (rather than the number of worker-owners), and they are provided by banks who have signed agreements with the Ministry of Labour. However, it is still too early to evaluate the impact of these reforms and so the discussion that follows concentrates on the arrangements during the period 1979–85 when the SALs first came to prominence.

Second, funds from the FNPT were not the only source of finance for these WTOs. The workforce commonly made use of redundancy payments and back payments of wages (provided by the Fondo de Garantia Salarial (FOGASA), a public fund that exists to provide these payments in cases where a bankrupt firm is unable to meet its obligations). In addition, further funds would be obtained from banks on normal terms.

Third, until the passing of Law 15/1986 the SALs did not actually exist under Spanish law, but were instead completely governed by normal company laws. However, in order to benefit from official assistance provided by the FNPT, the Ministry of Labour required specific conditions to be reflected in the statutes of SALs. Between 1979 and Law 15/1986 the requirements were:

- A minimum of 50 per cent capital had to belong to the workers. (Before 1979, 100 per cent of capital had to be held by workers; Law 15/1986 requires that this percentage be at least 51 per cent).
- No shareholder could hold more than 25 per cent of share capital (previously it could be as much as 35 per cent.)
- Shares had to be registered and could only be transferred to other workers in the company.
- Modifications to the above statutory conditions could only be made upon authorization by the FNPT.

Hence the existence of the FNPT and the evolution of the terms under which it operated enabled large numbers of WTOs to take place. Many of these adopted the SAL framework and during the years in question the growth in their numbers had essentially been proportional to the annual budget assignment made to the FNPT by the government. Some specific features of the FNPT scheme and the SAL form have created particular problems. First, although SALs have employed fewer workers than the source company the workforce is normally above requirements. One of the reasons for this is that the loans were being granted according to the number of employees in the company. Hence the number of workers to be recruited upon the incorporation of a SAL was determined more by the initial financial requirements than by production needs.

Second, the fact that SALs were not legally recognized until the passing of Law 15/1986 meant that there were conflicts between the company laws under which they were registered and the limitations placed on their statutes by the Ministry of Labour. According to company law, limits such as the FNPT required could not be applied to share sales or transfers. These ambiguities were often a source of some conflict and uncertainty.

In general, the financial problems of the SALs have been acute. Some of the reasons for this are to be expected in the context of WTOs (e.g. the need to replace obsolete equipment; the initial business plans being over-optimistic; shortages of working capital arising from difficulties in obtaining loans from banks and credit from suppliers). However, some of the problems have been particular to the Spanish context. For example, it was not uncommon for the source company's assets to be purchased at a value considerably below what they would be worth in the context of a viable business. Once a SAL was trading however, it would wish to value the assets more realistically to provide security for additional loans. Unfortunately, to do this left the SAL liable to increased tax, in line with the usual provisions of company law.

Moreover, in the early years of the FNPL system the procedure for incorporating SALs was through the issuing of new shares and their sale to the workforce. This had the effect of underwriting the company's debts to social security and tax agencies, which were still carried by the restructured enterprise. More recently, incorporated SALs form a separate company which purchases the trading activities of the source company – and the source company then goes into liquidation. The workforce thus acquires the assets of the company but not its debts. This method of SAL incorporation is known as the 'Catalan path' and since its development some of the older SALs have been allowed to overcome their difficulties by cancelling their debts to the Social Security and Tax agencies. Furthermore, the Catalan path has given rise to the creation of the so-called re-SAL, that is, the dissolution of a SAL as a result of the bankruptcy of the company, followed immediately by the creation of a new SAL. This can happen if the workers are owed wages by their company. This means that legally they have preference over other creditors with respect to the assets of the company – which they then use to set up the new SAL. ELSA, described in Box 1.2, took this route in 1987. Recently, co-operatives have begun to devise ways of carrying out the co-operative equivalent of this manoeuvre (see the case of MOSTA in Box 6.4).

Funding for Co-operatives and WTOs in Italy

In order to understand developments in Italy it is important to appreciate both the constitutional position of co-operatives and the extensive involvement of both regional and national government in the co-operative movement.

The important social function of co-operative and mutual enterprise was recognized in the Italian Constitution and in the first post-war law to reorganize the co-operative sector after the demise of Fascism. Apart from ensuring democratic principles (e.g. one member one vote), setting a minimum size for co-operatives, and establishing the principle of mutual enterprise, the legal framework created by these measures had several distinctive features:

- The number of technical and administrative members may not exceed 12 per cent of the total membership (only recently, with the passing of Law 49/85, has this number been raised to 20 per cent for rescue-co-operatives; with the passing of Law 44/86, it has been abolished completely for co-operatives of young people in the South of Italy); in practice this is often evaded, except in sectors like building where government controls are strict (to avoid domination by the Mafia);
- limits on the distribution of profits encouraged reinvestment; but in addition, a limit was set to the amount of such social capital held by the members (only recently raised to 30 million lire per person).

Such stipulations reflect a conception of worker co-operatives *as little more than an aggregation of skilled and unskilled labour* – a conception which is now at odds with the way the movement has developed and which still hampers the development of its financial institutions.

These post-war measures also recognize the importance of the co-operative associations which were assigned promotional and supervisory functions in relation to co-operatives (the role of the co-operative associations is described in more detail in Chapter 7). The importance of the co-operative associations in promoting and supporting co-operatives was reconfirmed and extended in the regional statutes of 1970. In addition, the Ministry of Labour grants financial help to the associations for their promotional activities and for their vocational training programmes. Similar financial aid is also provided by the legislatures of each region. Thus, the incentives and facilities made available to the co-operatives may be of general (tax relief, vocational training, etc.), sectoral, state or regional character. Within the context of regional aid to co-operatives there exists a variety of legal instruments designed to help them obtain credit, build up joint stock, organize vocational training, and to provide 'real services', and revolving funds aimed at specific sectors or types of co-operative (of young people, of people who have lost their previous jobs, of unemployed workers, etc.). Particular attention is paid to cases of WTO by the legislation of some regions (e.g. Lazio, Piedmont, Sardinia), but the present tendency is towards co-ordinating existing aid instruments by means of a legal framework, and directing economic resources towards co-ordinated projects.

Such was the general context in which a prolonged parliamentary and public debate led to the passing of Law 49/1985, the Marcora Law. This was designed to meet simultaneously requirements of a *conjunctural* nature (the maintenance of employment levels in cases of companies undergoing crisis) and of a *structural* nature (the reform of the co-operative sector and the provision of a secure credit system in order to facilitate the setting-up and support of co-operatives).

The first aspect is dealt with by the Law in the form of the Fondo Speciale per gli Investimenti (Special Investments Fund); the second in the Fondo di Rotazione per la promozione e lo sviluppo della co-operazione (Foncooper) – a special revolving fund for the encouragement and development of co-operatives.

The Fondo Speciale was intended to be available to:

- producer or worker co-operatives comprising workers in Cassa Integrazione Guadagni (see Box 2.2) or redundant workers. In order to set up these co-operatives the workers involved must invest a part or all of their severance pay, and they receive in return a maximum of three years of wages from the Cassa Integrazione Guadagni, as grants;
- finance companies, set up by the Co-operative Associations, at least 80 per cent of whose capital is owned by producer and worker co-operatives. The financial measure is designed to support, encourage and develop the setting-up of rescue co-ops.

Foncooper was intended to be available to:

- all co-operatives who initiate projects designed to increase productivity, employment, or technological and organizational innovation, to give greater competitiveness to their products or to restructure or reconvert their plant;
- producer and worker co-operatives comprising workers in Cassa Integrazione Guadagni or redundant workers and which present schemes similar to those outlined above.

This legislation has proved highly controversial. Moreover it contains somewhat contradictory elements with respect to its long-term goals, the extent of the finance provided, and in its operating criteria. As a result, and despite the fact that parliamentary, social and economic debate began in 1977, there have been long delays in devising the instruments required to implement the law. The co-operative associations have very mixed feelings towards it. In general, they would rather concentrate their efforts on the reform of the legislative framework for co-operatives. They claim that the legal framework, while guaranteeing as it does the principle of mutuality, social function and a new process of accumulation, should be reformed to place co-operatives in a position of parity with respect to the public and private sectors of the economy. To this end, they argue that a suitable instrument of financial aid is required in the form of a proper credit institution for co-operatives. This would overcome their problems in gaining access to the capital market, problems deriving from the fact that co-operatives may not issue debentures, shares or operate on the stock market.

In particular the co-operative associations are not in favour of the system of non-repayable grants. Rather, they would prefer to see a system of revolving funds designed to overcome the problem of under-capitalization (caused by the fact that co-operative members possess only limited capital), or temporary endowment funds, which the rescue co-operatives would be obliged to repay as their situations improved and which would thus become available for other co-operatives. Financial aid paid out in this way should be based on feasibility plans providing guarantees for the future of the enterprise. In particular, the expectations of the co-operative associations with respect to the recent Law 49 are:

- state support (to be regulated by law for the first time in Italy) for the creation of self-managed enterprises able to compete in conditions of potential parity with the rest of the economic system;
- the effective implementation by the co-operative associations of the law, in order to prevent it from being rendered ineffectual because of its internal contradictions: contradictions arising mostly from a confusion of the roles of Foncooper (for the development of new co-operatives) and the Fondo Speciale (for WTO co-ops);
- an exclusive role for the co-operative associations in the management of the Fondo Speciale: a role in which they would act as the only public agency supplying aid and 'real services' to all co-operatives. In this manner, the three main co-operative associations have constituted a single finance company, in order to participate in the formation of the WTO co-operatives' social capital (as provided by the law) and to provide the WTO co-operatives with the necessary 'real' aid.

The general principles underlying the position of the co-operative associations are also shared by the most representative trade unions (CGIL, CISL, UIL) who are also guaranteed a presence in the finance company formed to manage the Fondo Speciale.

A further criticism of Law 49 is that the finance provided is very limited in relation to the requirements of the co-operative movement. 180 billion lire has been set aside for both funds whereas, for example, the Lega (the largest of the associations) alone estimated a requirement of 80 billion lire for sixty existing or nascent co-operatives. Finally, the co-operative associations feel very strongly that the 'conjunctural' aspect (action towards companies in crisis) has prevailed over other structural measures involving all co-operatives. Since 1977, the co-operative associations have openly voiced the demands outlined above and have on several occasions expressed their fears of being relegated to the role of 'managing decline', with all their energies being devoted to coping with problems unloaded on to them from the private and public sectors.

In conclusion, the passing of Law 49/1985 had led to a wide variety of different, often high, expectations: the ambiguities in the interpretation of the law, and the limited managerial horizons of the workers (who favour non-repayable grants) make it difficult for the co-operative associations to satisfy all these different expectations. The associations, in fact, tend to think in global terms (revolving funds, temporary endowment funds, the overall development of the co-operative sector), and thus they occasionally find themselves in conflict with spokesmen for particularized interests (individual co-operatives, or the private sector, which tries to avoid the costs of restructuring). In short, the situation is currently quite fluid and it is likely to remain so until more of the uncertainties surrounding the implementation of Law 49 have been resolved.

Patterns of government support

Clearly, the extent of government involvement in WTOs varies very widely between countries. It is also clear that even within a country the response of public authorities can vary enormously from one case to another – depending on, for example, the extent of the finance required, local arrangements, the personalities involved, the proximity of elections, and so on.

Nevertheless, two different patterns can be broadly distinguished. In one, the political and the commercial support for the WTO are loosely coupled; in the other they are tightly coupled.

The 'loosely coupled' model has been common in Italy where it has been described as 'the ritual for companies in crisis'. The elements of this are:

- Public meetings promoted by the workers' council in association with the political parties and other bodies. These discuss the causes of the Italian industrial crisis and call on the authorities to act to safeguard employment in the factory in question.
- The owners and the workers' representatives are summoned to meetings with the prefect where both sides agree to discharge their responsibilities, the problems of the industrial sector are recounted, the desire for a new buyer is expressed, enquiries to Rome are prepared, and so on.
- Messages of encouragement, sympathy, solidarity etc. are received from social institutions, other workers' councils, trade unions etc.

The result of all this activity – which may take some time – is a gradual acceptance that the only way to preserve the enterprise and its employment is through a WTO – and a public commitment for this course has by this time been built up. It is only at this stage that the co-operative associations and advisors can begin serious work on preparing a business proposal. Hence the political commitment to support the WTO, based on a rather loose appreciation of the commercial possibilities, precedes the detailed technical planning, the calculation of financial requirements and so on.

By contrast, in the 'tightly coupled' model, the political support is dependent on the apparent viability of the project as represented in a detailed plan. But since, for the reasons set out earlier in this chapter, the commercial prospects of the WTO are likely to depend on the extent of a political commitment, this means that efforts to obtain the support of the banks and the public authorities are iterative, and proceed together in close conjunction. Thus, an initial proposal for the WTO is discussed with both banks and government officials. The responses are cautious but indicate the sorts of conditions that will have to be met, the additional information required, and so on. In due course a revised proposal is prepared and presented, and if it is seen as showing sufficient promise, the extent of support that may be provided is discussed along with a more detailed set of conditions regarding the further modification and elaborations of the plan that will be expected. This process continues until agreement is reached – or until it is clear that agreement cannot be reached.

Both these models can work effectively, though the 'loosely coupled' one may depend on the existence of strong co-operative associations that have the desire and the capacity to support the new enterprise, and the right and duty to step in and take over trusteeship if it is in serious difficulty. Where this expertise and experience is lacking, the 'loosely coupled' model is often disastrous. For example, in France, Spain and the UK there have been cases where a strong political commitment to rescue an enterprise has been made, and as a result WTOs were achieved. But the enterprise quickly ran into difficulties because important commercial considerations had been neglected.

On the other hand, the 'tightly coupled' model can also be abused. This happens when in the end the public authorities effectively use the un-willingness of the banks to support the project on a normal commercial basis as grounds for denying its viability and thus for withholding support (see the case described in Box 4.3). This position ignores the particular problems that WTOs face with the banking system. It also overlooks the possibility that a project may appear insufficiently profitable to justify the risks if funded on a normal commercial basis while still having sufficient prospects of profitability to justify a measure of public support – in other words, that it may very well be appropriate for public authorities to use a less demanding standard of viability than a commercial bank in assessing such projects (which is certainly not to suggest that viability is unimportant).

Box 4.3   A failed attempt

A plant of Schmalbach Lubeca GmbH, situated in the highly industrialized Ruhr area, had a peak employment of 350 in the 1970s. This had reduced to 130 in summer 1983, when closure was announced, to take place in July 1984. The product was small plastic containers of up to 5 litres. The main reasons for closure: reduced markets for the product and an overall rationalization and restructuring of the company and production.

Surprisingly, there was not much reaction from the highly unionized and experienced workforce; but there were immediate ideas for a WTO, initiated by some works council members and supported by the local trade union, IG Chemie-Papier-Keramik. Talks and consultation followed with the main company board in Braunschweig, with economists of a nearby university and with representatives of the trade-union-owned Bank fur Gemeinwirtschaft (BfG) to clarify the feasibility of, and further develop the plan for, the workers takeover. Further development was in co-operation and/or consultation with state and local governments, public labour administration and the local IG Chemie; the RKW gave additional economic advice.

First results were encouraging: positive commercial assessments by experts; generous support by the company (handing over large parts of the assets at little or no cost; implicit market agreements; promises for contract work during the first six months of trading); an encourging response by BfG; continuation of the old production; and solid contacts to old and new clients. By the begining of 1984, a carefully elaborated plan to restart the business three months after closure at the latest, with about fifty employees who would also own the company had been prepared. It also considered new activities such as container-recycling, and new products. The new company, Velberter Kunststoff Verpacking GmbH, was formally founded and registered in January 1984.

Self-management was not very strongly instituted in the legal structure of the new company: the employees, represented by three trustees of the registered association (called 'workers take over their firm') were only sleeping partners in the company beside the two managing directors as active ones. A lot of consideration, however, was given by the employees to the shaping of future production and work organization, payment systems and structures of decision-making.

All this was difficult, tiresome, and many of the employees did not really feel qualified to realize such a project, and they were sometimes near to giving up.

Nevertheless, the initiative was never seriously endangered by these difficulties. The main problem, and this became clearer and clearer, was that of financing. An estimated 3 million DM in total was needed, with a much smaller proportion of share capital which was to be repaid in by the employees, from their redundancy compensation payments.

In spite of two independently produced and positive commercial assessments by experts (one of them by an RKW member) the SPD state government decided to postpone their support decision until after the banks had made up their minds. And they (in return) asked the initiative for proof of profitable business during the next five years! – which of course could not be provided. By the end of February, BfG categorically refused any loans because they believed that there was no security for part of the capital needed (a risk, at most, of 1 million DM). The second potential creditor, a state bank (Westdeutsche Landesbank) produced an efficiency analysis, resulting in a negative forecast, and used this to justify not granting any loans. This was the signal for state government to declare officially, in April 1984, that they had decided not to support this WTO – one of those cases in which death took place before birth.

5 | Legal Choices in a Worker Takeover

A failed business looking to resurrect and reconstruct itself will, in most cases, have considered a number of options before a worker takeover becomes a serious item on the agenda. These other options – takeover by another individual or firm, or a management buyout – have the advantage that the new legal form adopted will be very similar if not identical to that of the failed enterprise – a limited liability company with conventional shareholding and a conventional managerial structure. While some WTOs attempt to exploit the advantages of such a structure for acquiring capital, most opt for a different legal form that strengthens their rights as workers. However, the choice of a legal framework that will better suit the requirements of the workforce may be problematic, requiring agreement to be reached quickly on a number of far-reaching issues. The underlying dynamic that governs this choice is depicted in Figure 5.1.

There has to be some degree of matching between worker objectives and the ownership structure devised or chosen.[1] Clearly, if the culture of the workforce is individualistic, a strongly collectivist structure and property relations would be inappropriate. They would almost certainly prefer a structure that allowed individual shareholding. On the other hand, if the

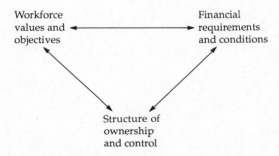

Figure 5.1 The choice of legal form as a matching process

WTO emerged from a long struggle by the workforce giving rise to a strong sense of solidarity and egalitarianism, then more collectivist property relations would probably be sought.

Whether the preferred ownership structure would also be feasible is another matter, of course, and this brings in the third consideration – finance. Smaller WTOs requiring limited sums of money are likely to have a greater freedom in allowing the matching of worker objectives and the ownership structure than larger WTOs where the cost of restructuring is high. In these cases it is more likely that co-op sources will be inadequate (except possibly in Italy) and conventional sources of finance will have to be brought in on conventional terms. They will want to influence the ownership structure and the risk/benefit equation in their favour and may require board representation as long as their money remains in the project. The workforce may then have to modify its objectives and, for example, accept that only partial worker ownership is possible.

In very general terms, therefore, the legal form chosen by a WTO has to provide a structure of ownership and control that is compatible both with the values and objectives of the workforce and with the financial realities of the project. Furthermore, these broad questions often bring with them a host of complicated technical considerations concerning, for example, the voting rights, transferability and redemption rights of shares, the terms of loans and the taxation implications of different legal forms and provisions.

The purpose of this chapter is to explain the main legal forms that are used, the reasons why they are chosen, and some of the problems associated with them. To this extent, the chapter continues the examination of the practical issues in achieving a WTO started in Chapter 3 and it also extends the analysis of the financial problems of WTOs outlined in the last chapter.

However, a further purpose is to prepare for a consideration in later chapters of some of the policy issues raised by WTOs and the forms of employee ownership associated with them. Hence, the discussion starts with a review of the advantages and disadvantages of each of the main forms of worker ownership and worker co-operatives.

Forms of worker ownership and co-operation

Company law provides a framework for commercial activity with limited liability that originates in the idea that rights to control and to the benefits arising should be proportional to the capital invested. The underlying principles of co-operative law are less well understood. It also provides limited liability but is designed for associations conducting commercial activities *for the mutual benefit of members* in accordance with the following six co-operative principles:

(i) *Open membership* – no discrimination on grounds of race, gender, politics or religion.

(ii) *One member one vote* – as democratic associations, ultimate control resides with the membership.

(iii) *Limited return on capital* – interest need not be low or unvarying, but capital loaned has no open-ended right to the surplus.

(iv) *Members benefit in proportion to their participation in the co-op* – on a equitable basis related to work done or membership, rather than capital invested.

(v) *Education and social objectives* – a commitment to personal development, education about co-operation or other social objectives.

(vi) *Co-operation with other co-operatives* – acting for the benefit of the movement as well as other co-operatives.

The benefit that an association is formed to provide can, of course, take many forms – saving and credit facilities (credit unions), residential accommodation (housing co-operatives), processing and marketing facilities for farmers (agricultural co-operatives) and so on. Where the principle benefit is the provision of employment – or of a particular *kind* of employment – and the membership is based on those employed, then the co-operative is usually known as a workers co-operative (though the terms *producers co-operative* and *industrial co-operative* are also used). The difference between worker co-operatives and conventional companies is neatly captured in the slogan '*labour hires capital instead of capital hiring labour*'.

Although the contrasting basic principles from which co-operative law and company law arise are both quite clear, each has developed a complicated range of possibilities. This is particularly true of company law which is generally quite flexible, allowing, for example, different types of shares with differential rights of control and benefit. Indeed, in the UK, a variant of company law allows for companies limited by guarantee (rather than shares) and this can be used to constitute bona fide worker co-operatives as happens quite often.[2] In a similar way, the principles of co-operation have been interpreted in rather different ways in different countries, and considerable choice may exist over the arrangements, for e.g. membership, capital contributions and repayments. Hence, both company law and co-operative law are broad families whose members may differ considerably even if they spring from a common stock. And they may be used in different ways to construct worker-owned and controlled enterprises. A discussion of two different forms of worker-owned companies and two different types of worker co-operative will illustrate the range of possibilities – and will highlight the key issues in the design of legal forms for workers' enterprises.

A company with individual share ownership

This is often the simplest form of worker ownership to arrange, requiring no more than the purchase by members of the workforce, of a controlling interest in the enterprise. Such worker ownership is fundamentally unstable, however, unless additional changes are also introduced.

In the first place, even if to begin with the shares are equally distributed, this will be undermined by the arrival of new employees who do not automatically become owners. Second, and more fundamentally, those owning the shares may wish to sell them to outsiders (in order, for example, to realize a capital gain) or they may leave the enterprise and take their shares with them (e.g. on retirement). In these ways, workers who are not owners, and owners who are not workers, will gradually (or suddenly) appear and the character of the firm as a worker-owned enterprise will be lost.

If worker ownership is seen as an inconvenient or purely as an expedient arrangement (rather than one with positive advantages), then the fact that it is bound to be temporary will not matter. Indeed, the possibility of the shares eventually appreciating in value may be an attraction for the workforce, or sections of it. However, as the discussion in earlier chapters of the aspirations of workers attempting a takeover has shown, there will often be a desire to establish a more democratic and egalitarian form of organization on a permanent basis. In such cases, the fact that this form of worker ownership will be subject, sooner or later, to a process of *constitutional degeneration* (Cornforth *et al.* 1988) is a serious problem. Moreover, the obvious solution to this problem – which is to require those leaving the firm to sell their shares, and those joining the firm to buy shares – will often face a number of severe practical difficulties, especially if the enterprise is at all successful. Some of these difficulties are illustrated by the case in Box 5.1.

With this form of worker ownership, the more successful the enterprise, the more difficult it is to prevent degeneration (and vice-versa) – because newcomers cannot afford to buy the shares; and if the firm is obliged to buy them, then it risks being critically *de-capitalized* when a number of long-standing worker-owners leave or retire within a short space of time. This problem can also be encountered in certain forms of co-operative.

Box 5.1   The case of A/S Samfundsteknik

Samfundsteknik was started in 1970 owned on an equal basis by two consulting engineering firms. It produces consultative services concerning sewerage, planning of development areas, road construction etc. to the Danish local authorities. The firm expanded in spite of hard times for firms of this kind in Denmark. The economic success led to a conflict between the two owners. One wanted to withdraw capital and invest it elsewhere, the other wanted to consolidate the firm. The conflict turned into a deadlock in which each of the owners wanted to get rid of the other. The employees, especially the departmental managers, were very frustrated, as no constructive decisions could be made. They formed a group with the intention of taking over the firm. This was not easy, as one of the owners was unwilling to sell his shares. By a series of complicated legal transactions the group succeeded in buying the firm in 1977.

At that time the firm had 60 employees, and 20 of them, who were mainly professionals, bought the shares in joint-ownership, each owning 5 per cent. Thus the firm may be characterized as being only partly employee-owned. The takeover had nothing to do with a traditional job-saving action, as Samfundsteknik was financially successful. Neither was it rooted in the labour-movement co-operative tradition or in the alternative grass-root movement of the late 1960s. It may be described as a middle-class action with the intention of securing the independence of the professionals enabling them to do their job as it was defined by themselves and their clients.

To achieve this, they had to prevent any external control while at the same time ensure that none of the employees, nor a small group of them, took over control. As a consequence, two principles were instituted: (1) any employee-owner who left the firm should sell his/her shares to the firm, and (2) the employee-owners should have equal shareholding.

In the following years, the firm continued to expand and in 1979 – two years after the takeover – the employee-owners decided to increase the share capital as well as the numbers of owners by 50 per cent. As a result of this, new owners bought equal amounts of shares. The financial success continued in the 1980s. This, however, caused some problems: (a) how could the owners enjoy the return on their shares without developing too sharp a difference between the two groups of employees, owners and non-owners; and (b) how could new owners be found who could afford to buy shares, the value of which had increased six times?

New owners were wanted not only because the number of employees had expanded, but also because some owners had left, selling their shares back to the firm, and in Denmark a firm is only allowed to own 10 per cent of the shares – a fact which meant that some of the employees had to buy shares at a certain time.

In 1982 they tried to solve some of the problems by giving up the principle of equal shareholding, thus making it easier to find new owners. Then in 1984 the firm expanded the share capital for a second time, inviting new owners to buy. At the same time, it was decided that all owners had one vote, without regard to the size of shareholding. This was primarily a management action with the intention of encouraging the most attractive among the professionals to buy. But a small 'revolution' took place as non-professionals, with lower status, bought shares in the firm. This 'revolution' was not only supported by the non-professionals, but also by some of the professionals and should be regarded as something else than the middle-class drive, described above, which was the background of the takeover in 1977.

However, the importance of this 'revolution' should not be overestimated. The general idea was still to enable the employee-owners to continue their professional activities without external or unwanted internal control.

By 1985 the number of employees had risen to 230, spread all over the country in small independent departments. 62 of the 230 were owners, a slightly smaller proportion than at the time of the takeover. However, the firm is still concerned about counteracting this trend towards degeneration, caused by the financial success of the firm.

A company with shares held collectively

This arrangement requires the formation of a second legal entity – such as an association or trust – which buys the shares in the trading company using gifts or loans from the workforce or from sympathetic sources. The employees of the trading company constitute the membership for the association, though external supporters may also be allowed to join. The management of the company is thus appointed by and accountable to the office-bearers of the association (as the shareholders) who, in turn, are acting on behalf of the workforce. Since there are no individual shareholdings, employees who join the company do not have to *buy in*, and those who leave cannot take any shares with them, and so the problem of degeneration (or alternatively of decapitalization) does not arise (see the case of IKP in Box 2.4).

On the other hand, it also follows that members of the workforce do not have the same continuing individual financial involvement in the performance of the enterprise – an involvement which is one way of promoting a broader understanding of and commitment to it. This may not be important for the founders who will usually have a substantial psychological investment in the success of the enterprise, whether or not they have a financial stake as well. But the position of those who join later is rather different and it is often argued that without an individual financial stake these later employee-owners will not take the role of owner seriously (Oakshott 1978).

Another possible problem is that those who risk their money in loans to set up a worker-owned firm in this way, and who may then forgo part of their wages in the early years in order to secure its future, will not be entitled to realize any part of the capital gain that they have made possible. Some people fear that this presumes too far on the idealism of the workforce and may act as a disincentive to the formation of worker-owned firms. Others do not see this as an issue and would expect the founders to be rewarded in different ways.

This 'two-tier' arrangement can also have advantages if complete worker ownership is not desired or possible. In such cases the workforce can enter into a partnership with one or more external sources of capital who buy some of the shares of the company. If the enterprise succeeds, the external investors are likely to receive a greater return on their funds (and may be able to realize a capital gain on their investment) than if they had been provided as loans; and they will normally be entitled to some share in control (e.g. by the appointment of one or more directors). This obviously makes it somewhat easier to attract external capital, while at the same time the fact that the employees' shareholding is held collectively makes it easier for the workforce to exert its maximum influence on strategic issues and on the manner in which the company is managed.

A workers' co-operative

The basic idea of a workers' co-operative has already been described. This form ensures permanent employee ownership and also ensures that enterprises using it will be eligible for support from other co-operatives and from movement organizations; and they will also be eligible for any legal advantages conferred on co-operatives. On the other hand, worker co-operatives have some difficulty in attracting external capital other than as loans.[3] The issue of financing for worker co-operatives is difficult and controversial, and as the last chapter showed, it remains unsolved even in Italy where co-operatives are recognized in the constitution and the movement is so strong. Suffice to say that worker co-operatives vary in terms of whether, to what extent, and on what terms, they allow external shareholdings.

Worker co-operatives also vary in terms of the nature and extent of the shareholding required of members. In most worker co-operatives in Europe members are required to buy a specific number of shares in the enterprise and the value of members' share accounts will fluctuate in line with the performance and net worth of the co-operative, and this is seen as one way of encouraging members to consider the longer term impact of decisions on the fortunes of the enterprise as a whole. However, this arrangement also leaves the co-operative liable to the problems of degeneration and decapitalization which beset worker-owned companies based on individual shareholding: if the co-operative is successful and reinvests its profits, the value of the shareholdings may increase to the point where new workers cannot afford to join – and the co-operative finds it embarrassing to redeem the shares of retiring members.

These problems are avoided in the more collective form of worker co-operative that has been favoured in Britain over the last decade. This type of 'common ownership' co-operative avoids the problems of individual share accounts by requiring members to buy only a single nominal share which is, in practice, no more than a membership card. The assets of the enterprise (built up on the basis of loans and retained earnings) are owned collectively and those who leave are not entitled to any share of those assets. Broadly speaking, therefore, this form has similar advantages and disadvantages to a company whose shares are held collectively – except that the enterprise can enjoy any benefits associated with being a co-operative.[4]

On the other hand, this arrangement, which also precludes any external shareholding, does have the disadvantage that nominal shareholdings mean a nominal equity base, with members' financial contributions appearing on the balance sheet as loans. In consequence, such enterprises cannot offer equity (i.e. security) for external loans, and they will appear very highly geared (implying, e.g. a heavy burden of interest payments). It can be argued that in practice these effects on the financial structure of the co-operative are not really significant (because they do not affect the underlying position). Nevertheless, the 'common ownership' form does seem to accentuate the problems of attracting external finance, especially in the early days of a co-operative.

Since these two forms of co-operative have complementary weaknesses and strengths, efforts are often made to promote a balanced combination of individual and collective ownership within a co-operative framework – as, for example, within the Mondragon group of worker co-operatives. Such schemes have obvious attractions, but soon become extremely complicated.

The principle characteristics of the main forms of worker ownership and worker co-operatives that have been discussed are summarized in Table 5.1. But it must be stressed that this table is a simplification of the main types – each of which can be developed in a range of different ways.

Table 5.1   Principal forms of worker ownership and worker co-operatives

	1. A company with individual shareholding	2. A company with shares held collectively ('two-tier' arrangement)	3. Co-operative with individual shareholdings	4. Collective 'common ownership' co-operative
1. Conditions for sharing ownership	Purchases of shares	Membership of association (open to workforce and possibly others)	Membership (open to employees who buy shares)	Membership (open to workforce, nominal shareholding)
2. Control by/ accountability to	Shareholders, in proportion to their investments	Association, as in constitution	Membership – one person, one vote	Membership – one person, one vote
3. Distribution of surplus	Proportional to shareholdings	To the association (hence as agreed by members)	In relation to members' earnings, or as otherwise agreed	In relation to members' earnings, or as otherwise agreed
4. Access to accumulated wealth	Sale of shares by individuals	Retained by the association; not available to members	Reflected in share accounts	Not available to members
5. Form(s) of external capital	Loans or equity	Loans to the association or operating company; equity in operating company in case of partial worker ownership	Loans and possibly restricted forms and amounts of external equity	Loans
6. Possible advantages	Allows individual capital gains/ losses. Temporary form. Simple, familiar to banks etc. Allows external equity and partial worker ownership	Permanent arrangement. Can allow some external membership. Avoids problems of individual shareholding. Can allow external equity and partial ownership	Permanent arrangement. Mutual status and support from co-op agencies. Individual capital stakes. May allow restricted external equity.	Permanent and complete worker ownership and control. Workers more likely to join. Avoids problems of individual share holding. Mutual status and support from co-op agencies.
7. Possible disadvantages	Unstable – liable to degeneration or decapitalization	Can be complicated. No individual capital stake – ownership can become a formality. Possible problems in attracting finance	Degeneration/ decapitalization problems if co-op successful. Problems in attracting finance	No individual capital stake – ownership can become a formality. Severe problems in attracting finance. Partial worker ownership not possible

Variations between countries

Having outlined the main forms of worker ownership and worker co-operatives, the next questions are 'Which forms are actually chosen, and for what reasons?'

In **Germany** no WTO has chosen the legal form of a co-operative society. This seems to be because co-operative law is difficult to adapt for this purpose without offering any clear advantages. In Germany the co-operative associations require those applying for membership to sit a series of strict examinations over an extended period. Moreover, the considerable social distance between those involved in the co-operative associations and a workforce attempting a takeover means that the associations would be reluctant to accept a WTO as members.[5]

Instead, the GmbH form of company is almost always used. This usually involves the shares being held collectively by a staff association – though membership of the association may be opened to representatives of the community as a way of promoting more public participation and support (see the case of AN in Box 3.3). The formation of a staff association has other advantages in Germany where the law plays a major role in defining rights and responsibilities in industrial relations: certain activities are forbidden to the leaders of a WTO if they also hold positions in the works council; in addition, a works council cannot negotiate with a state body and, hence, the need for a new organization of the workforce to be created will be particularly urgent. (This contrasts starkly with Italy, where WTOs are so normal, that the parties involved are often content to proceed in negotiations on the basis of informal agreements while trusting that legal niceties can be resolved in due course.)

Another advantage is that the staff association provides a vehicle for maintaining organization and mutual support among the workforce if the company that is being taken over has ceased trading – or, indeed, if the WTO attempt is unsuccessful. This form has also been used in Denmark, but there arrangements with individual shareholding are also common. Danish law does not provide for worker co-operatives and so this possibility is simply unavailable.

By contrast, a co-operative form is the automatic choice in **Italy**. This is because of the substantial benefits associated with this form, especially in the context of a WTO – support from strong co-operative associations and access to special funds for co-operatives, tax advantages and, in certain sectors, a degree of market support through public purchasing contracts. The form of a worker co-operative usually involves significant individual shareholdings by members. The situation in France was similar to that in

Italy, with the co-operative form carrying obvious advantages (e.g. not paying local property taxes) and usually being based on individual share-holdings. However, legislation in 1984 provided individual and corporate tax incentives for employee ownership and so the co-operative form is no longer the automatic choice. The poor public image of worker co-operatives (partly resulting from the Manufrance fiasco) is probably another factor in the reduced use of the co-operative form. It seems that France is becoming more like the UK by having fewer WTOs and more management, or management-led, buyouts.

In the **UK** WTOs have at one time or another used all the main legal forms. However, the collective (common owneship) form of co-operative has been used most frequently. It is hard to believe that this has resulted only from the spontaneous emergence of collective co-operative principles among those who have mounted WTOs. A more likely explanation is that the role played by professional advisers, often from local co-operative development agencies, who have tended to favour this form, has been very important; and that adopting this form, for which model rules were readily available, ensured that the legal formalities were completed quickly and cheaply – no trivial matter in the urgency and turmoil of many WTOs.

In recent years, the advantages and disadvantages of this form have been considered more seriously, both within the Industrial Common Ownership Movement and elsewhere as part of a wider debate about co-operative financing. As a result, two trends are now apparent. The first has involved various attempts to overcome the difficulties that common ownership co-operatives face in attracting external finance by creating quasi-equity or more secure terms for loans (e.g. non-voting preference shares, debentures). The second trend has involved attempts to tackle the financial problems more fundamentally by promoting model rules that involve individual shareholdings, or by promoting what have been called, perhaps inaccurately, *equity participation co-operatives*. These work as follows: some of the shares of the trading company (which is not a co-operative) are held by a co-operative of the workforce and some by the source(s) of external capital. Since company law is very flexible, the entitlement to profits and the extent of control associated with the shares can be defined in whatever way is acceptable to both parties, and need not be the same for both parties. The arrangement can, therefore, be temporary with the co-operative gradually buying out the external party. Such schemes are essentially a form of partial ownership with the shares held collectively – though by a co-operative of the workforce, rather than an association of some other type (see column 2 in Table 5.1).

Equity participation co-operatives are thus similar to the employee share ownership trusts which have also been promoted recently by Unity Trust, the new banking arm of the trade-union movement. Although these developments are potentially relevant to WTOs – especially larger or more capital-intensive ones – it is not yet clear what advantages and disadvantages they possess in practice. Overall, though, the trend is clearly towards a wider range of legal forms being more readily available to WTOs in the UK.

In **Spain** some WTOs form co-operatives and others form SALs – limited companies with individual shareholding – and although there are many of both types the latter form seems to have been preferred. The measures made available by the Ministry of Labour in order to create SALs and co-operatives in the context of WTO are practically the same. There are, however, more tax incentives for worker co-operatives than for SALs. So why have workers in businesses undergoing crisis preferred to adopt the SAL form?

One answer would be that the egalitarianism and democracy of the co-operative form does not appeal to most workers. In fact, *one person one vote* among shareholders and a striving for consensus (rather than voting according to the number of shares held) seem to be common practice in SALs, as the case of Equipos Industriales in Box 5.2 illustrates. In addition, the SALs promote themselves as providing a modern and genuine form of industrial democracy (though quite how they will avoid the problems of degeneration or decapitalization still remains unclear).

Box 5.2   Equipos Industriales

Equipos industriales trades under the name of 'Thomas', the English version of the Spanish Tomas, which is the name of the old family owners of the business. The company make factory sheds, overhead lifting gear for factories and structural steel work. They are located in the Cornella suburb of Barcelona.

They have 130 employees and were converted in 1983. When the original founder of the business died, his son took over and wanted to change the firm and sack workers, but this was obviously going to be difficult and following a union initiative proposing a conversion, he eventually sold it to the workers. He still has some formal role and attends meetings, but is himself an old man now.

The company used to have a commercial and technical office in Barcelona and management had, at one point prior to the conversion to a SAL, wanted to close the Cornella plant (presumably to reduce the business to a consulting firm using sub-contractors). However, since it was turned into a SAL, the company has moved the offices to the factory instead, so it now works on one site.

The Catalan SAL federation (FESALC) played an important part in advising the workforce and the owner concerning the transformation. They also put in a general manager in the early days of the SAL. He was for some time a communist union official who now works with the SALs; he has since returned to FESALC. The basis of the conversion remains rather obscure since it was another case of a one peseta transfer. At the time of the conversion some of the workforce objected to the arrangements that were being made. However, most of the workforce became shareholders, though as one said, 'The shares are nothing; the profit is the job.'

Most of the technical managers stayed at the conversion and relationships with management have now changed – as one activist said, 'We know them better now.' In addition, the supervisors are no longer seen by workers as 'the kings' they used to be. As far as managers are concerned, they think that the employees now work more willingly than they used to.

Equipos Industriales appears to have been performing reasonably well since its conversion and when the opportunity to buy the freehold of their factory site came up, they wanted to take it – particularly since the price was very reasonable. However, to do so, they needed to increase the share capital of the company in order to provide the basis for additional borrowing. Each member already had shares worth 258,000 pesetas (about £1,250) and they were having to consider whether to purchase a further shareholding of this magnitude. This decision was partly occasioned by the belated arrival of redundancy money paid as a result of the closure of the old firm. This issue was discussed at some length in an assembly of about seventy shareholders.

The discussion of this issue in the assembly raised the question of the basis for voting in SALs. It was accepted that even if some members did not subscribe to the new issue of shares, everyone would still have equal voting rights. Although this practice could have been written into their internal rules, it was not. Hence, officially the position remains that the voting should be according to the number of shares, but in practice, this SAL, like many others, follows the co-operative practice of one vote regardless of the size of shareholding. The assembly meeting came to no clear conclusion but it was agreed to proceed on the basis that, when matters had been formalized by the junta, each individual could decide whether to subscribe the additional funds or not.

Another explanation for the preference for the SAL form may lie in the negative opinion that many workers had of Spanish producer co-operatives – excepting of course Mondragon – during the Franco government. These co-operatives were usually small, with elementary technical processes, existing under precarious conditions, with many of them benefiting from governmental assistance because of their ties to the government. However, the co-operative movement in Spain has been growing rapidly in recent years so, again, this negative image of industrial co-operativism during the dictatorship can hardly have been an important factor in the preference for the SAL form.

The co-operators have another explanation why the SAL form is often preferred – namely, that the trade unions (and the consultants to whom WTOs turn for advice) recommend it. The reasons for this seems to be that the unions have closer links with the SALs and more of the workers in SAL enterprises maintain their union membership. But this still rather begs the question of why the SAL form should have come to be preferred. A number of factors seem to have contributed, with an important one being the advantages that Spanish laws grant them as workers and shareholders. SAL workers continue to be considered as hired workers, maintaining all rights they originally had under the Spanish labour system, which are basically as follows:

- The power to appeal to a court for their work rights from a company in which they are shareholders, as well as workers.
- The right to receive benefits from FOGASA, the Wage Guarantee Fund.
- The right to receive financial and assistance benefits provided by law for jobless workers. This is a point of enormous importance, because until 15 June 1985, the date on which Royal Decree 1043 extended unemployment protection to working partners of producer co-operatives, co-operators had no right to unemployment insurance, due to the fact that the recognized legal relationship between the co-operative member and the co-operative was of a corporate, and not a labour, nature. Bearing in mind the birth pangs of a new enterprise and its uncertain future, it appears logical that in WTOs prior to June of 1985, this was an element that would greatly affect the choice of legal framework.

Another consideration may be the fact that the SAL form allows external parties to hold share capital in the businesses, thereby making it easier to attract finance into the enterprise. Finally, there are fewer restrictions on the transfer of shares under the SAL form; and the worker-shareholders have rather less responsibility vis-à-vis third parties.

Overall, therefore, the fact that more WTO use the SAL form appears to reflect idiosyncrasies of Spanish employment and co-operative law rather than a clear ideological preference. In the light of the wider European experience this exemplifies a more general point about the historical and cultural specificity of the legal options available to those attempting a WTO. Earlier it was suggested that the choice of legal framework for a WTO was ultimately a matching process in which the structure of ownership and control had to be compatible both with the values and objectives of the workforce and with the requirements for securing adequate financial support. However, the fact that WTOs use particular forms in different countries, even though in most cases a wider range is available, indicates that other factors are at work. It is clear that in practice those advising a WTO play an important part in determining which legal form will be chosen. Moreover, the choice facing the workforce is often heavily conditioned by the contingent advantages and disadvantages of different frameworks in particular countries. In consequence it may be easy to decide which basic form will be used and the only questions will concern more detailed issues within that form.

Wider issues

The preceding discussion has suggested that the key considerations in the choice and design of a legal form for a WTO are, first, the degree of individual versus collective ownership that is preferred; and second, whether the enteprise will be wholly or partly worker-owned, that is, whether and on what basis there will be external shareholders. These two

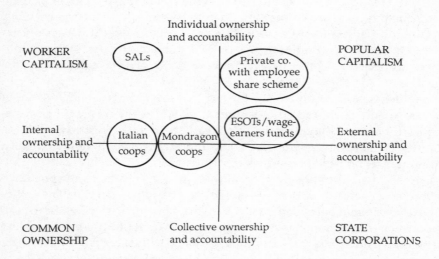

Figure 5.2 Dimensions and types of economic democracy

dimensions relate to broader debates about economic democracy, as is clear from Figure 5.2.

Figure 5.2 locates in terms of these two dimensions some of the forms of partial and complete employee ownership, and relates them to different conceptions of economic democracy.[6] One interesting point about this view of the issues is that it immediately calls in question the superiority of the pure 'polar' types (worker capitalism, popular capitalism, common ownership and state corporations) that have often been the most strongly advocated. What is wrong with the centre of the grid? It has already been suggested that a combination of individual and collective ownership has some definite advantages and a strong case can be made for a combination of internal and external accountability being preferable to either one or the other. In fact, the co-operative movements in Italy and (especially) Mondragon both manage to ensure a significant measure of external accountability to the wider co-operative movement. The practical advantages of this are fairly obvious in providing another possible source of error-detection and correction when, for example, a co-operative is not tackling its difficulties vigorously enough. Hence, quite apart from the need to provide reasonable terms for external capital, there are grounds for having a measure of external accountability – though obviously much depends on the nature of the external parties, and on their involvement not jeopardizing the workforce's *psychological* ownership of the project.[7]

Finally, the variety of different legal forms used for WTOs raises one other question: is it still helpful to think of co-operatives as a particular legal form distinct from others? Or would it be more helpful for those involved in WTOs to accept that worker co-operatives are simply one of a range of legal forms that ensure substantial employee ownership and influence on decision-making? It can be argued, for example, that a sentimental attachment to the ideas of the co-operative movement places an artificial barrier between different forms of employee ownership that actually have a great deal in common.[8] The counter argument is that often the idea of co-operation still provides a powerful expression of workforce aspirations – and, of course, in countries like Italy, where there is a strong co-operative movement, it carried a host of very practical advantages. This issue, and the increasing fiscal support for employee ownership in many countries, suggests two different scenarios for worker co-operative movements. In one, worker co-operatives would take advantage of these new measures to increase in size and numbers, and at the same time strengthen the co-operative identity by networking and inter-trading among co-operatives. In the other, there would be a gradual dilution of the co-operative identity as worker co-operatives discovered the scope for mutual assistance and sharing of experience in the broader networks and associations of different types of employee-owned firms (Laville and Mahiou 1986).

6 After the Workers Take Over

This chapter reviews the experience of the enterprises established as a result of a WTO. Such enterprises commonly start in a mood of optimism or even exhilaration, with the workforce feeling (justifiably) that effecting the take-over was itself a substantial achievement. Nevertheless, the commercial situation of the enterprise will often be precarious, with enormous and unfamiliar problems needing to be tackled. The great variety of different circumstances of WTOs makes it hard to generalize about the course of events thereafter. The most that can be hoped for, and the aim of this chapter, is to identify the more common issues that WTOs face, and the patterns of development that often arise.

Overview: phases and outcomes

The building up of an enterprise once it is clear that a WTO attempt will succeed is usefully considered in terms of two phases. The recovery phase is essentially concerned with making sure the new business can keep going, that it can obtain the customers and resources it needs, and manage the production, so that it is no longer losing money. The development phase is distinguished by efforts to strengthen and consolidate the enterprise – by trying to achieve greater autonomy in the market, for example, or by introducing new production methods.

The character of the recovery phase, which usually lasts for several months at least, depends greatly on the circumstances surrounding the WTO. If it is a 'phoenix' and the workforce have had to develop a detailed plan for the new enterprise, the recovery stage is obviously a matter of implementing that plan as fully as possible, and the same will be true in 'rescues' for which there has been the time to prepare carefully. Often, however, a 'rescue' is a hastily arranged affair and decisions to proceed with, and to support it are made on the basis of a general appraisal of the commercial situation rather than detailed business plans. This is particularly true in Italy where WTOs are more widely accepted. Hence the recovery stage is often a matter of improvising and may display the following pattern:

- Initially, after it is clear the WTO will proceed, the major preoccupation is restarting production and making the co-op's presence felt on the market. This has a symbolic significance; it demonstrates that the co-operative is a reality. Commercial and production issues seem to prevail: finding customers and producing the goods.
- Thereafter, problems concerning the amount of finance available move to the fore as shortages of working capital become apparent (hence the importance in these early days of stocks of raw materials or semi-finished goods). Attention shifts to the need to negotiate credit with suppliers and to ensure promised financial support is quickly made available.
- In due course more specifically organizational problems become important: functional specialization, the introduction of methods of management control, and the need to maintain social cohesion (concerning wages, management structures, etc.).

These activities will usually be carried out in collaboration with the advisors supporting the WTO. In Italy this involvement of external parties is particularly noticeable as the WTO may be able to take advantage of measures that have been developed to aid WTO and other co-operatives. These range from provision of facilities for renting premises or purchasing plant and equipment, to facilitating access to credit, to agencies providing planning, marketing, and book-keeping services, and so on. Hence these instruments are not only financial in nature, but also offer 'real services' which facilitate the acquisition of managerial and organizational skills – absolutely essential given the intense learning process that WTO co-operatives undergo. These real services may be provided by public or private organizations of various kinds, but the most important factor in the success of WTO has been the organizational network of the co-operative associations described in more detail in the next chapter.

In general, the recovery phase is dominated by the urgent need to restore profitability – or, at least, to break even. Hence a series of short-term or tactical steps are taken which have the effect of exploring the more immediate possibilities in terms of both the market and the production system. In doing so, a rudimentary management team also evolves.

The development phase is marked by a recognition of the need to strengthen the co-operative's market position and the formulation of longer-term strategies to achieve this – whether through plant modernization, new product development, direct marketing (rather than the subcontracting on which many WTOs have to rely), collaboration with other organizations, the negotiation of a new financial support, or some combination of these. In practice the two phases may not be clear-cut. Some WTOs, like Northwest Pre-Cast (see Box 4.1), move very rapidly from recovery to development. Others may struggle to stabilize their commercial situation for months or even years because losses can only really be avoided if fundamental weaknesses in the market position of the enterprise are tackled. Nevertheless, the two phases are clearly apparent in the development of many WTO enterprises (e.g. ELSA, Box 1.2; Lake School of English, Box 2.1; CLG Box 6.2; Lithosphere Box 7.2). Moreover, the three characteristic outcomes of WTOs relate directly to their success in these two phases. These three outcomes are collapse, marginality and consolidation.

Collapse refers to cases where the recovery phase is incomplete and unsuccessful. The failure may happen gradually or it may happen suddenly – as when a promised contract is cancelled; but the enterprise never achieves viability.

Marginality refers to WTOs that accomplish the recovery phase but are unable to undertake the development phase successfully. Such cases are common.[1] Like many other small and medium-sized enterprises, they are trapped in a poor competitive position with precarious profitability (e.g. as sub-contractors, or because of obsolete equipment, or because they produce mature products with declining markets). In any year a proportion fail; but many continue for years. Some WTOs become marginal enterprises for other reasons: their competitive position is potentially sound but they fail to use it to full advantage because of poor organization. The enterprise then becomes trapped in a vicious circle as poor economic performance leads to dissatisfaction, low commitment, conflict, and people leaving if they are able to.

Consolidation refers to those cases where the development phase is successfully undertaken. The WTO achieves a 'workers' turnaround' and produces a competitive, profitable and expanding business.

What proportion of WTOs achieves each of these different outcomes? This is very difficult to estimate because of the general dearth of statistics and information on WTOs. Moreover, where figures are available they are simply in terms of survival rates. For example, in France[2] 63 per cent of WTOs founded in 1981 (figures for subsequent years are not available) were still viable in 1986. This figure is higher than that for 'new-start' co-ops (only 46 per cent of those founded in 1981 were still operative in 1986), and significantly higher than the estimates for small and medium-sized companies (two-thirds of such companies are thought to fail within their first three years). The available figures from Spain only refer to SALs and are complicated by the fact that a significant number of re-SALs (see Chapter 4) have been created from the SALs set up in the period 1976–81. This creates problems in estimating the number of failures during the quoted period because legally the re-SAL is another enterprise, although most of its assets and workers come from the former one. If the re-SALs are not considered as new enterprises then those closely associated with the SALs estimate that 50 per cent of SALs formed during the period 1976–81 survived into the mid-1980s. Since 1981 the SALs have performed better and an estimated 70 per cent are thought to be surviving for five years.

Beyond these rather limited figures – which are, nevertheless, sufficient to challenge the popular view that WTOs are particularly unstable – one has to rely on the estimates and impressions of those who have been involved with WTOs and the analysis of summary information on known cases. On this basis it seems that generally about 25 per cent of WTOs result in 'collapse', and about 25 per cent achieve 'consolidation'. The remainder can be classi-fied as 'marginal', though of course some of these will fail in any given year. Such a pattern is quite compatible with the survival rates quoted above. It seems, too, that these proportions vary somewhat between countries. Denmark appears to have had an unusually high proportion achieving 'consolidation' and in Italy 'collapse' is less common because of the safety net provided by the co-operative associations and the support they can mobilize.

Reducing costs

Whether a WTO aims to serve the same markets as the old firm or hopes to develop new ones, it is usually essential to find ways of reducing costs. There are two main areas in which substantial cost reductions are often achieved – overhead costs and production costs.

Savings in the former are particularly significant where the unit has been subject to standard head-office charges. It is not uncommon, too, for the enterprise to benefit considerably from the ending of inappropriate central policies on for example, purchasing and pricing (Red Dragon stores in North Wales (Thomas and Thornley 1989), illustrates this point; similar advantages are reported for management buy-outs). Overhead costs can also be reduced by moving to smaller premises. Reductions in the number of managerial staff and in the level of salaries and fringe benefits provided to them is another source of savings – one that can sometimes be very substantial, as the case of Northwest Pre-Cast in Box 6.1 illustrates.

The second main area for cost-reductions, that of production, is where WTOs have their potential comparative advantage (in relation to other

Box 6.1   The case of Northwest Pre-Cast – Part II
(*Continued from Box 4.1*)

Northwest Pre-Cast continued to trade profitably and to expand. The bank and LEL were prepared to lend more money and the co-operative was able to buy the site. By the end of 1987 the annual turnover was about £650,000 and still rising. The co-operative employed 37 people.

The most obvious reason for this success was that the WTO had reduced massively the managerial overheads of the enterprise. At the end of the 1970s Tayban had an office staff of twenty-seven with seventeen company cars in the car-park. At the end of 1987 while doing well over half of the turnover of the late 1970s there were seven in the offices (although Jim thought they were understaffed and would need to recruit two or three more in due course) and three small Ford Escorts made up the car fleet. (The members agreed to provide these 'company cars' on condition that the staff concerned gave other workers lifts to and from work.) It can also be assumed that the senior management salaries were far lower than what Tayban's top managers would have been paid (indeed, Jim is not the highest paid employee of the co-operative).

The members of the co-operative now concentrate entirely on what they know best. They are entirely production-oriented and hardly promote themselves at all. The paradox of a firm which does no marketing but that is receiving a steadily increasing number of orders with which it can barely cope is best understood if one realizes that their production effort is also their marketing. This is a trade in which quality, reliability and delivery dates are crucial. By concentrating on these, Northwest Pre-Cast have built up a reputation that has guaranteed them work in the future.

This was possible because the workforce was highly skilled. But it is also a matter of motivation and how much it costs to supervise them. The workforce must not just know how the work should be done, but care about how it is done, and be prepared to work long and hard as well. This is where the co-operative framework is crucial; the productive workers are respected, trusted, kept well informed – and left to get on with it.

To be sure, they are also well rewarded for their efforts; wages have been increased substantially. But the commitment they show also clearly reflects their psychological ownership of the enterprise and the strong bonds that tie them: it is theirs – and a source of pride, a demonstration of their collective achievement. In short, Northwest Pre-Cast is successful because it utilizes its key asset – the skilled workforce – to maximum advantage, while keeping supervisory and management overheads to a minimum.

Another important factor has been the tight but skilful financial control. This has enabled the co-operative to grow rapidly despite severe restrictions on its working capital and difficulty in increasing its trade credit. At this point the explanation for Northwest Pre-Cast's success has to acknowledge the import-ant support it received from LEL and Lancashire CDA, who stay in close touch with the co-operative. As Jim Stamper said of his LEL contact, 'If we are going to be late with a repayment he knows we aren't in difficulty or frittering it away – it must mean we need it to be able to expand, to buy materials, say, for a big order. . . . He understands the business; he's not just a banker.'

One matter that the co-operative has not really worked out is a satisfactory way of handling its own decision-making processes. Jim Stamper held the key management position as well as being leader of the co-operative, and commit-tee meetings have rarely been held. Instead, the co-operative relied on a combination of general meetings and extensive informal consultation, to keep people informed and make decisions. The general meetings, which non-members also attended, started off as monthly occasions, beginning half an hour before the end of the working day, and running over into members' own time if necessary. Gradually, however, the meetings became less regular, being called whenever something came up that needed discussing. The general pattern was that production always took priority and members were reluctant, or just too tired, to meet after work. So informal processes were relied on but intermittently these produced decisions that were, or appeared, unacceptable. When this happened grumbles started. Presently, they either subsided as more information was demanded or filtered down; or someone called a meeting to 'clear the air' – and to sort out how such issues should be handled in the future. In this way managers have been reminded that consent cannot be taken for granted, and the members have learned more about the complexities of management. Moreover, important precedents – e.g. on how disciplinary matters are handled, on how managerial appointments are made, on rights to information and to call meetings, were being set. Hence although the democratic processes were haphazard and the co-operative still depended heavily on Jim Stamper's personal authority to hold things together, quite fundamental changes had taken place.

By the end of 1987, however, such arrangements were widely felt to be unsatisfactory. The co-operative had grown too large; the informal processes had become unreliable (a source of 'rumours') and the character of the meetings had changed (with people less willing to speak their minds). More-over some members felt morale was suffering and tensions between different areas were beginning to re-emerge. For these reasons there was a widespread view that the co-operative would have to have more, and rather different, meetings. This had led to regular weekly 'production meetings' of the section heads being held; and a proposal that the shop floor have its own regular meetings had also been accepted. In addition the co-operative had finally appointed a production manager to help co-ordinate work on the shop floor and Jim Stamper was trying to arrange for another person to take over his role as chair of the co-operative. The need to regularize and strengthen both managerial decision-making and participation in the co-operative had been recognized.

takeovers or buy-outs). This is the area about which the workforce have the most influence, knowledge and experience.

However, this potential comparative advantage may not be realized; it depends entirely on the extent to which the workforce have accepted both psychological ownership of the enterprise and the realities of its commercial situation and are prepared to collaborate in tackling intensely difficult decisions. Hence, the importance of the workforce being involved fully from the beginning of the takeover process, and ensuring that a climate favourable to continued learning is maintained.

The scope for production cost reductions will depend on the quality of the previous management and on technological limits but arises in the following ways:

- reductions in staffing levels, consequent on e.g. the closure of unprofitable lines, increased labour flexibility, increased work rates, a reduction in supervisory staff (with self- and peer-monitoring being substituted), and the 'screening out' by the workforce of less motivated and productive workers at the time when the WTO is being prepared.
- wage reductions, often as a result of, or in conjunction with, reduced wage differentials;
- improved working methods: many conventional enterprises, especially larger ones, fail to enlist the intelligence and knowledge of the workforce in devising production methods. A WTO provides the motivational and organizational context for this latent ability to be realized – and the results have sometimes been very important. The case of Aire Habitat in Box 7.3 provides an example.[3]

The first two of these ways of reducing labour costs are the basis for trade-union anxieties about 'self-exploitation'. This term deserves some comment because it is commonly used of those working in WTO enterprises – indeed, practically any reduction in terms and conditions of employment will prompt this charge from trade unionists and those on the Left who are opposed to WTOs. The problems with such charges are, first, that they very frequently ignore the longer term financial reward that may clearly result, or the other benefits (e.g. better child-care arrangements; changed social relations at work) that those involved value. Second, such criticisms often confuse the problems of firms and sectors: for example 'cut, make and trim' sub-contracting in the clothing industry is a notoriously hard way to earn a living, and WTOs in this sector have had no monopoly on low wages and poor conditions.[4] Third, the term itself is emotive, logically confused, and reeks of 'we know what's really in your interests' paternalism.[5]

Nevertheless, these points certainly do not mean that WTOs are beyond criticism regarding their terms and conditions of employment. In particular there are occasions when a workforce is putting enormous effort for very low or occasional wages into trying to save an enterprise with no credible prospect of recovery. This pattern may be sustained by a refusal to accept the failure of a project in which they have invested such hopes (and by the absence of other employment prospects). So to this extent what is called 'self-exploitation' can be a problem, particularly in certain sectors (like textiles), even if it is not nearly as widespread as some have suggested.

Strategic choices

The key strategic decisions for a WTO, as any other business, concern what to produce and for whom. In the context of a WTO this usually means deciding how far to change the product-market strategy of the old business, for example:

(i)   whether to continue with the same product-market profile, relying on the advantages to be derived from the greater productivity of co-operative work;
(ii) whether to change partially the product-market profile for example, by concentrating on particular segments, or by aiming to improve competitiveness through product development;
(iii) whether to convert, to a quite radical extent, the activities of the company by renewing the product, the market, the production technology, and so on.

The most straightforward cases are obviously those where the first of these options looks feasible: the combination of a financial restructuring and cost reductions may be sufficient to ensure profitable operation, especially when the production is not complex, and the competitive position is basically sound.

However, there are many reasons why a WTO initiative may have to consider new products: they do not have permission to continue with the old products; the market for the old products is declining; or the existing products are not in line with their political beliefs (military production, for instance). In these cases the second and third options must be considered. As the earlier discussion of recovery and development phases indicated, this is seldom a tidy sequence of diagnosis, planning and implementation. In searching for a new entrepreneurial formula WTOs commonly experience the following difficulties:

- inadequate systems of financial information and control mean that available resources may be draining away, the profitability of different activities may be unclear;
- the enterprise may be so under-capitalized that the costs of entering new markets, reinvesting to reduce the cost advantages of competitors, or of introducing product improvements are prohibitive;
- management adopt a series of desperate stop-gap measures in order to ensure some work is available and in the hope of 'buying time'. For example, small sub-contract orders, or selling goods through trade-union branches. At best such measures may make a contribution to overheads; at worst, they generate a pattern of short-term and ineffective management which makes any attempt to tackle the strategic problems even more difficult;
- the workforce's agreement to difficult decisions may be hard to achieve and their commitment to the implementation of such decisions may be weak.

Despite these difficulties a significant number of WTOs are able to identify new opportunities and mobilize the necessary resources. Examples are Duncans of Edinburgh, Box 3.4; the cases of CLG in Box 6.2, SCOOP, Box

---

Box 6.2   The case of CLG   Part II
(*Continued from Box 2.2*)

The first months were extremely difficult: after months of idleness, without customers, without capital and without managerial staff, recovery seemed impossible. At first the workers regarded this as a period of sacrifice to be borne to keep the firm going until a new owner could be found. But after the first positive results were achieved, the idea of self-management as the prosecution of workers' struggle and as an alternative to working for an employer, gained ground.

   Particular attention was paid to factory democracy, of which various experimental forms were tried out. In general, it was organized as follows: the workers' assembly acted as the body that effectively ran the co-operative. It comprised five work groups, each made up of members representing all the production departments and each dealing with a particular problem. The administrative board had no decision-making powers but was merely an instrument for co-ordination and implementation, and in each production department the co-operative members were responsible for their own work organization. This was subjected to a number of changes over time. Initially, the departments stayed as they had been under the previous management, and managerial duties were carried out by a co-operative member acting as co-ordinators of the workers in his department, but with no decision-making powers of his own. This system of factory organization lasted for three years and was then changed because, although it directly involved the individual members in the running of their departments, it did not provide them with a global overview of problems concerning the production process in its entirety.

From 1979 work was organized into a 'planning and technical unit' and two 'production units', each responsible for the management of the complete production cycle. Each of these three units was co-ordinated by a highly experienced member of the co-operative.

Members' wages were fixed by the assembly on the basis of the collective labour contract, which set out three wage levels according to age. There were no other increments: wages were the same for both workers and office staff. Only a small number of co-operative members with managerial responsibilities were paid a special fixed allowance for their hours of overtime.

The previous firm had employed 80 people. By the mid-1980s about sixty people were working in the co-operative; a reduction resulting from the introduction of new technology, mostly during the first four years of activity. A heavy investment programme was embarked on, strategically aimed at shifting production to medium-high quality, for which there is a solid and steady market, and at replacing traditional photography with electronic apparatus.

As always, the co-operative faced considerable difficulties in finding finance, but support from other workers and public opinion helped to attenuate the problem: the buildings were leased, the investment programme was set in motion by a number of leasing options, a local bank granted a loan on favourable terms to provide working capital, the co-operative members postponed their wage payments for the first eight months and the co-operative's-most important customer (Mondadori), thanks to the intervention of its workers' council and the graphic workers' trade union, agreed to monthly cash payments for major orders.

In the years that followed, CLG relied on bank financing, loans from co-operative members, finance from the Lega and various reserve funds set up with its own means. Since 1979 wages have been paid regularly and the co-operative's initial problems seem to have been overcome.

By the mid-1980s CLG had a sales volume of 3 billion lire. In its field it may be described as a 'large scale' company, since the specific nature of its product (photographic separation) requires a large amount of work in a very short time (something that smaller sized firms are not able to do). Moreover, the high quality of its product had given the co-operative direct access to the market, of which it controlled a good 50 per cent at home, as well as capturing business in Europe. The high profitability of the product permitted such speedy recapitalization that in six years the firm had been able to buy both the factory plant and the buildings.

4.2, MOSTA, Box 6.4; some of the short Italian cases in Box 3.1; Lithosphere, Box 7.2. The willingness and ability of these enterprises to take substantial commercial risks is striking.

The development of new products, however, is particularly difficult for WTOs. It is a long and costly undertaking and a WTO is usually not able to finance its own research and development activities. Government schemes to promote technological development mainly favour high, hard and large technology (and large companies). Royalty payments in respect of products developed elsewhere and produced under licence can be quite expensive, and the development of 'technology exchanges' is in its infancy so that such exchanges as there are can hardly respond to the needs of WTOs. Finally, the marketing of new products is often difficult and expensive and raises unfamiliar issues for the workforce.[6]

For most WTO, therefore, new product development is not a serious option. On the occasions when it has occurred (e.g. the case of AN in Box 3.3) it has been achieved by depending heavily on contract work while at the same time setting up working groups to look for and develop new product ideas and, eventually, build prototypes; and seeking all possible subsidies for new products, and new product development (with as much public support as can be generated).

Management forms and management skills

A newly formed WTO enterprise has to devise a management structure for its activities and this raises a host of questions: will the new organization be similar to the old one? How much authority will be given to technical managers? How can the activities best be divided to form work groups? What meetings will be held, and how often?

The size of the rescued enterprise affects the choices that are made. In larger units where functional specialization is quite fundamental to the organization this division of labour is usually accepted and it is a matter of adding on new forms of participation in order to plan and tackle problems. In smaller plants it is easier to be more innovative and often work groups responsible for a combination of productive and managerial/administrative tasks are formed. In any event, the fundamental problem is the same: how to combine a division of labour and clear allocation of responsibility, with participation by the workforce – both on the shop floor and at the 'top' of the organization.

Whatever forms are chosen, a WTO must still find people with the capabilities to perform the essential managerial activity. This is very often problematic for the following reasons:

- key managers may have left, and those that remain may be ineffective (poor quality management is a common feature of firms that have been in decline over a period of years – being both cause and effect);
- sympathetic and suitable managers may be hard to recruit (especially given the uncertainty, and perhaps an egalitarian wages policy);
- the workforce will commonly underestimate the importance of skills and activities they are unfamiliar with. At worst, there will be widespread hostility towards the conventional managerial roles or personnel, on grounds both of cost and ideology.

Hence, rescued enterprises tend to be 'under-managed' in terms both of quantity and quality, particularly in the areas of marketing and finance. Such problems are not uncommon among small and medium-sized enterprises. (There is a sense in which only the most successful can afford to be well-managed.) However, they tend to be more severe after a WTO, and the low status and role ambiguity of managers may accentuate the difficulties.

In some cases these problems produce a managerial vacuum – an example is provided by the WTO bakery in Scotland which traded profitably for six months on the basis of a particular hot pie. Advisors persistently warned that a summertime product was needed. This problem was ignored as the leader worked very long hours with his colleagues producing the pies. When the warmer weather came, demand fell away sharply, it was too late to identify a suitable alternative, and the co-operative collapsed a few months later.

Another common pattern, especially in small plants, is for a former shop steward to assume the role of general manager or managing director. The problem is one of transition from being a leader in the struggle to becoming a co-ordinator of the general management of the company. As far as the workforce is concerned such a position evokes contradictory reactions: the leader enjoys a certain gratitude for services previously rendered, but if the culture of the organization is not also changing the new role can be considered by the other employees as a kind of betrayal, and lead to serious conflict. The main problem however is simply that the former shop steward may be unable to learn and adapt his or her behaviour quickly enough to perform the role adequately – the case of TCS in Box 6.3 provides an example.

This case also illustrates some of the difficulties WTOs face in recruiting managers externally. Not surprisingly, the workforce will want someone who is not just competent but sympathetic to the aspirations of the WTO and prepared to manage in a participative manner. For this reason, and because the absence of suitable managers was so often a factor in the

Box 6.3   The case of TCS

The TCS co-operative (Tolerie Cablage de Seyssinet (Seysinnet sheet metal and cables) in the Isere) was established after the Rabillond company, which employed seventy-four people, filed a petition for bankruptcy in 1981.

After a four-and-a-half month occupation, the worker co-op was started up by nineteen people, on the initiative of CGT union officials (the former owner set up a rival non-co-operative business not long after).

The idea of a co-operative had first been advanced by an engineer who was to have become its managing director, but who left over a disagreement on salary before the enterprise got under way. The workers were, however, sustained in their efforts by the many contacts they had made within the civil service and among local councillors. They were able to raise a large initial capital (800,000 frs. out of their redundancy money and loans from the regional council) and received assistance from the local authority, which bought the buildings and lease-purchased them back to the company.

Although there were difficulties with the receiver, who overvalued the stock, the main problem encountered was over leadership of the co-operative. At first, the union leader who had directed the takeover operation established himself as chairperson/managing director, but he turned out to be authoritarian and incompetent. The functions of chairperson and managing director were then split, but things eventually got so bad that the original chair/MD had to be dismissed. Another problem was the desperate lack of commercial expertise. After making an unfortunate mistake with one appointment, the co-operative took on a commercial manager who was better paid than the other employees but efficient. Thanks to him, the co-operative passed from craft production methods to small-scale mass production. They also engaged an accountant to complete the administrative team. She became chairperson of the board, while a shopfloor worker performed the managing director's role.

The co-operative abandoned the polyester activities of the old company in order to concentrate on sheet metals and cables. It invested in computerized machinery and increased its workforce to more than thirty.

Its financial position is sound and its commercial prospects are good.

We may say that after some difficult patches, TCS has achieved a balance both in its functioning as a co-operative and in its production. Without doubt, one of the keys to this success lies in the cohesiveness and motivation of the workforce. All have had training in management; five of the six members of the board are shopfloor workers; they are able to combine prudence in decision-making, particularly about growth (workers have only been taken on very gradually), with determined action in the interests of the co-operative (dismissal of the former leader, employing managers from outside, product specialization etc.).

problems and failures of WTOs, CG-SCOP in France tried to organize a pool of 'relay managers' to assist WTOs. This has faced many difficulties. Managers are generally reluctant to join enterprises that are commercially vulnerable, quite apart from the additional doubts and uncertainties that most managers feel about the idea of a WTO. A key issue for managers in a WTO is maintaining the solidarity and commitment of the workforce as the enthusiasm of the first few weeks inevitably starts to fade. The danger is that there will be a return to old attitudes and a deterioration in management – worker relations. However efforts to make the new values permanent and build a collaborative form of management face major obstacles.

In the first place intense production pressures and long hours of work may undermine morale. More seriously, they make it difficult to afford the time for meetings required to resolve disagreements consensually, and to ensure a continuing appreciation of other people's views and circumstances. Secondly, the 'old' values may still be embedded in the production technology and organization, in the form of repetitive, highly routinized work and a clear separation between those who plan and control, and those who are operators. To the extent that the experience of responsibility, discretion, problem-solving and control at the level of the work group provides a foundation for an involvement in enterprise decision-making, this constrains the scope for institutionalizing the new values – especially if the capital and training costs of a more progressive production system are high. Moreover, the social divisions associated with fragmented labour generate conflict and undermine the cohesion of the workforce. Thirdly, with employees often expecting much greater influence in day-to-day decision-making, the role and responsibility of managers can become confused. While it may be accepted in principle that 'managers must manage', they are usually accountable to the workforce and they may be unclear as to the extent of their authority (this is especially true when the workers' leader effectively combines the roles of shop stewards' convenor and managing director). Such problems tend to be particularly acute in larger enterprises with a history of an authoritarian style of management and poor industrial relations. In such cases, old suspicions and stereotypes are likely to reassert themselves and those involved may lack any model or experience of a more participative style of management.

Democracy and self-management

While a desire for greater employee influence occurs in practically all WTOs (and this conditions the way managerial activity is conducted), in some cases this leads to more thoroughgoing attempts to develop democratic organizational structures and self-management. In these WTOs the formal accountability of managers to shareholders, or to an elected committee of the workforce, is seen as insufficient. Instead, democratic practices may permeate the organization, taking one or more of the following forms:

- talking-democracy
- voting-democracy
- electing-democracy

In talking-democracy, the employees attempt to arrive at a consensus as to problem definition and solution. In voting-democracy, most of the decisions are reached by voting among the employees. Both forms are direct in the sense that the employees personally participate. This is in contrast to the third form, in which the employees elect representatives as management, directors, etc. to look after their interests. In most WTO enterprises there is usually a combination of the three forms, but the weight attached to each varies. In every case there is an employee assembly which often meets several times a year (and up to once a week). Attendance is often greater than 50 per cent – up to 100 per cent – and important problems such as capital expansion, new investment, hiring and firing of staff, and long-term policies are discussed. The management and board of directors are also elected here, which provides the element of representative democracy. The workforce may also become directly involved in decision-making through section meetings, working groups and the like.

Needless to say, the sudden introduction of a variety of forms of direct expression can have a dramatic effect on the organization. After years of being tied up by the company's command structure, by competitive work and pay conditions, by work-organization which disconnects everyone from the over-all process, by a works council and the trade-union system which is based on representation and delegation much more than on grass-root and individual initiative – developing the capacity for self-management is a difficult and often tiresome learning process. Self-management and autonomy can be interpreted in very individual, private terms. People then refuse to be integrated in and subordinated to the complex organization of the new company. The uncertainty of the individual roles and positions within the new organization and fears resulting from this lead to inflexible attitudes, rivalries, or cliquish groupings: the essence of the new independence, for some, seems to result in being late and casual. Carelessness, sloppy work and disciplinary problems may spread quickly. Self-management tends to become more and more identified with those negative phenomena – until the majority of the workforce ask for a strong regime with clear-cut structures and responsibilities.

However this is by no means inevitable and where a significant proportion of the workforce – and especially its leaders – are committed to self-management, it can certainly be made to work, as the case of MOSTA in Box 6.4 illustrates (see also the case of CLG in Box 6.2 and Lithosphere in Box 7.2).

Box 6.4   The case of MOSTA

MOSTA makes heavy equipment and is based in Barcelona. In the 1970s a French company tried to take over the group of companies of which MOSTA was a part. As regards MOSTA itself, the main assets which it wished to control was the sales network based on an office in Madrid – it was quite prepared to close down the production unit. The Madrid office was close to the relevant government ministry, and to the headquarters of many of its customers, namely the distributors and wholesalers; the companies and utilities who are ultimate clients for much of the equipment; and the big contractors who equip factories. MOSTA have a niche in this market, which is basically dominated by multinationals.

As a production unit the company had been badly run down before the workers took it over in 1980. Union activists initiated the process. Many skilled workers left at the time of the takeover, and in addition voluntary retirements reduced the numbers from 170 to 110. The conversion came about as a result of something of a struggle; lawyers had thought a co-operative would be impossible, but the workers committee insisted that this was the legal form they wished to use, even though few of the rank and file members knew about co-operatives at this time. During the transition the co-operative also lost the support of the union which disapproved of the economists who were advising the co-operative on their feasibility and business prospects. In consequence the members stopped paying their union subscriptions, but went ahead with the feasibility study on their own. The co-operative has also had problems in relation to other Spanish firms. One asked if it was a co-operative and when it was told that this was the case, it wanted nothing more to do with it.

The general manager of MOSTA left after falling out ideologically with the president. (Interestingly, he left to work for a SAL in the machine tool industry employing 190 people in a nearby town. He says he prefers it there because the SAL is more 'manageable'.) However, he has not been formally replaced in MOSTA as general manager; instead, the president is acting as general manager. He is a very serious and idealistic person who has refused a salary increase, despite his very considerable responsibilities. As such, the president heads a management group which often has to take decisions on its own; it has to be light on its feet, by the nature of the market it is working in. Indeed, a fair amount of wheeling and dealing with the customers takes place on the phone and requires spot decisions. Tender wars, for example, are common and they may have to sell under cost to large companies to get the publicity of the deal and to get the approval, too, of the technical standards by the ministries. The introduction of self-management has had to ensure that rapid decision-making on such matters was still possible. The culture and organization of the factory have changed considerably since the workers took over, though it is still seen as problematic. 'We all think ourselves masters, now' was one comment that encapsulates both the extent of the changes and the difficulties that remain.

The assembly of members plays an important role in decision-making. For example, an assembly lasting five hours was held in 1987 in which the major topic (taking up three hours) was an ingenious plan to restructure the finances of the co-operative. Despite all the difficulties it is clear that MOSTA has done well to stay in business. Currently it is involved in new product development in collaboration with a Swiss company, with the aim of better utilizing new technology.

Note: MOSTA is not the co-operative's real name.

Patterns of development

The size of the enterprise taken over has a considerable bearing on the way it develops – simply because size is so important for the division of labour and functional organization.

Larger WTO, right from the beginning, preserve their functional organization, and their economic decisions are dictated by a desire to maintain employment levels. Such WTO have direct access to the market and seek to increase their share of it by keeping to the same product even if it is relatively mature (through careful marketing and by keeping costs down). At the same time they try to diversify production by extending the product range or by entering into collaborative arrangements with other manufacturers. These WTO function in the main like conventional companies insofar as they delegate to a group of skilled administrators (consultants or career managers) the task of defining company strategy. However, the fundamental basis for the strategy is fixed: employment levels should be maintained. Hence, company strategy is not based on seeking out potentially the most profitable investments, given the state of the market; it is based on the selection of markets and policies capable of making the existing human resources and other available assets productive. Nevertheless, major investments are often necessary in order to continue using the labour resource competitively. One outcome of these efforts may be that the enterprise is returned to private hands. This can also occur with smaller enterprises; but it seems more common with larger ones, either because their capital requirements are greater or because it is more difficult to achieve meaningful and widespread involvement by the workforce. In such cases the effect of the WTO has been to preserve employment by rationalizing the activities to a point where they are again attractive to private capital.

A very different logic is common in the smaller and medium-sized WTOs. In these, a rejection of the previous functional organization, and a search for as much parity in the division of work as possible, tend to occur. However, it is recognized that some functional specialization is indispensable, and the evolution of the management and organization reflects decisions regarding the market and the pressures it imposes. The organizational patterns are therefore more complex and varied. Subcontracting to a limited number of large firms is initially vital to the rescue of almost all those WTO that base their strategy mainly on the price factor and this may be sufficient to achieve recovery. Characteristically, this recovery process is sporadic, conducted by trial and error, and strictly dependent on internal social dynamics that lead directly to the growth of a managerial system drawing uopn the human resources of the most committed members of the enterprise. This is augmented in some cases by specific skills recruited from outside. At this point WTO may be quite successful in terms of profitability, while continuing to occupy a marginal position in the market. This arises because, by their very nature, they possess characteristics that make them competitive in areas of little interest to private capital (where profit margins are too narrow or uncertain). In consequence, as we have seen, a significant proportion of these WTO are not able to escape from a half-hidden 'shadow' economy, and from a precarious dependence on the medium and large-size companies for which they perform ancillary functions.

However, most WTOs do make some efforts to develop the enterprise beyond this point. When this happens the maturation of the enterprise often goes through the following stages:

- The search for greater autonomy directs the WTO towards product diversification and finding a wider range of customers for its products and services, and also towards gaining direct access to its own market.
- In this way, organizational and managerial complexity increases, and the limitations of the members' expertise and of their being production-oriented become increasingly apparent.
- A more functional organization is adopted for practical and efficiency

reasons, although idealistic elements oppose the internal hierarchy (introduced to improve coordination), greater management authority and graduated pay scales.

- In order to meet its requirements for personnel with specific skills, the WTO may either seek external consultation, hire personnel more or less in sympathy with its aims, or develop the professional skills of its members in a relatively organized fashion.

Characteristically, therefore, there is gradual reversion to a rather more conventional pattern of management. The workers expectations of influence decline; various practices and bodies designed to express worker concerns cease to function; the authority of newly appointed or internally developed managers increases; the commercial stabilization of the enterprises both reduces the need for major change and provides greater material rewards to compensate for reduced social satisfactions; staff turnover and recruitment dilutes the body of the workers who remember the 'great days'; memories fade.

Superficially, this process corresponds to Miester's (1974) life-cycle model of producer co-operatives which results in the social degeneration of the enterprise and its dominance by management. There are four stages in this model. In the establishment phase a conflict develops between direct democracy and badly developed economic functions. In the second phase some conventional organizational principles are introduced to secure the survival of the co-operative but the conflict between idealists and pragmatists is still present. In the third phase a form of representative democracy is introduced instead of the direct form. This is because of the market pressure on the management system, pressures which are no longer resisted. This leads to a greater gap between management and the others. In the fourth phase the management gains full control of the enterprise and the degeneration process is completed.

This simple sequence is based on a conflict between democracy and efficiency, and while it does describe the course of some WTO enterprises the majority of cases appear far more complicated – or, indeed, quite different. In the first place not all the developments towards a more conventional form of management reduce the influence of the workforce: or represent a retreat from democracy (see the case of CLG in Box 6.2). More importantly, even when there is a clear decline in employee influence and involvement, this need not be permanent – as the case of Northwest Pre-Cast in Box 6.1 illustrated. In other words, a degeneration of democracy may be followed by a later regeneration. A clear example of this occurred in one Danish WTO where the workers developed a direct democracy immediately after the takeover (about 10–12 employees were involved). However the weekly general meetings seemed to produce more problems and conflicts than they solved, and after a year or so, when the enterprise was in serious difficulties, they appointed three people to take care of the management in collaboration with the board. The direct democratic element disappeared; old members left the firm, and new ones were taken in without involving them in the decision-making process. Some of the new members were not even told that the firm was more or less collectively owned by the employees. But after two or three years they decided again to introduce meetings for all employees, while still keeping the element of the representative democracy. Hence the process in some way resembles the life-cycle-model developed by Batstone.[7]

Two other patterns of development also occur. One displays a growth of democracy and is illustrated by the case of IKP in Box 2.4. These enterprises start at a moderately democratic level, but then through various learning processes develop and improve the employees' capacity to manage the enterprise. This requires that the distinct subcultures found in enterprises that have existed for several years, are altered and 'softened up' so that the employees can move from 'political' decision processes towards more dialogue-based processes in which they can learn from each other. This improved capacity makes them able gradually to take over a greater and greater part of the traditional managements power without the enterprise's survival being jeopardized, and without them forgetting their more idealistic aspirations, for example, for greater equality among the employees. As there is seldom agreement as to how far one can go with democracy, the process does not occur without some use of various power bases.

Finally, there are cases of stable democracy. These tend to occur in smaller enterprises where the workers have chosen a form of democracy which suits their aspirations and which has a rather good fit to the demands of the production process. This means that there are few contradictions between the ideals and the requirements from the market. Those contradictions which always show up are tackled by learning processes by the workers so that in the long run they are able to maintain a stable democracy. The Lake School of English (Box 2.1) and Reklame (Box 2.3) provide examples.

A lack of information gathered over a long enough period means most WTOs cannot be classified in terms of these different patterns of development and so it is difficult to judge how often each arises. Only in Denmark have WTOs been closely studied in this respect and there the degeneration of democracy has taken place in 6 cases out of 14. In the establishment phase of the worker takeover they all developed a degree of democracy which was later abandoned in favour of a traditional management. However, this transformation did not follow the course predicted by Miester. It happened, in all six cases, because the ownership degenerated. The firms either needed capital or employees – and the problems were solved by attracting either external capital (and control) or new employees (who did not become owners). This emphasizes the point that even if employee ownership does not in itself guarantee organizational democracy, it is (in the absence of major changes in property rights) a necessary condition for its development and maintenance in the longer term.

Conditions contributing to success

Three factors stand out as particularly important for the long term economic and social success of WTO enterprises.

The first concerns the characteristics of the workforce. Often, successful WTOs are based on the efforts of a cohesive homogeneous group of skilled workers even if a range of other employees are also involved. These characteristics reduce the number of differences and disagreements that arise, and help contain those that do. Moreover, such a workforce seems more likely to contain employees with both the latent ability to undertake managerial work and the self-confidence to do so.

A second factor contributing to the success of WTOs is a leadership which is competently committed to both social and commercial objectives and which can balance short- and long-term considerations. This may be provided by a single individual, or by a group. What must be avoided is an (other than temporary) dominance by either type of objective; or a failure to integrate the different objectives (which leads to conflict and inconsistency). A common pattern in Italy is for an older generation of workers' leaders to make up a board of management to whom managers are accountable. These leaders then negotiate terms and conditions of employment and any disputes with a fresh generation of shop stewards. The former group effectively argues for longer-term commercial interests of members; the latter represents their immediate or sectional concerns. But both groups share a common experience in and commitment to the labour movement (Holmstrom 1989).

The third factor which produces successful WTOs is the existence of effective and continuing external support. When this is available it is usually provided by the organizations of the co-operative movement (and more recently also by the SAL federations, in Spain). This is not simply a matter of access to finance – vital though that is. In Italy WTOs have received advice, orders, and managerial personnel from other co-operatives, or co-operative consortia. On occasions, in Italy and France, the enterprise may be merged into another co-operative either permanently, or in order to build it up again for a secure and independent future. Moreover, the integration of the WTO enterprise in the networks and associations of an established co-operative movement can provide:

- realistic models of participative management;
- a chance to recruit capable and committed managers;
- support for the social ideals of the enterprise;
- advice and training in co-operative organization;
- the opportunity to learn from peers who have faced similar experiences.

7 | The Support for Worker Takeovers: Structures and Strategies

Earlier chapters have highlighted the important role that external actors often play in the WTO drama. The main ones are trade unions, co-operative movement bodies, and government departments and agencies. Where the WTO option is generally considered by one or more of these bodies to be worth exploring, then they are likely to support, or even promote, a WTO attempt by the workforce. This can greatly increase the chances of an attempt succeeding, and can also affect the longer term prospects for the enterprises created. Nevertheless, support for WTO has frequently been controversial, and the best ways of providing it are seldom obvious (except perhaps with hindsight).

This chapter reviews the range of attitudes towards the WTO options that are held by these external actors and compares the structures and strategies used by them to provide support.

Before proceeding, however, one other important provider of support should be mentioned: the independent sympathetic professionals. These appear in every country and often play very important roles as long-standing advisors to WTOs. In Germany an informal network of these 'free professionals' has compensated for the relative weakness of the worker co-operative movement there. In Spain they are often to be found working in the small practices of professional lawyers, economists and accountants which are common in Spain and which provide advisory and management services to small and medium-sized businesses. Some of these *gabinetes de assesoria de empresas* are themselves SALs and wish to support industrial democracy. For example, one practice in a suburb of Barcelona has a close relationship with the Comisiones Obreras – the local communist trade union. The union may send shop stewards round to the *assesoria* if a firm is in trouble; the firm may then pay for a feasibility study for a conversion to a SAL, or the *assesoria* may do it itself, free, in the hope of gaining later business. They also help worker takeovers (and new start co-operatives) in finding official support. Comparable independent consulting partnerships exist in France, Italy and the UK. Sympathetic professionals are also found in universities and colleges.

Trade union attitudes

With the exception of Italy where, despite some tensions in relation to WTOs and co-operatives, the trade unions and co-operative associations are linked in various political federations, the dominant attitude of the trade unions towards WTOs in the 1970s was outright scepticism. This is partly explained by the difficult historical relations between trade unions and co-operatives: conservative 'petty bourgeois' traditions in the co-operative movement in Germany, compromises with fascist power in Spain, the clash between marxist and the anarcho-syndicalist approaches to co-operatives in France.

More importantly, the WTO option was not easily reconciled with many established trade union strategies. In Denmark the labour movement has traditionally adopted a centralized approach which is reflected both in the preference for trade union (rather than worker) buy-outs of enterprises in crises, and in the current proposals for economic democracy based on central funds. Similarly, the ideological and institutional attachment of the labour movement in the Federal Republic of Germany to co-determination in industrial relations has been incompatible with strategies of self-management and autonomy. Likewise, the fundamental commitment of trade unions in the United Kingdom to collective bargaining has meant that a management buy-out has commonly been seen as preferable to a WTO which would threaten conventional collective bargaining. More specifically, common trade-union arguments against WTOs have been that:

- Supporting attempts at WTO can undermine the fight against closure (and privatization).
- WTOs can lead to splits in the labour movement – as when workers elsewhere in the same industry feel their jobs are being threatened by support for workers in a WTO (e.g. the response of workers at Small Heath, Birmingham to the Meriden co-operative; similar situations have occurred in Spain).
- Support for a WTO will involve collaboration in job losses, wage reductions and the violation of other trade-union principles (e.g. concerning craft skills and job demarcations); in general, WTO are seen as producing marginal enterprises in which market pressures force 'self-exploitation'.
- Support for WTOs diverts scarce skills and financial resources away from trade unions' primary responsibilities; and diverts attention from the responsibility of governments to maintain employment.
- Enterprises arising from WTO do not usually survive for long. Traditional

approaches to the regulation of enterprises and the labour market have proved more effective, historically.

Such arguments generally ensured that mainstream trade-union movements were at best doubtful or indifferent, and at worst hostile, towards WTO. Co-operatives were commonly regarded as a distraction from major problems: class struggle and opposition to capitalism. Moreover, much of the *defensive* WTO experience (e.g. the 'Benn Co-ops') in the 1970s could be seen as confirming these views.

Nevertheless, during the 1980s, rising levels of unemployment and the failure of traditional strategies for saving jobs prompted a more positive reconsideration of the WTO option within the labour movements of all the countries studied (except, so far, Denmark). This led to varying degrees of support being provided for WTOs. In some contexts this involved a close commitment by the trade union giving them de facto status of main actor in WTO attempts. This dramatic change in posture resulted from their seeing new opportunities, or being forced to accept them, in changing political and economic conditions at local and national level. The clearest example occurred in France where the communist-oriented union, CGT, changed its analysis and attitude toward the social economy (particularly regarding co-operatives) mainly as a result of the changes (such as nationalization, decentralization, new employee's rights) that occurred in France after the arrival of the left-wing government in 1981. According to GCT, 'This new situation modified the balance of power in favour of the workers.' However CGT saw clear limits to the extent of the changes and firmly rejected as an 'illusion' the idea of a third sector, between the public and private sectors.

Co-operation (in production) was a means by which the CGT tried to find a solution to the general economic crisis, by implementing social changes that it considered to be appropriate. In the long term, this co-operation was seen as offering a 'possibility of enlarging a particular form of socialization within the framework of a mixed economy'.[1] In this perspective, the development of the co-operative sector contributed to the industrial strategy of the trade union in the following ways: it was a means of struggle to maintain and develop employment, in spite of the employers' failures; it strengthened the industrial structure and preserved the domestic market; it contributed to a modification of social relations; it expanded the consciousness of the workers and developed their management skills.

On this basis, the CGT searched for 'the best possible method and means to start a systematic and vast action'. This was done by creating first, a trade-union sector for the social economy; and secondly ADITES, 'a techno-political structure' – in effect, a small agency charged with participating in the actual operations of relaunching and starting enterprises of a co-operative or similar form. The CGT considered that the difficulties arising during a WTO required judgement and special consideration for each individual case: the co-operative solution was not the only one. The objective was to create 'authentic and efficient enterprises which would be well managed and based on democratic principles'. The CGT held the view that a three-cornered power struggle usually existed within such enterprises – between the elected management bodies, the appointed managers and technical experts, and the trade unions. However, although recognizing that the three power bases existed, the CGT was reluctant to accept such a situation and explicitly aimed to place the union in overall control – organizing the workforce and supervising management activities. Moreover, the CGT was opposed to any of the attempts to introduce more radical forms of organization that often arise in WTO – elements of direct democracy, or efforts to transform social relations within the enterprise.

There is no doubt that the CGT put pressure on both government bodies and the co-operative movement during the first three years of the socialist government and more financial support was provided as a result. However, the support of the CGT for WTOs during this period was permeated by its hierarchical and adversarial assumptions and inseparable from its broader strategy in the new climate created by the arrival in power of the left. This political dimension was often allowed to overshadow the concrete problems posed by particular WTOs, with political considerations overriding a more reasoned approach to particular situations.

Changes in the political circumstances (the governmental austerity program, the confrontation between the socialist party in government, and the communist party which abandoned the government) did not facilitate collaboration between the CGT and government bodies over WTO. In fact, this collaboration was directly questioned during particular operations, such as Manufrance. Hence the CGT curtailed its policy of support for WTO and sought instead more classical solutions (e.g. purchase by another company). The CGT justified this shift by blaming the failure of WTO co-operatives on financial and governmental bodies.

While this case is unique in that trade-union policies have changed very sharply and at a national level, there have been other cases of very directive intervention by trade unions. In the UK, for example, the Transport and General Workers Union was closely involved with the 'Taunton Shirt Co-op' which eventually failed (Thomas and Thornley 1989). This failure exemplifies many of the classic traps trade unions may fall into in a WTO – especially the centralization of control in a manager/shop steward alliance to preserve the trade-union investment at the expense of member involvement; and inadequate business skills (in particular, in this case, marketing). This type of 'controlling' support has been highly disappointing in its results and is quite quickly abandoned, though, like some congenital defect, it still emerges from time to time.

Happily, most trade-union support has been more limited and more pragmatic, taking the following forms:

- advising and assisting with (or financing) expert analyses of business prospects;
- legal assistance;
- organizing;
- taking part in (or taking over) negotiations with politicians, potential creditors etc.

This kind of support has resulted from the pressure by local trade unionists when directly confronted with the concrete problems of maintaining jobs and work communities. These local initiatives have gradually affected the national positions of at least some unions so that now trade-union attitudes and activities in relation to WTOs are far more varied and complicated than in the 1970s.

In Germany, at least 7 out of the 17 member unions of the German Trade Union Federation (DGB) have had to deal with WTO in sectors controlled by them. But neither DGB nor member unions have produced anything near a clear policy statement: most of them have, officially, ignored the subject. The same is true for unions outside the DGB. Only the metal workers union (IGM), with about 50 per cent of the known WTO cases occurring in their organizing areas, has considered the problem. IGM head office was instructed by the 1983 Union Conference to produce a policy statement on the subject which was concluded and published in March 1985. It is so well balanced 'that those in favour of and those against WTO can refer to it' as one IGM official put it. This policy statement is based on the understanding that the worsening employment crisis must lead to unconventional trade-union responses; and that resisting further job losses in an effective way will not be possible within the terms of the present (industrial relations) law.

Essentials of the statement are:

- Support for WTO must not absolve either the 'mother' company (in the case of plants and subsidiaries) or the state from their responsibility to provide employment. Hence the state should provide financial support for WTO on the grounds that it makes more sense to invest money to create (or save) jobs than to finance unemployment.

- WTO should lead to long-term job savings. This requires that company purposes are defined differently, 'stressing labour market and socio-political points of view and not paying excessive attention to company profitability'. This aims at a new kind of overall economic budgeting, and at dealing with WTO attempts as elements of regional and structural policies.
- The financial position of employees must not be jeopardized, for example, by employees providing money to the old company to prevent a closure; or by employees investing large sums in their own WTO enterprise at considerable personal risk.
- Certain trade-union standards concerning payments, holidays, working conditions, etc., shall be observed (no union support for 'self-exploitation').
- More workforce influence, in the sense of extending co-determination rights.
- Trade-union support of WTO shall take account of the chances of success or failure and this requires a close study to discover what has really caused the closure.

What trade unions actually do is not always consistent with their official pronouncements (or silences). In practice, almost no takeover initiative in Germany has been developed without trade-union support, mainly provided by local or regional officials. Head offices, usually, are more cautious and certainly more 'diplomatic'; they prefer to observe developments while providing no more than tacit consent.

In Great Britain local officials usually operated in isolation without national union guidelines or support, and without adequate resources and skills to carry out the feasibility studies and the negotiations for a takeover. Nevertheless, once they became seriously involved the experience was often fruitful, for example:

- USDAW negotiated with the large supermarket chain Fine Fare over their divestment of several small retail stores. Eventually three co-ops were set up and Fine Fare gave the co-ops *better* terms than they offered for stores divested to management buyouts.
- TGWU negotiated with Dunlop in setting up Bootle Co-operative Installations.
- NGA were prominent in setting up Parados Graphics Co-operative.
- TGWU gave considerable support to the setting up of Liverpool Boatmen Ltd.

As in other countries the question raised by such local initiatives have received considerable attention and it is clear that attitudes are now changing at the centre. Three large unions (the AUEW, TGWU and GMBATU) have produced policy statements supporting co-operatives under appropriate conditions – with 'new starts' receiving a stronger endorsement than WTO. The first two of these unions have special branches in London for workers in co-operatives – a development that would have been practically unthinkable even five years ago. In addition the Trade Union Congress has produced a policy statement, though its position is more cautious. Its main reservations are:

- low wages undermining other TUG wage agreements;
- recognition of the need to restructure the business (and not save all the jobs);
- recognition of the need to acquire sound financial/marketing information on the business;
- a wariness of parent companies trying to sell unprofitable companies that have no 'turnaround' prospects;
- possible loss of redundancy payments and other rights;
- a concern that co-ops may be used as a strategy to ease the path of privatization; they discourage using the co-op option in such situations, *even as a last resort*.

However, the statement did recognize the importance of working with co-opertive support organizations in promoting WTO and other co-operatives.

Such policy statements are more a reflection of changing attitudes and the continuing debate (see Table 7.1) than an indication of current trade-union activity. In practice there are considerable differences both between unions, and within unions, with the attitudes and policies at national level tending to be more conservative than at district/regional level. This is especially clear where unemployment and local economic initiatives have stimulated new thinking in particular localities – for example, the involvement of AUEW and TASS in co-operatives and WTO in Sheffield. The differences between unions are largely accounted for by the extent to which WTOs are an issue for them. Those unions whose members are in small businesses are more likely to be confronted with the issue than those in nationalized industries. Privatization could force other unions to become involved but so far political opposition to privatization has obscured WTOs as a possible response.

Elsewhere broadly similar developments have taken place. In Spain in the 1970s the main trade unions were opposed to the operation of the National Labour Protection Fund which enabled WTOs to take place. They felt that the formation of SALs entailed the transfer of an increasingly heavy respon-

Table 7.1 Principal reasons for trade unionists supporting or rejecting an involvement with WTO and co-operatives

---

Advantages and hopes

- Strategy against closures
- Strategy against unemployment
- Extension of industrial democracy (challenge to managerial prerogatives)
- Extension of work reform
- Extension of Labour movement presence in small firm sector

Disadvantages and fears

- Low wages and poor terms and conditions
- Possible undercutting of prices in conventional firms (and consequent threat to other jobs)
- Only some jobs saved
- Clash with traditional principles – unfamiliar strategy demanding new skills
- Financial risk – where loans are made
- May undermine opposition to privatization
- Incompatible with occupational base of trade unions
- Greater administrative problems of organising in small firms/co-operatives
- Undermines collective bargaining and protection of workers
- Cultural clashes with co-op movement – e.g. demands for reform of TU sexist and racist practices
- Diversion from class struggle against capitalism
- Collaboration with different class interests associated with co-operative movement.

---

sibility to workers during an economic slump. If the company purchased by workers was subsequently forced to close, the workers could not join together to resist the closure since it would be seen as their own failure. However, these attitudes were not always shared by trade union members and significant numbers were becoming involved in WTOs. The CCOO Confederal Congress held in 1982 produced a change in the position of this union towards WTOs, in which they were shortly joined by the UGT. Indeed, in 1983 these two unions – the one communist- and the other socialist-oriented – were instrumental in establishing FESALC, the Catalonian Federation of SALs, partly in order to avoid inter-union rivalry in the area of SALs. They still have an agreement which shares representation on the FESALC committee between the two unions. In general the union attitude is now fairly favourable towards SALs, but they have no clearcut policy: their position is basically pragmatic – to evaluate each case on its merits.

The French CFDT, which has always been better disposed towards self-management, has come to comparable conclusions: it approves a change to a co-op status only if it is likely to lead to social progress within the enterprise: improvements to working conditions, work relations, implementation of a democratic structure, and so on.

Overall therefore the picture of TU support for WTOs is varied and changing. Increasingly, national trade-union organizations are expressing a more balanced approach to WTOs. Some are still emphasizing the dangers but others go further and link their support to the positive opportunities that WTOs present for improvements in the quality of working life and workers' participation. In the mean time, the officials of other trade unions continue to be involved in WTO attempts without having any guidelines from their organization.

Co-operative movement support for WTOs

While the presence of worker co-operatives and worker-owned firms in itself lends credibility to the idea of a WTO, the actions and attitude of co-operative movement bodies are very important. However, support for WTOs is a controversial issue within worker co-operative movements – largely because of the risk of failure and its effect on the movement (and its image). Higher risks are faced by less well-established movements, particularly where they fail to develop appropriate strategies and structures, as a brief review of the experience in different countries illustrates.

The Italian co-operative movement embraces all the main forms of co-operation (not just worker co-operatives). It is most easily described as a *network* which comprises three different types of organization:

- the individual co-operative
- the co-operative consortium
- the co-operative association

The *individual co-operative* may operate on the market without necessarily being enrolled in a co-operative association, and without having relationship with other co-operatives.

The *co-operative consortia* are formed by a number of individual co-operatives which together carry out one or more shared activities in a particular sector. Here the term used is 'consortium-enterprise' in so far as it manages at first hand its productive activity. By contrast, the 'service consortium' does not act on its own behalf but only and exclusively in the name of, and in the interests of, its associate co-operatives, and in activities designed to obtain better services rather than profit (purchasing or marketing consortia, for example). A consortium may group together a number of co-operatives in a small area, or at a regional or even national level.

These consortia may belong to one of the *co-operative associations* (there are three main ones with differing political orientations) which represent, protect, assist, regulate and guide the individual co-operatives that belong to them. As legally recognized bodies they also have the power to step in as trustees where a co-operative is failing. There also exist a number of national organizations, which take the form of limited companies and whose stock is owned by co-operatives and other economic entities.

Thus, a co-operative may be linked to others in at least five different ways:

- in a provincial sectorial grouping
- in a regional sectorial grouping
- in a national sectorial grouping
- in a regional association of co-operatives from different sectors
- in a national association of co-operatives from different sectors

It should be remembered that these various groupings are not only concerned to represent the interests of the individual co-operatives. Today, they have increasingly taken on the role of providing co-ordination and strategy formation for a 'grid-iron' organization, an organization whose main strength is its ability to establish or re-establish enterprises extremely rapidly, and to plan their growth by means of operations involving assistance, collaboration and inter-trading among different elements in the network.[2]

The co-operative movement continues to increase in importance and size in the most traditional geographical areas of co-operative activity, where the organizational network is most firmly established, and where it possesses sufficient autonomous assets to be able to provide guarantees for bank loans. The strength of the movement in such areas should be emphasized: for example in Italy, there is actually a continuum between *worker* and *co-operative* takeovers. Some WTO occur as a result of interventions by the co-operative associations: the closure or divestment of an economic unit may be seen as providing an opportunity to make a strategic investment at a low price. Thus, if the enterprise in question can be readily integrated into a network, strengthening the market or geographical position of the association, it may encourage and support the workforce in mounting a takeover. This increases the economic coherence of the movement. But it can also be seen as an 'aggressive' strategy, uncomfortably similar to a capitalist one.

An example of this is provided by Consorzio Produttori Laterizi (CPL), which arose when a company in crisis was saved by the setting up of a company comprising 'natural persons' (the workers) and 'juridical persons' (six producer and worker co-operatives in the same sector and in the same geographical area). A manufacturing consortium was thus constituted. Further evidence of this trend is provided by the concern shown in one report (Cespe 1986) over the tendency to be found in the larger co-operatives to purchase or to set up limited companies 'when this proved convenient'.

The strength of the movement is also evidenced by the ability of the co-operative associations often to arrange the transfer of workers from a co-operative in crisis or that is closing, to other co-operatives in the sector or locality, thus avoiding having to make them redundant.

It is this strength and dynamism which has enabled the Italian co-operative movement to support WTO financially and in terms of real services on a continuing basis. Such support is not provided automatically or in every case and WTO are seen as imposing a burden on the movement even if they also provide opportunities. There is also concern over the problem of marginal enterprises in a movement which it is often said operates *a due velocita* ('at two speeds'). Nevertheless, within the constraints of its available resources, the movement has successfully supported large numbers of WTOs, many of which are themselves now contributing to the strength of the movement.

By contrast, in France, where there are far fewer worker co-operatives and they are not closely associated with other branches of co-operative activity, attempts to support WTOs have been more problematic. Most worker co-operatives are members of CG-SCOP. (Membership is not compulsory but it opens the way to some potential advantages among which is the 'co-operative quarter' that is allocated to co-operatives in certain areas of public purchasing.) CG-SCOP has the job of disseminating information to co-ops, organizing and representing them, and supporting their internal and external development. It comprises:

- A classic structure of representation: every three years in a national conference, workers' co-ops vote on policy and elect the members of the national council, who in turn elect the Federal Bureau and appoint the general secretary of the Federation.
- National and regional services, co-ordinated by the general secretary, whose job is to disseminate information, give assistance and organize training. There is a Federal Expansion Fund (Fonds d'Expansion Confederal), which provides financial assistance in the setting-up, development or rescue of co-ops (funded by one-third of subscriptions paid to the

Federation by co-ops). In addition, since 1981, the Development and
Support Office does work requiring specific skills and tries to provide
'relief managers'. There is also a Promotions and Exports Office.
- At the regional level the progressive establishment of regional 'technical'
  delegations with paid workers alongside the regional 'political' unions –
  which are mainly responsible for selecting candidates from the co-ops for
  the national council. The 'technical' delegations respond to the local
  development needs of co-ops and assist their growth. As at the national
  level, the main work of these delegates is to support the creation of co-ops
  and to ensure continuous managerial and other assistance to those
  already in existence.

At the local level, co-ops are trying to set up exchange networks. This is
hindered by their limited numbers in relation to the diversity of their
activities and preoccupations. Nevertheless, there are federations of co-ops
in the building and graphics industries, and in metallurgy, while groupings
are being formed in information processing and in the furniture trade.

On a more ideological level, the revitalization of co-operation has led to
questions and debates illustrated by the recent establishment of a network of
small co-ops affiliated to the Federation: faced with the institutionalization
of a movement where democracy is not a major issue, and with a pyramid
structure which does not fit their needs, these co-ops advocate co-operative
radicalism, springing from actual co-operative practice (in relation to information, training and facilitation), and more horizontal, decentralized forms
of organization, based on the establishment of local groups, the proliferation
of interco-op exchanges and the opening up of co-ops to their environment.

In relation to WTOs the problem for CG-SCOP was to develop a consistent
policy and the means to carry it through that was realistic in relation to the
available resources. Confronted with a rapid growth in the number of
(mainly small) co-operatives (see Chapter 2) CG-SCOP began to stress,
particularly in its policy for the establishment of new co-operatives, the
importance of the organization of systematic support for medium-sized and
industrial projects. In this way, during the 'fervent and innovative' Congress of 1981, the movement explicitly looked at WTOs as a means of
furthering its development. The number of WTOs increased sharply and
although the government provided increased financial assistance in 1982,
this was insufficient to meet the demands both of the existing co-operatives
and of further WTO attempts.

In 1983 CG-SCOP tried to adopt a more selective attitude towards WTOs
and the conditions required for their success – covering for example, the
quality of equipment, market forecasts and the capacity of management. But

it still lacked the resources and the experience to prevent an embarrassing number of failures. By its 1984 report CG-SCOP's attitude had hardened further. Although acknowledging that its growth was largely due to WTOs, it said, 'Many of the WTOs occurred under unreasonable circumstances, *and often without consulting the movement*. The inevitable and expensive failures did and will continue to affect the image of the movement' (emphasis added).

CG-SCOP subsequently shifted its strategy primarily toward the consolidation and development of already existing co-ops, and toward the conversion ('mutation') of healthy enterprises, usually those whose owners were retiring – though it did not completely abandon the promotion of 'new starts' and 'well prepared take-overs of failing enterprises'. In practice this new strategy encompasses a much more rigorous policy towards WTO projects involving a large number of employees. It also means that WTO projects involving less than thirty persons are treated like 'new starts' (i.e. starting with a small number of employees and building up employment gradually). CG-SCOP report a reduced demand for WTOs from employees, in comparison with the great popularity that WTOs enjoyed in 1982–4. Since 1986, it appears that the movement has become even more oriented towards 'new starts' than it was previously.

In retrospect this brief account suggests that the co-operative movement, confronted with an unprecedented expansion and diversification, did not succeed in clearly defining its strategy. It was drawn into the classic pattern of over-promotion and under-resourcing to which left movements and governments are prone, and more generally it tried to take advantage of every apparent trend or opportunity to build itself up (variously, 'new starts' associated with local employment initiatives, WTOs, and later 'conversions'). It had no clear conception of the place of co-operatives in the French economy, and so its ambitious reactions effectively prevented it from opposing, in due time and with sufficient firmness, some of the pressures brought to bear by other actors (such as the state and trade unions). Despite these difficulties, which meant some WTOs were supported or promoted on a quite inadequate basis, it remains the case that other WTOs during that period, and many since then, have been successful.

The lessons from other co-operative movements are far more limited. In Spain both the worker co-operative and SAL movements have been experiencing a period of rapid growth, but the development of their support structures has lagged behind the increasing number and variety of worker co-operatives and SALs. These support structures have been developed furthest in Catalonia, where FESALC (the Catalonian SAL federation) is able to assist WTOs with legal advice, in negotiations, in obtaining local and national government support, and by providing managerial support (see the case of Equipos Industriales in Box 5.2). FESALC itself has received substantial government funding. FCTAC, the Catalonian federation of worker co-operatives, tries to provide similar services but it is also heavily involved with 'new start' co-operatives. It now has a number of local offices and is trying to promote 'consortia' in sectors like building and textiles where co-operatives are strong. Most of these developments are too recent to be able to evaluate their impact on the incidence and performance of WTOs.[3]

In Great Britain, the workers' co-operative movement doesn't have social or commercial links with the other more strongly developed sectors of the co-operative movement. Its representative body is organized on a national basis and poorly resourced, providing a forum and a source of information, promoting experimental training and trying to initiate inter-sectoral collaboration. In addition, sections of the movement have been reluctant to commit resources to the support of WTOs, which they saw as leading to crippled enterprises made up of reluctant co-operators. Hence, although some help has been given to WTOs, these were not a priority and its efforts have mainly been oriented towards the needs of 'new starts'.

In Germany the traditional co-operative associations have not wanted to have any involvement with WTOs but on occasions help has been provided by what can be called the new co-operative movement – the renaissance of co-operative ideas and practice, fertilized by the 'alternative scene' and explicitly including producer co-operatives. New organizations and other support structures have been developed besides numerous co-operatively organized projects with commercial, social, educational, ecological, cultural and other purposes.[4] Politically, this 'scene' is loosely associated with the Greens and the SPD. With its growing infrastructure and the expertise of many individuals closely connected with it, substantial support has been provided, often in a quite competent manner. While their financial means have been very limited, they sometimes played a key role in giving advice and organizational support as well as informing the public and raising 'sympathy capital' – usually in close collaboration with committed union oficials. Of course, the relationship between the workers involved in a takeover and those from the new social movements who were offering support did not develop without conflicts – quite different worlds, ideologically and socially, were trying to collaborate. All those concerned have had to learn a great deal about each others' concerns and views. But these problems have not been insoluble, as the case of AN (Box 3.3), which was quite clearly influenced by the ideas of the new co-operative movement, illustrates.

Table 7.2   Policy measures and initiatives relevant to WTOs

Pro-active initiatives and measures:

- Publicity and information dissemination
- 'Early warning' systems to give notice of firms that are in difficulty
- Promoting dialogue between the trade-union and co-operative movements
- Formulation of policy guidelines and strategies

Initial enabling support:

- Funding for feasibility studies, advisors and other preparatory expenses
- Assistance with premises
- Funding and facilities for preparatory courses and meetings
- Assistance with negotiation and lobbying of third parties

On-going support:

- Training courses for members and managers
- Facilitating secondment/recruitment of managers
- Purchasing contracts for products or services (including training, work experience, etc.)
- Rate relief
- Tax relief
- Reinvestment tax incentives

Infrastructural enhancement:

- 'Standing arrangements' with independent agencies for funding feasibility studies when required
- Regular financial support for independent agencies
- Creation of roles/departments for co-operative and other enterprise support
- Creation of semi-independent agencies
- Procedural changes to speed up WTO support
- Training for co-operative support staff
- Research and dissemination on new model rules, taxation practices etc.
- Promotion of co-op support networks, conferences etc.
- Promotion of networks between sources of product ideas and unemployed/co-op and labour movements

---

State support for WTOs

State support for WTOs has not been limited to the financial measures discussed in Chapter 4. As Table 7.2 indicates, WTOs have been assisted in a wide range of other ways. Most of these initiatives have occurred as part of more general efforts to develop local economic strategies or to support the co-operative sector, and hence many measures have occurred only in particular localities or regions rather than nationally. Moreover, in very few areas indeed have a significant proportion of these measures and practices become effectively institutionalized. At least initially, support for WTOs has always been ad hoc – it has usually been accidental (as when WTOs have been able to use measures designed for rather different purposes), or reluctant (as when an administration was giving way to political pressure), or impromptu (hastily devised and implemented). Not surprisingly, therefore, such efforts to support WTO have been characterized by a number of common weaknesses:

(i) Expecting too much, too soon

Hastily prepared measures, limited time horizons, and over-ambitious policies have resulted in what is seen as an unacceptably high proportion of failures. This was the experience at a national level in France between 1982 and 1984, after which the policy on WTO was reversed. The underlying misconception in such cases is the failure to appreciate the essential social dynamics of a successful WTO and the commercial pressures to which they are subject. The short-term concern to preserve employment has undermined longer-term prospects for self-reliance and economic regeneration. Local authorities in both France and Britain have also intervened in this way. Similarly in Britain WTOs have sometimes been seen as a vehicle for pursuing a range of other social objectives – for example, concerning equal opportunities and model employment practices – with insufficient regard to the commercial constraints and pressures affecting the enterprises, or the time and support required to institutionalize such values in an effective way.

(ii) Too reactive, too late and too slow

Support agencies frequently wait until approached by workers from a failed business. They don't usually have an early warning system for identifying possible candidates and in general they don't actively promote the WTO option. In consequence they tend to be confronted with the 'last resort' possibilities which are the highest risk. In addition support provided from local governments has the disadvantage that it is bureaucratized, often requiring the co-ordination of several departments to ensure that, for example, premises, finance and advice are provided quickly and to schedule. There are horrendous tales of WTO projects sitting in a series of lengthy departmental queues while customers, suppliers and workers gradually lose patience and their money. This situation is compounded by the fact that state support is not just channelled through the local state, or regional governments; many labour market policies are administered through national agencies. Arranging a co-ordinated response from several layers of government to an 'unusual' project can be very difficult.

(iii) A mismatch between the requirements of WTOs and the services offered

In Germany and the UK especially, many of the quasi-autonomous agencies created to support local employment initiatives are heavily oriented towards the promotion of small new enterprises by the unemployed. For example, most local co-operative development agencies in the UK make this a priority. As a result they lack the skills or resources to handle the related, but generally much more complicated and urgent problems posed by a WTO.

However, there have been some exceptions: the Scottish Co-operative Development Committee has consistently made the support of WTOs a priority and has been moderately successful in doing so. Their approach is summarized in Box 7.1.

Box 7.1   The Scottish Co-operative Development Committee's Approach to WTO

The Scottish Co-operative Development Committee (SCDC) has the most extensive experience of WTOs of any of the co-operative support organizations in the UK. Its approach has three elements:

(i)   measures to obtain early contact with enterprise closures;
(ii)   providing assistance to the work force in considering the WTO option and in trying to achieve a WTO;
(iii)   supporting the new enterprise in a variety of ways after the takeover, often for a prolonged period.

As well as some general publicity with trade-union officials, SCDC has promoted the idea of WTO with a range of economic development officials in local government and in the Scottish Development Agency. The officials often hear of impending closures and notify SCDC when a WTO may be an option. These arrangements operate informally by telephone agreement and at standard rates, so that there is no delay.

The first task is usually to inform the workers and their leaders about the co-operative option. This is a frank description of what they can expect – it is not a matter of 'selling' the idea, which may be abandoned at this point. Thereafter it is a matter of working with potential members to assess the feasibility of a cooperative. This will involve cycling through the following activities in progressively greater detail:

(a)   Analysing why the business closed.
(b)   Searching for products/services for the co-operative and identifying customers.
(c)   Identifying whether the necessary factors of production are present or could be acquired. This will frequently involve negotiations with the previous owner, or the liquidator if the business has gone into liquidation.
(d)   Assessing the human resources of the co-operative. Identifying how many people the new business can employ, whether people have the necessary skills and commitment, and working out how the co-operative will be managed.
(e)   Working out the financial resources that the co-operative will need to get off the ground, and identifying ways it can be raised.

If the prospects are reasonable SCDC may then help in mobilizing public support for the co-operative in order to help persuade the previous owner or other relevant organizations to help the co-operative. They will also be closely involved in preparing the business plan in order to raise external finance and backing. If this succeeds they then help to implement the plan and get the co-operative off the ground.

Because of the need to slim the business down, and the additional time for planning and preparation that is available, SCDC generally favour 'phoenix' co-operatives rather than 'rescues'. One experienced former staff member has estimated that for every ten occasions when they make contact with the workforce of an enterprise that is being closed, on roughly five occasions the discussions will be very quickly abandoned (usually because of a combination of poor prospects and workforce reservations); on a further four occasions the option will be seriously explored but will not in the end be achieved; and on only one occasion will a co-operative start trading. When a WTO cannot be achieved it is usually for a combination of reasons, but the absence of people able – or with the confidence – to undertake managerial roles commonly contributes. On occasions, SCDC has attempted to overcome this problem by seconding one of its own staff into the co-operative on an interim basis.

Once the new co-operative is established, SCDC development officers will stay in close touch, providing further advice and assistance especially during the crucial early years. SCDC has encouraged such co-operatives to lease from them (at a very modest charge) a simple micro-computer with a basic accounting package prepared to the co-operative's requirements, for which initial training is provided. They believe this is often instrumental in promoting a much more positive attitude to financial information and management generally.

(iv) A failure to provide 'second stage' support

Agencies (and governments) have often failed to appreciate the importance of support for WTO enterprises being available after recovery has been more or less achieved – in order to carry through the development phase and sustain the social progress of the enterprise. Quite apart from the financial resources required, such support would require greater expertise than many of the agencies possess. Despite this, there are exceptions – such as the case of Lithosphere in Box 7.2, which indicates the sort of sustained improvement in performance that such support can bring about, and which prompts interesting speculations about what might be possible if such support were generally available for the more entrepreneurial WTOs.

Box 7.2   The case of Lithosphere

In 1979 the Charity Commissioners instructed the charity War on Want to dispose of its in-house printing department, because it judged it really to be a commercial operation. The six staff (four full-time, two part-time) who were made redundant bought the equipment with a five-year interest-free loan of £30,000 from War on Want, and, using their redundancy payments as working capital, set up Lithosphere Printing Co-operative in April 1980. At this point they had an annual turnover of about £90,000. They worked in cramped premises with quite limited equipment and it was very hard to do more than survive. The members realized that somehow they needed to undertake a major development.

By good chance they heard of a sympathetic bank manager in a not-too-distant suburb and moved their account. In early 1982, with a turnover of about £130,000 and a staff of eight, they were able to arrange their first expansion. They moved to premises three times larger and took a seven-year lease on an £80,000 two-colour press. This was a huge risk – and the members had to guarantee the financial arrangements personally, putting their homes at risk – but it worked out. Towards the end of 1983 they were in a much stronger position (with a turnover of about £330,000 and twelve full-time staff) when the Greater London Enterprise Board (GLEB) indicated that it might be prepared to provide finance for strategic investments to strengthen the co-operative presence in particular sectors, one of which was printing. Lithosphere sought advice from the British Print Industries Federation and with the help of a consultant prepared a comprehensive proposal for another major expansion. GLEB accepted the proposal and provided a £200,000 loan on very good terms – thereby allowing the co-operative to purchase a four-colour press and to replace a great deal of now obsolete equipment. Again, the investment was successful and the co-operative extended its market from the trade unions and community groups it had originally served, into educational publishing work. Two years later its turnover had risen to about £550,000 and it was employing about twenty full-time staff.

In 1985 in the wake of this continuing expansion the co-operative again sought outside advice, this time from a print industry management consultant. He reported favourably on their performance but identified a number of ways in which they could strengthen their management structure and practices. By happy coincidence it was at this moment that Lithosphere had the chance to join an experimental training scheme for co-operatives jointly promoted by ICOM and GLEB. This provided further advice and resources, as well as an impetus, to carry through both the training and the reorganizations identified by the print industry consultant. Perhaps even more importantly, this training scheme brought members in contact with many other co-operatives, not just in London, but in France and Italy as well. The effects of this were electric: it was 'a tremendous inspiration – it really opened our eyes . . . we saw what could be done'. So the experimental training scheme generated a renewed commitment to both expansion and co-operative working. A range of courses were put on with the objective of increasing shop-floor business understanding and confidence – so all members could play a full part in the monthly meetings.

In early 1989 the co-operative had an annual turnover of about £1,200,000, employed thirty-three staff, and was undertaking another large and risky investment – this time largely on the basis of its own resources (in the form of a £200,000 loan from the co-operative's own pension scheme).

(v) No evaluation of support and a lack of learning

The absence in any of the countries studied of any systematic efforts to assess policies of support for WTO is striking. This may be understandable in the northern countries, where there have been fewer WTOs, but it is astonishing that, for example, in Italy only one book has been published on the subject (Irecoop 1985) and that was based on presentations to a colloquium rather than any empirical studies. In consequence, it is impossible to compare the effectiveness of different methods of support for WTOs or to compare the costs of support for WTOs with other efforts at employment creation or preservation; and major errors in support for WTOs have had to be painfully rediscovered even when firms in the same industry were involved (e.g. textiles).

Despite these weaknesses there is no doubt that state support has been very important. Moreover, the weaknesses have been increasingly recognized and in areas with considerable WTO activity the support policies and instruments have been, and still are, evolving steadily. The general picture, therefore, is one in which more extensive and better delivered state support is now available in countries and regions where WTOs are accepted, and where the co-operative movement (and SAL federations) along with their political supporters and labour movement sympathizers have been strong enough to influence governments, whether locally, regionally or nationally.

Methods of support and intervention

In Chapter 3 it was pointed out that a conventional consultancy approach to the support of WTOs was inappropriate and ineffective. Likewise, directive 'top–down' interventions by external actors were more likely to stifle than to stimulate the workers' psychological ownership of the project and the vital commitment, mutual aid and self-reliance that this generates.

In general terms, it is appropriate for those advising WTOs to adopt a more 'bottom–up' approach – to attempt to involve as many of the workers as possible and to aim to facilitate their own problem-solving and learning.[5] There are several reasons for this. In the first place, the crisis of possible closure promotes new relationships among the workforce and a confused desire that 'things should be different from before'. A participative approach is in tune with this feeling, and demonstrates an appreciation of the concerns of the workforce and thus strengthens the advisors' relationship with the WTO. Secondly, there are all the economic reasons (discussed in Chapters 3 and 6) why it is important for the workforce to be actively involved in a WTO. Finally, the actual take-over process is also critical in laying the foundations for democratic management in the future.

This is not only a question of how to organize the 'superstructure' of a company (its statutes and procedures, leadership and industrial relations structures, communication and control systems, delegation of respon-sibilities and power etc.). To be sustained, democratic management must be embodied in the productive structures of the company, anchored in collab-orative and responsible work practices, and represented in an organic integration of functions and roles, as well as in enlargened role boundaries. The problem is that co-operative rules (and those of other forms of worker ownership) generally rely on the mechanisms of representative democracy to give the worker-members managerial decision-making powers. Over time, this arrangement produces marked differences in levels of involve-ment and competence among the membership, to the extent that the accountability of the leadership and the empowerment of the workforce are undermined. Hence, as Chapter 6 implied, to avoid degeneration it is important for the representative procedures to be complemented by ele-ments of direct democracy oriented towards the lived daily experience of work, and in working arrangements that encourage an appreciation of the contribution of others in the enterprise.

However, it is also clear that attempts to promote widespread involvement also face many difficulties and pitfalls. For example, the abandoning of existing structures and excessive egalitarianism can totally confuse and discredit the whole process. Another problem has arisen where help is provided by strongly ideological sympathizers. These may have excellent campaigning and leadership skills, but their role in the project may become confused – are they advisors, or project promoters? These volunteer helpers may take over, to a certain extent, the roles of the workers concerned and promote developments in which the workers are faced with the real risks of the market but without, for example, sufficient financial support.

Such problems are certainly not inevitable however. Where advisory support has been effectively and participatively provided, it seems to use the following methods:

- having an explicit contract with the workforce, the objectives of which are defined for a limited period of time, and periodically renegotiated;[6]
- accepting the need for the delegation of specialist tasks (for example drawing up a financial plan) while consulting everyone on essential decisions by regular 'feedback' sessions, presenting different scenarios;
- providing all the workers with channels of direct expression appropriate to their cultural background and organizational experience.

Such methods can avoid the dangers both of unstructured participation and of calling in experts at an early stage to solve the pressing economic problems (and putting off considerations of internal organization until later). How these general principles are applied in practice obviously depends on the size of the enterprise, the time available and the extent to which the workforce wishes to participate. In a small business undertaking a 'phoenix' it may be possible for the development advisers to work with the whole membership, the group itself regulating the extent to which different members participate. An example is provided by the case of Aire Habitat in Box 7.3.[7]

In a larger enterprise, where there are greater differences in levels of skill and more marked cases of dependence on particular individuals, the bulk of the technical planning work will be concentrated in the hands of the few. But at the same time, it is possible for groups to form homogeneous work teams, from the same workshop or division, to discuss the work (job content, working conditions, product quality, etc.) and the modifications to be introduced. The greatest problem is often time. In the UK some co-operative support organizations have made their loans to WTOs conditional

Box 7.3   The case of Aire Habitat

In December 1980, M. Prudhomme's companies were put into liquidation following the owner's arrest for fraud. Most of these companies were based at Nozay in the Paris region (though two small branches had also been set up at Lyon and at Rouen). The first company had been formed in 1974 with six employees, but the group grew rapidly, reaching 280 employees by the time of the crisis. The business specialized in the conversion of attics, a gap in the market that M. Prudhomme had been able to exploit by perfecting a technique that he had patented. Conversion of lofts was negotiated on the basis of an inclusive price per square metre. The enterprise enjoyed quite a good reputation as regards working conditions. There were no unions in these companies, which always had fewer than fifty employees in order to avoid having works councils.

By December 1980 these companies had already been in difficulties for several months. In a continuous state of expansion, the Prudhomme companies were kept going by some clever accountancy. However, in September 1980 the problems worsened, a receiver was appointed, and plans for restructuring were agreed with M. Prudhomme. This meant dismissing 120 staff. But there was no great reaction to this news because the employer saw each one individually to tell him that he would be re-engaged at a higher wage later on. Later M. Prudhomme was arrested (for other reasons) and the companies were put into liquidation.

The premises at Nozay were occupied. People could not understand why a business that was doing so well (its order book was full, amounting to 800,000 Frs.) should be closed. Eight workers started a CGT union branch; local authorities, councillors and trade unions supported the movement and began to study the possibility of a takeover. There was no mention of a co-operative at that stage. All efforts were directed to finding a new owner who would take back most of the employees. However, losses were assessed at between 50 to 60 million francs, and so no one was in a hurry to buy the company.

Gradually the movement fell to pieces. Some of the executives started their own small business, the client file disappearing, most inopportunely, at this moment. In the end it was a group of only ten people (shopfloor workers and supervisors), who were rather bewildered and somewhat sceptical about the experts they had met up to that point, that came to a meeting with a group of advisers in March 1981 on the initiative of a local councillor.

After this first contact with the leaders of the occupation, a framework for the involvement of the advisory group was quickly established. It defined the arrangements for a joint study of the case. The eleven workers interested in resuming work agreed to collaborate with a group of advisers (one commercial and two mangement consultants) with a view to starting up a new business.

The demand that the whole of the group should be involved in this process itself reveals the dual objective of the advisors' exercise:

1 to provide the technical management skills (in the widest sense of the word 'management') that people starting a business must have in order to control the future of their project;
2 that they chose to seek to equip everyone with those skills followed from another consideration – the desire to lay down the conditions for real democracy in the enterprise.

The process that was set in motion was not aimed at creating a whole host of bosses in the same company, but at creating the condition for collective management by making a distinct break with the prevailing division of labour. It took fifteen days' training (over a three-month period) during which the following were accomplished:

- informing the members about co-operation and arriving at the definitive constitution of the group (all shareholders except for a secretary and a commercial manager, who were taken on later);
- setting up the finances of the project (based mainly on a capital of 280,000 Frs., each co-operator acquiring 20,000 Frs. worth of shares, the money being drawn against the sum of their unemployment benefit under the Act of 22 December 1980);
- acquiring a legal status for the co-operative;
- planning the organization and operation of work, including administration and advertising; negotiating the first contracts.

When the 'Aire Habitat Co-operative' was formed on 1 June 1981, the company's strong points seemed to be the gap in the market; the quality of workmanship provided by a group of good skilled workers, and the awareness of the need for strong management. Nevertheless, they faced the difficulties and uncertainties inherent in any new enterprise (the time required to reach the point of profitability; possible mistakes in assessment of the market; suppliers' terms for settlement); and some of the group were unwilling to remain attentive to management problems.

The early months were very eventful. *Economically* 'Aire Habitat' on the whole achieved its forecasts. The order book filled up and the wages were paid (6,000 Frs. net for all the worker-shareholders; 7,100 Frs. for the managing director; 5,000 Frs. for the secretary). It is a long way to the two-year point beyond which one usually reckons that a business is established, but one can show a certain optimism over the way the group proved its management qualities – for example, in the considered way it adapted its business plan to the situation which actually arose.

Socially this initial phase was also very rich. The period of occupation at the premises had started to break down the divisions between different categories of employee (shopfloor, office workers, productive workers, non-productive,

French, North African and Portuguese, executives, foremen, skilled workers, unskilled) and this process continued, despite setback and difficulties. Three instances illustrate the progress.

1 At first the group itself took on the work of door-to-door selling, but because of the difficulties they encountered, they decided in July to take on a salesman. However, this was not a return to the old methods: the salesman worked to a catalogue prepared by the co-operators; and they have also given up the idea of a price based on square metreage.

2 The group was able to reach a workable, if inegalitarian compromise to neutralize certain issues (e.g. family ties) which threatened to upset the balance in the group.

3 A group of 'non-productives' got together following a dispute with the 'productives'. This dispute, which was overcome in September, marked an advance in the life of the group because, until then, most of the 'productives' had preferred to leave matters of management to the rest. By threatening not to pay their share of the capital, some shareholders created a situation in which roles could be redefined. From then on there was to be a profound change with regard to the technique inherited from the previous business which had been considered as one of the project's essential assets. Realizing their power, the 'productives' were able to apply their knowledge and gradually modify the technique that had until then been imposed on them; and they reviewed with the customers certain projects which they considered from experience to be badly conceived and thereafter 'Aire Habitat's' distinctive approach developed as part of a process in which the co-operators were able to regain their autonomy.

(The co-operative continued to be successful: five years after it was formed it employed twenty people and its turnover had quadrupled.)

on members of the co-operative undertaking specified training (which may take the form of organizational development work with a consultant) in the months folowing a WTO (Barnsley Metropolitan Borough Council, undated). But whenever it takes place it is always hard to reconcile the inevitable period of experimentation and apprenticeship with the urgency that characterizes the first steps of a WTO enterprise.

The dilemmas of support

This chapter can be summarized by pointing to a number of dilemmas that are inherent in any attempt to support WTOs.

The first is that between realism and encouragement: any policy to support WTO is likely to have the unintended consequence of encouraging attempts on an inappropriate basis, or of raising false hopes, where the prospects are poor. Conversely, it is essential for those who assist the workforce in a WTO attempt to confront them with the requirements of pursuing such a course. But this must not be done in a way that is unnecessarily discouraging. Such a balance may be particularly hard to strike if those concerned are under pressure to 'do something'.

The second dilemma arises over the competing priority of social and economic concerns. This appears in the extent of the solidarity it is reasonable for co-operative organizations (e.g. in Italy) to show towards WTOs, given the financial support they may require. It also appears in the tension between efficiency and democracy in the organization of WTOs: can the enterprise afford activities that do not directly contribute to economic recovery, or practices that may be socially desirable but less efficient? The problem is that these activities and practices can also make an essential contribution to the economic recovery and longer term success of the enterprise (by sustaining motivation, promoting wider understanding, bringing on individuals to accept managerial responsibility, etc.).

Finally, there is the dilemma of the helping relationships – how to provide assistance without on the one hand encouraging a relationship of control and dependence, or on the other hand allowing the project to fail unnecessarily. A WTO is a collective learning experience. While a great deal can be learnt from sympathetic advisors, there are limits to how far and how fast it is possible to develop a practical understanding simply on this basis. Moreover, the scope for that most vital of all forms of learning – learning by the correction of errors – is likely to be strictly limited by the precarious financial situation. Hence a reluctance to insist that particular problems are faced may lead to costly mistakes jeopardizing the enterprise with which the advisor has come to identify. He or she will wish to protect her personal investment – quite apart from all the other considerations. On the other hand, efforts to prevent failure may easily be counterproductive: insisting that particular issues are tackled may undermine the relationship, leading to a rejection of the advisor; or it may lead to dependence with the advisor exercising informal control and finding it increasingly difficult to withdraw. This dilemma is also implicit in the provision of financial support. Where public funds (or guarantees) are provided for a WTO, the danger arises that the workforce may see itself as being rescued, rather than being rescuers. The ethic of self-help may only extend to the engineering of political support, and not to commercial reconstruction. The obvious solution is for such support to be provided on unambiguous terms, either as a once and for all contribution, or in relation to pre-determined performance targets. Thus the workforce will know where they stand, and any further assistance must be earned. In practice, however, the uncertainties associated with a WTO may make it difficult to develop sufficient contractual clarity on a realistic basis – and so the door may be left open for assistance, and thus dependence.[8]

8 | Prospects and Possibilities

For some, the most important message of the WTO experience described is simple: like other successful organizational innovations it keeps alive the hope of evolving on a more general basis ways of working and organizing that enhance the roles, influence and status of ordinary working people, that allow them to contribute and realize more of their creativity and intelligence – and that remain efficient and competitive. Viewed in these terms WTOs are at least providing a little fuel to keep a dream burning. But do they have any more practical significance? Might they, even, provide some small part of the means to realize such a dream? And do they offer anything to those with less encompassing concerns?

Having reviewed specific aspects of the WTO phenomenon, this final chapter returns to some of the wider questions raised at the start of the book. It assesses the significance – now and in the future – of WTOs, the different reasons why they may be supported, and some of the outstanding questions concerning how that may best be done.

WTOs and job preservation

Since WTOs are, first and foremost, about job preservation in a context of company closures and high unemployment, the first question to consider is whether they are likely to have any continuing significance at all, whether they deserve much further attention. Endearing they may be, but, it can be argued, in countries where WTO are common, they already receive some special treatment and make their contribution to economic life; while in countries where they are rare, policies of support would only take effect slowly and uncertainly, and hence they are hardly a priority for the scarce time and attention (not to mention resources) of public authorities. More significantly, WTOs are clearly children of economic recession and restructuring. So by far the most likely scenario for WTOs is that they will simply fade away. On this view, the gradual recovery of the European economy means a reduction in the number of failing and bankrupt enterprises, a gradual decline in the unemployment rate, a slackening of public support for employment creation measures, and hence far fewer new WTOs being attempted and successfully carried through. At the same time, the existing WTO enterprises will die out gradually, or be taken over: the marginal ones would be in danger of this anyway but many will be further weakened by a more competitive labour market (e.g. as key workers drift away to much better paid jobs becoming available elsewhere). The stronger ones, those that had achieved consolidation, will survive longer,[1] but, as the founding cohort retires, they will tend to lose their distinctive character.

This is not a critical view of WTOs: arguably, it accepts them for what they are without becoming sentimental – an essentially counter-cyclical micro-economic response, worthy of some support and promotion at the *start* of a period of high unemployment, but not when the *end* of one may at last be in sight.

There is obviously some truth in this view and it cautions against exaggerating the continuing significance of WTOs. Nevertheless, it is vulnerable to two counter-arguments. In the first place it considers WTOs simply in terms of job saving and creating, and neglects other reasons why they may continue to be supported (these are discussed presently). Second, this view is too sweeping: many regions, industries and marginal groups have yet to benefit significantly from the present economic recovery. In many parts of the UK, and of Europe more generally, the local (or regional) economy remains in recession and unemployment rates remain depressingly high. In such areas job saving and job creation remain high on the political agenda. The demographic forecasts for the 1990s suggest some attenuation of the problem – but very few think there is much prospect of it going away. Indeed, a number of recent studies (e.g. by the UN Economic Commission for Europe; by the French Government Commissariat du Plan) have suggested the problem may very well get worse again (Eme and Laville 1988). In addition, the intensification of international competition in the 1990s is likely to precipitate further economic restructuring, which, even if the economy is growing overall, is bound to hit some regions and localities hard. In such areas even a modest level of WTO activity (that may seem trivial in terms of national economic output) could bring substantial local benefits. So even if job saving and creation (and, on this basis, WTOs) are becoming less *generally* relevant (which is debatable), they will still remain highly relevant in particular areas and regions.

Given, then, that the public interest in job preservation measures – for example, local employment initiatives, local economic strategy – is likely to continue in many areas, policies of support for WTOs will be well justified on this basis. As earlier chapters have shown, the number of WTOs in an area does respond to policy initiatives. Comparatively modest amounts of public funding are often able to facilitate substantial investment by the workforce, the banks and other parties. Compared to the jobs created in many other LEI projects, the number of jobs saved in WTOs is often high. In general, the time and resources committed to WTO support appear to generate more jobs than an equivalent effort spent on 'new starts'. The survival rates of WTO enterprises, as far as they can be estimated, do not support the popular view that these enterprises soon fail – indeed they seem to compare favourably with the survival rates of other small businesses.

Such observations suggest that in countries like the UK where they have been comparatively rare, WTOs and measures to support them warrant considerably more attention than they have generally received. Whether this will be forthcoming is another matter. But even if it is not, one can easily foresee a continuing role for WTOs as part of what may be called the 'fringe economy' in depressed regions and areas, including the inner cities.

Increasingly, the mainstream economy (of large companies and the more successful small and medium-sized enterprises) is bordered by a *complementary*, and in significant measure, socially supported, sector of embryonic and marginal businesses, community-based economic projects, small co-operatives, and the like. This fringe economy, with its apparatus of start-up grants, soft loans, advisory services, low cost facilities and premises, training services and (increasingly) a measure of market protection – via ideological or local sympathy, or the procurement policies of local authorities and the more socially responsible large companies provides both a safety net and a launching pad. It represents a decentralized social and economic response in areas where capital has closed down and retreated, abandoning sections of the population; but it sometimes also encompasses activities where private capital is not yet confident of a high enough return to be willing to invest.[2] As such, the fringe economy is continually shifting and changing: some of its constituents grow strong enough to enter (or re-enter) the mainstream; others may not particularly wish or expect to, being more concerned to earn a modest living with like-minded people and in a congenial manner. In some areas economic regeneration may render the fringe economy unnecessary; in others it grows rapidly, or looks set to become an established and substantial part of the local economy.

If this prospect has some validity then it provides a second possible scenario for the future of WTOs. They will remain a feature of the fringe economy. The majority will live out their days there; a minority will use it as a launching pad and enter the mainstream. In terms of job preservation, both outcomes may be considered successful and worthwhile – barring, of course, the minority of cases which collapse soon after they have been set up.

The left critique of WTOs

Quite how desirable one considers this prospect to be is another matter. The 'left critique' of WTOs provides one basis for a hostile assessment. In essence, this view argues not just that wage levels but also the internal arrangements of WTO enterprises, like other enterprises, are largely determined by external, especially market, forces. Hence in taking over failed enterprises, and faced with peculiar problems in obtaining finance, WTOs will normally face a precarious commercial existence with low wages, long hours and poor working conditions. Nor, if they wish to survive, is there much prospect of organizational democracy: competitive pressures will demand the most efficient – capitalist – organization. Workers' control in any meaningful sense is simply not a possibility.

Of course there will be a few exceptions – enterprises that stumble on particular market niches and that are able for a few years, perhaps more, to maintain more democratic working arrangements. But these will be exceptions, and cannot be used to hold out a different prospect for the vast majority. This majority must conform to the dependent and marginal role of most small firms, a role that fits the requirements of large corporations in a modern capitalist economy (Rainnie 1985). In short, the ideal of prosperous and autonomous co-operatives is naive, because (quite apart from other considerations) most small firms are neither of these things; hence support for WTOs means the promotion of false hopes, low wages, poor working conditions and demoralization.[3]

One response to such observations is that if one is considering WTOs simply in relation to job preservation/creation (the grounds on which most are undertaken) then it is a bit severe to damn them for not also achieving economic consolidation and organizational democracy. Of course a substantial proportion of small and medium-sized enterprises can be considered 'marginal', but those that die are generally replaced with others – and they still contribute substantially to employment. In short, the critique is not particularly relevant.

Many of those willing to support WTOs in relation to job creation will be uneasy at simply side-stepping the criticisms in this way. So it is worth asking whether they are justified by the recent European experience, and is that experience illuminated by the left critique? In some measure the answer must be yes: the marginality of many WTO enterprises noted in Chapter 6 is clearly consistent with this view and the analysis of small firm/large firm relations in the modern economy helps to explain why the image of the prosperous and autonomous small firm (or co-op) does not match their actual circumstances in so many cases. On the other hand, the description and analysis in earlier chapters also provide a basis for questioning important features of this perspective.[4] The weak points are as follows:

- This perspective seems to underestimate the potential for the 'consolidation' of WTOs; as Tomlinson (1982) has pointed out, Marxists sometimes mirror neo-classical economists in their attribution of rationality to the untidy processes of economic life. They, too, seem to assume that if a plant is threatened with closure it must be unprofitable. As Chapter 2 and several of the cases demonstrate, this is simply not the case. Moreover, being dependent on large firms does not necessarily mean one cannot prosper (as cases like Northwest Pre-cast demonstrate). Put another way, the left critique spoils a fair point concerning marginality by overstating it.
- The idea that, with few if any exceptions, significant changes in management practices in WTOs will be either temporary (with degeneration following inevitably) or impossible, seems likewise to be a quite considerable overstatement. To be sure, the development of new ways of working and more democratic forms of organization is far from straightforward – but a good number of WTOs seem to have achieved this, and arguably those that have tried and failed were unsuccessful for reasons that were at least as much socio-cultural as a matter of market forces.
- It virtually ignores the non-material benefits for individuals and communities that are commonly associated with WTOs; and it tends also to exaggerate (e.g. through fast and loose charges of 'self-exploitation') the significance of a temporary or permanent decline in material benefits and working conditions that may well occur – which is not to deny that low wages are a serious problem in many of the marginal WTO enterprises.
- The critique generally assumes that WTOs will create enteprises isolated from others sharing similar values and experience and that there will be little or no effective external support to assist them. The possibility of gradually building up networks of comparable enterprises and supporting agencies (thereby redressing to some extent at least the weaknesses such enterprises otherwise face) is often ignored or seen as unrealistic.

Overall, therefore, the left critique is more convincing if it is not pressed too far – if it is taken as pointing to some of the difficulties to be overcome, rather than as grounds for not advancing policies of support for WTOs.

The support of WTOs: some basic principles

The preceding sections have suggested that on simple job preservation/job creation grounds there is a strong case for supporting WTOs. They do not, of course, provide 'the answer' to concentrations of high unemployment, but considered as one instrument among others they have a contribution to make. If this is accepted then the experience of WTOs that has been discussed also indicates some of the principles that should govern any attempts to provide such support, for example:

- WTOs should have equal access to measures for enterprise creation and recovery available to other forms of enterprise; administrative, legal and fiscal anomalies that obstruct WTOs should be removed wherever this can be simply arranged (Holand *et al*. 1986).
- Any support for WTO must recognize that the workforce are the central figures in the project. WTO are achieved through and because of the workforce. If the workforce is not interested in a WTO – and they may have good reasons for rejecting the option – then the idea cannot sensibly be pursued. Their perspectives, concerns, needs and potential contribution must be central throughout the planning and negotiations to support the project. Likewise, they are responsible for the success or failure of any adequately funded venture.
- Financial support for a WTO should not be an entitlement. It must always be justified in relation to the prospects for developing a viable enterprise. It should be provided as far as possible on a contractual basis that allows additional support to be obtained where past results and future prospects warrant it.
- The financial support provided for WTOs should be commensurate with the other support services available, and vice versa. Money without real services is foolhardy; support agencies without access to finance are pointless.
- Advisory support for a WTO is not the same as normal business advice, nor is it, in general, well provided by conventional business advice agencies. Such agencies may well have a contribution to make in providing specialist back-up to a WTO and its advisors. But they commonly lack or fail to appreciate the social committment, specialist information and extent and style of workforce involvement required.
- Given the extreme urgency affecting most WTOs, it is essential that the provisions of any government measures are clear, and that they can be effected quickly. A complicated generous programme will be less useful than a simple strict programme.
- Support for WTO should be limited to small and medium-sized

enterprises. Because of the difficulties described in Chapter 3, rescues of larger and more capital-intensive plants and enterprises should be considered exceptional and undertaken only under very favourable circumstances.[5]

Such principles are, of course, fairly well established in Italy and Spain, and in some measure also in France. However in countries with less experience, like the UK, their acceptance would still constitute a considerable advance.[6]

Beyond job preservation: restructuring and economic pluralism

The preceding principles, which assumed a job creation/preservation rationale, can be considered a 'minimalist' position regarding support for WTOs. More extensive support may also be advocated, but it is important to recognize this will generally be for rather different reasons than simple job preservation. Two other rationales for supporting WTOs are worth distinguishing.

The first sees WTOs as a means to assist the processes of economic change and restructuring. The rationale for this objective is based on two propositions:

(i) Restructuring that arises *within* a declining enterprise is very much preferable, both socially and fiscally, to restructuring that results from the closure of one enterprise and the opening of another, often in a different region.

(ii) WTOs can succeed where others have failed or are unwilling to try. Even if (inevitably) WTO enterprises are marginal to begin with, they can consolidate and develop.

Clearly, this objective is far more ambitious than simple job-saving. A job-saving policy might have a time horizon of, say, 3–6 years, and be considered successful even if the enterprises created were economically marginal. But support efforts intended to promote economic restructuring would aim to ensure that wherever possible WTO enterprises were able to escape their marginal status and secure a longer-term future. It is clear especially from the Italian experience that the financial resources, the expertise and the experience required to achieve this are very much greater.

The other rationale for supporting WTOs sees them as a means towards what can be called *economic pluralism* (Hodgson 1984) – the creation or strengthening of a worker co-operative or worker-owned sector within a mixed economy. The very substantial contribution that WTO enterprises have made to the growth of the worker co-operative sectors in Italy and

Spain, and the emergence of the SAL phenomenon in Spain, suggest that support for WTO can be an effective means of promoting 'economic pluralism'.

In practice these two objectives are closely associated. A dynamic sector can hardly be based entirely on marginal enterprises. In addition, the development of a worker co-operative sector with its own infrastructure (or equivalent secondary organizations for employee-owned firms) increases the prospects for economic restructuring through the continuing support they provide to WTOs. Clearly, the pursuit of these objectives implies more vigorous policies than those outlined for the 'minimalist' position. By implication, the potential for restructuring and economic pluralism is unlikely to be realized by policies simply concerned with job preservation.

The crucial requirement is for assistance in achieving the second, development, stage and what was referred to as consolidation. This in turn implies resourcing the infrastructure of the worker co-operative/worker-owned sector in such areas as:

- sectoral collaboration and joint ventures;
- consulting and advisory services;
- training and cultural support for both workers and management;
- the development of institutions for co-operative financing.

Given that some, doubtless imperfect, bundle of policies was gradually put together with these objectives in mind, one can envisage a third scenario for the future of WTOs in countries like the UK and Germany. This would involve a gradual build-up in the number of what would initially be small worker co-operatives and worker-owned firms. To begin with they would almost certainly be concentrated, as in France, in particular sectors, but there might also, be as in parts of Italy and Spain, concentrations in particular geographic areas. They would be supported and represented by a number of intermediary bodies capable of promoting commercial collaboration and providing common services. These arrangements would not, in themselves, resolve the problems of marginal enterprises; but they would give some purchase on it. Those enterprises that showed they had some prospect of successfully undertaking a development phase would have the financial and other support to do so, with many becoming much more substantial enterprises in the process. Others would at least have some assistance in making the best of their difficult circumstances, helping them to survive with dignity for as long as possible and, if need be, to bow out gracefully.

This scenario is much more ambitious and longer term, and doubtless opinions will differ on how attractive it is. Nevertheless, it does seem worth considering. One set of arguments would concern the general benefits widely believed to be associated with employee ownership – providing a less adversarial context for employee relations, enabling a modest diffusion of wealth and power, encouraging greater commercial understanding and efficiency.[7]

For those on the left this scenario would have somewhat different attractions: at a minimum, it would combine economic efficiency with bringing a progressive influence and some social ownership into the area of small and medium-sized enterprises – where the trade-union and labour movements usually have little if any presence. More ambitiously, and with a longer timescale, such a scenario holds out the prospect of developing the kind of powerful collective entrepreneuralism that is evident in the Italian co-operative movement and in the Mondragon co-operatives. Such arrangements do not ignore market forces, but are able both to temper them where necessary and to take advantage of them where possible, through elements of decentralized planning, inter-trading and solidarity that are grounded in a vigorous social movement. To this extent the scenario may even be seen as offering a way to achieve that holy grail of the left – something that might reasonably be called socialist, and that would also be popular and practical.

Policy issues for economic pluralists

Needless to say, to realize such a scenario would involve addressing a number of difficult issues. Many of these concern the problems of worker co-operative and worker-owned sectors in general and really go beyond the scope of a book on WTOs. What follows, therefore, is a brief survey of some of the main issues that are being, or would need to be, addressed wherever serious efforts are in hand to use WTOs as a way of developing economic pluralism.

The locus of support

Where should the support for worker co-operative and worker-owned sectors be located – in the trade-union and labour movement; in agencies sponsored by local or national government; or in secondary organizations representing the enterprises themselves (cooperative associations, SAL federations etc.); or in some combination of these?

The potential benefits of close ties between the co-operative and trade union movements have been emphasized by a number of writers (Thornley 1981; Cornforth 1982) and it is clear that the general support of trade unions, and often their specific assistance, are important in many WTOs. It is clear, too, that attitudes in trade unions towards worker co-operatives and worker ownership have been becoming more favourable. The main counter-arguments are that one should not underestimate the conservatism of trade unions,[8] that they tend to be too controlling in their support, and that it would be very difficult for them to keep separate their traditional role in representing workers to management, from a new role in promoting the longer term prospects of a workers' enterprise. Interestingly, where trade unions have played an effective part in supporting workers' enterprises (as in the Welsh TUC initiative and in the SAL federations) it has been done at arm's length, by promoting and supporting independent agencies. This seems like a sensible principle to follow.

Local or national government, or its agencies, provide another possible means of delivering support services, and especially where others are unable to do this effectively (for example, because the secondary organizations are weak), they become an obvious candidate. Ease of access for co-operatives to other government programmes may be a further advantage. On the other hand, state involvement has sometimes brought problems of bureaucratization and the involvement of staff lacking appropriate expertise (often because a novel policy is administered through traditional structures and procedures). It also brings dangers of sudden changes in political commitment, of short term political pressures, of dependence and the gradual co-option of an embryonic movement. So as with trade unions, close and continuing state involvement will generally be undesirable; but this does not mean there is no role for the state and its agencies.

Secondary organizations are most frequently advocated as the appropriate base for support services – particularly by those in and associated with workers' enterprises, of course. The case is strong: the staff of these organizations are most likely to have the information, expertise and experience needed, and as regards WTOs their interests – in achieving successful long-term outcomes – are most likely to ensure both that reasonable prospects are recognized and that poor prospects are discouraged. The only problems are that in some countries these organizations do not yet exist (and hence LEI and new social movement networks may have to provide the support instead), while in others there may be two or more of them in competition.

Arguably the latter is as much an opportunity as a problem. While WTOs, and worker enterprises more generally, may have much in common, they also vary quite considerably in their ideologies and purposes. Hence a measure of choice as regards who one turns to for support is surely desirable (if not always feasible). This certainly exists in Italy and Spain where the state and the trade-union organizations are also involved. Such considerations suggest that there is no one best location for WTO and worker enterprise support – it will depend on how well developed the secondary organizations are, on the attitude of trade unions, and so on – but that pluralism will be an important principle to promote.

State support: positive action or positive discrimination?

The preceding discussion raises the broader question of the part played by the state in promoting economic pluralism, and the extent of state intervention that is needed. At a minimum, the state has three roles in relation to the support of WTO.

(i)   Guaranteeing equal access – e.g. in relation to information, government programmes, etc.
(ii) Enabling not directing – e.g. providing resources to support those who choose the WTO option and can meet its requirements (revolving loan funds, capitalizing unemployment benefit, as in France and Spain, etc.).
(iii) Co-ordinating and reviewing support for WTO – e.g. promoting networks and collaboration among the interested parties, the evaluation of policies and practices etc.

However this rather begs the question of what constitutes equal treatment.
    One argument is that the workforce of a closing plant or enterprise is so disadvantaged in its attempts to mount a WTO in relation to other interests (creditors, asset-strippers, mother company etc.), and so obstructed by a general lack of understanding of WTO (among banks, suppliers, customers, trade unions, receivers, etc.) that only government measures to legitimize and facilitate WTO will prevent failures in the market for enterprises and allow the full benefits of this option to be realized. Such measures might include:

- extensions to employee rights to information in the context of plant and company closures;
- modifications to receivership law which are currently framed entirely in terms of creditors and shareholders rights;
- under specific conditions the introduction of a 'right to buy' for the workforce.[9]

However, it can also be argued that this will not be nearly enough: historically, worker co-operative sectors have only prospered in protected environments providing preferential access to finance and/or product markets, the latter via government purchasing or consumer co-operatives.[10] The counter-argument is that although these have helped at particular times that does not mean they were, or remain, essential requirements for the development of economic pluralism. Nor, indeed, are they wholly desirable as they introduce a significant element of dependence. Needless to say, the economic significance of such assistance is hard to assess, so how much support and protection these sectors need, and for how long, remains unclear.

Legal and financial questions

Earlier chapters described some of the legal and financial issues that are pressing in different countries and these vary considerably in line with the different legal and institutional patterns that have grown up. However one very basic issue is shared by WTOs and workers' enterprises generally in all the countries studied – the problem of access to capital, and the basis on which funds are lent to such enterprises. This problem does not only arise at the time of the WTO – it is also one of the obstacles to undertaking the development phase and achieving 'consolidation'. Put crudely, the argument is as follows: on the one hand there is the view that the demands of co-operative movements fly in the face of normal financial principles and practices. For WTOs in particular, it is patently unreasonable to lend, or to expect others to lend, substantial sums of money, unsecured, to an enterprise whose record of management is at best non-existent and at worst one of failure. The opposing view is that such 'normal' (or capitalist) principles are clearly inappropriate as they severely disadvantage worker owned enterprises, which the record shows can be successful and socially desirable. So these sectors require separate financial institutions, operating on a basis that respects the principles on which these enterprises are founded.

Not surprisingly perhaps, arguments on these lines sometimes obscure the possibility that both sides have a pretty good case and the way forward lies in respecting both perspectives. The trouble with ignoring normal financial principles (involving, in the case of high risk investment or loans, performance related returns and the chance to affect the management of the enterprise) is that loan funds will tend to run down, and there will certainly be no build up of the movement's resources. Some enterprises are bound to fail, but the co-operative movement has no way of sharing in the prosperity it helps to facilitate in other cases. Put another way, *who pays for the risk*? Either there is effectively a continuing state subsidy, or the cost is borne by the successful co-operatives – and a mechanism to ensure this is required. Moreover, without such a mechanism one can have reservations about the equity of arrangements under which, in effect, members of established worker co-operatives have the advantage of the 'free' capital accumulated by their predecessors and bequeathed to them. Besides, it is not clear that these normal financial principles are necessarily incompatible with co-operative princples.[11] At this stage the discussion can become very technical – concerning for example the respective merits (both commercially and in terms of political values) of different forms of quasi-equity (e.g. non-voting preference shares), equity participation co-operatives, supervision by contract etc. But these financial and legal questions actually point towards the more general issue (already raised in Chapter 5) of the desirability of these enterprises being wholly owned by (and solely accountable to) their workforces. Arguably, this is the more fundamental issue.

Autonomy and interdependence in a social movement

The ideal of the autonomous community of producers which decides its own future, administers its own affairs, and enjoys the rewards of its own industry and enterprise, seems to pervade the thinking of movements for workers' enterprises (co-operatives, SALs etc.). It is an image dripping with positive connotations – solidarity, self-reliance, direct participation, accessible and accountable leadership, mutual respect, craftsmanship. . . . The issue is: how realistic is such an image? Earlier in this chapter the notion of the prosperous and autonomous small firm was criticized on the grounds that it ignored some common patterns of small firm/large firm relations. The structure and dynamics of markets severely circumscribes the autonomy of

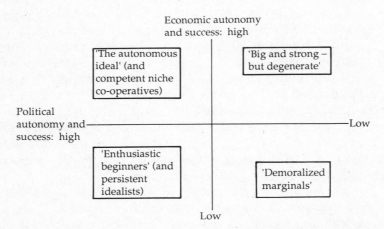

Figure 8.1 Dimensions of autonomy and types of worker enterprise

many 'independent' enterprises and leaves them vulnerable to changes in products and productions processes. Even if one believes such pressures only constrain (rather than determine) organizational form,[12] such enterprises are clearly less adaptable by comparison with *groups of enterprises* enjoying access to greater human and financial resources, and the benefits of scale, diversity and market power. The problems can be crudely represented as in Figure 8.1.

WTOs and other workers' enterprises often start with high ideals but precarious finances ('enthusiastic beginners'). They aspire to the 'autonomous ideal', and may move some way towards it – for a time; a few, indeed, may be in the right place at the right time and grow strongly – though if they become very large the nature and extent of democracy that is possible changes, and the tendencies towards degeneration are likely to increase.[13] Most are not sufficiently successful to fail in this comfortable way: sooner or later, unable to escape their marginality, or unable to prevent the erosion of a comfortable niche, the shifting forces of the market wear them down (and they become 'demoralized marginals'). These stereotypes provide a very simplified picture, of course. Many WTOs and other workers' enterprises are 'in-between', both economically and socially; and as Chapter 6 indicated, tendencies to regeneration can counteract degeneration.

Nevertheless, if this is accepted as a map of the space within which co-operatives often move then the experience of the more successful worker co-operative movements (Italy, Mondragon) suggests that one way of improving their prospects is for small and medium sized co-operatives to collaborate in order to increase their economic strength (Jordan 1986; Cornforth *et al.* 1988). But there is still a price to pay (and it must be paid in advance) – a definite loss of autonomy. So even if these 'integrated systems' allow a group of co-operatives to move generally 'upwards' (so that they are spread around the centre of the grid, and above), they may well appear initially as politically doubtful (as well as complicated, difficult and risky). The success of the Italian co-operative consortia has been widely admired by co-operative officials and others elsewhere, and there are reports of the worker co-operative movements in France, Spain and the UK all attempting in different ways to imitate them. The achievements to date appear distinctly limited.[14] Perhaps this is because it is a slow and difficult process to get started – but perhaps, too, the commitments to equality and democracy have a side-effect of making co-operatives more concerned with internal processes, and less outward looking. Such speculations aside, the point remains that the deep-rooted attachment to the idea of an autonomous workers enterprise co-exists uneasily with aspirations to build the sort of cohesive movement that the economic realities seem to require. Of course, in terms of good intentions, this is not an issue – co-operatives and co-operators can easily claim a commitment to the wider movement. The point is that the constitution of most co-operatives is built on the principle of autonomy, whereas the principle of relatedness, of mutual responsibility within the wider movement, has no such institutional foundation or expression. Hence, one is entitled to question the feasibility in most circumstances of building a coherent economic sector on such a basis.

The implications of this discussion are that in important respects the autonomous ideal may actually be a liabilty for workers' enterprises. Yet this ideal, or at least the values so often associated with it, are usually the distinguishing concerns of such movements' leaders and activists. They are what inspire commitment and provide a common bond in a whole range of ways that are vital to the success of the enterprise. Take away those concerns, and would there be a movement at all?

This presents a serious dilemma for economic pluralists: either they maintain the principle of autonomy (and insist on internal accountability only), in which case they must also accept its implication – a fairly restricted scope for economic pluralism;[15] or they decide that autonomy is not after all such an essential principle, and pin their colours to a rather different mast – one based more on interdependence and some sharing of control. This dilemma is really a version of the issue of 'purity versus compromise' which faces all social movements.[16] Perhaps, however, the stronger movements also show the way forward – through a pluralistic approach. In Italy a broad spectrum of types of enterprise encompassing a variety of different orientations are prepared to collaborate sufficiently to ensure their own economic strength – even as they compete fiercely on political grounds. In this way there is still room for 'purists', but within a much broader and stronger movement than they could ever achieve on their own.

Conclusions

The idea that WTOs may be a vehicle for promoting economic pluralism raises a number of broader issues concerning the prospects and policies for worker enterprises more generally. In particular there are difficult questions concerning the role of the state, the financing of such enterprises, and whether they will be willing, in the event, to surrender some of their autonomy in order to build a stronger and more coherent economic sector. So although the Italian experience (especially) does support the idea that WTOs can help build up movements of workers' enterprises, there are also grounds for caution, and some rather substantial obstacles to be overcome.

In fact this conclusion is a general one and applies in relation to the other hopes that people have of WTOs. They do indeed provide opportunities for individuals, for workforces, for public authorities, for co-operative movements and the like – but the opportunities are not easy or straightforward. Substantial benefits for all these 'actors' will often be available – but for all of them, too, there will be pitfalls, dangers and costs. So even if it is accepted (as this book has tried to demonstrate) that the unduly negative popular image of WTOs (in terms of rescues, failed businesses, self-exploitation, etc.) is unwarranted, opinions can still differ on whether and to what extent they merit support and promotion. Whether policy-makers are prepared to face the difficulties and risks in pursuit of the opportunities will probably depend, ultimately, on the value they place on the idea of collective entrepreneurship[17] as an alternative to a predominantly reactive, oppositional, work culture – for in the end this is what makes WTOs distinctive, and what they represent in social and political terms.

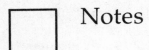

Notes

Chapter 1

1 The 'Benn co-ops' have been extensively discussed with Eccles (1981) providing a fascinating and detailed account of KME – but also see Tynan and Thomas (1984) for an interesting account of workforce reactions. Fairclough (1986) presents a Marxist analysis of Meriden Motorcycles, and a similar line of argument is developed by Clarke (1979) in respect of KME. Coates (1976) includes material on all three cases and is interesting as a period piece that conveys the aspirations of many in the labour movement at the time. Bradley and Gelb (1983a) include an extended case study of the Scottish Daily News and this book also provides far and away the most careful comparative analysis of 'defensive' and 'financial' WTOs (though they do not use these terms) including case studies of employee buy-outs in the US, as well as an account of Manuest. Other useful accounts of the employee buy-out phenomenon in the US are to be found in Russell (1985), Stern and Hammer (1978) and Woodworth *et al*. (1985).

2 The UK provides the clearest case: there had been hardly any WTOs in the years before the 'Benn co-ops' were set up following a wave of factory occupations in the early 1970s. No other *clear* cases of large defensive WTO have occurred since then, but there have been many 'participative' WTOs, especially from the late 1970s onwards. In France the picture is more complicated but the upsurge of WTOs that followed the advent of the left government in 1981 included many quite ambitious schemes that displayed several of the characteristics of defensive WTOs. Since then WTOs have corresponded much more to the 'participative' type. The changing social climate is also very clear in the Italian case if one compares trade union and workforce attitudes during the militant factory occupations in the early 1970s with those a decade later. The shift from 'class struggle and resistance to capital' towards 'solidarity through collective enterprise' has affected the size and nature of the WTOs that have been attempted. A fuller discussion of trends in WTOs within countries is given in the country overviews in Chapter 2.

3 The first two quotations are from interviews carried out by members of the Open University Co-operatives Research Unit. The third is taken from Webster (1984).

4 See, for example, Bradley (1986), Bradley and Gelb (1985), and Bradley and Gelb (1983a).

5 His suggestions suffer from the shortcoming that the rationale behind them cannot really be declared. To maximize the efficiency gains under workers ownership and management there must be a widespread belief – founded, ultimately, on actual possibilities – that economic recovery can be achieved. But to support a WTO while admitting one does not believe this actually to be the case, would seriously undermine it. For example, it is hard to imagine such a venture attracting significant financial contributions from employees and the local community; or stimulating a willingness to adopt labour-saving production measures. Nor would it be endorsed by co-operative associations whose support is so important; it would risk draining their resources in the most adverse circumstances, with the inevitably high proportion of failures attracting adverse publicity. But if the rationale for the policy is not made explicit, then it is likely to be politically unrealistic. A policy whose declared intention is to facilitate 'workers turnarounds' cannot result in a significant proportion of 'failures' without being seen as a waste of public funds – even if, in fact, such 'failures' fall within the range of acceptable outcomes. Such seems to be the lesson from the UK in the mid-1970s and France in the early 1980s.

6 As evidenced by the OECD's programme on local employment initiatives in Europe and by the numerous reports of the European Commission's 'Programme of research and action on the development of the labour market'. For the UK a useful survey of the field is provided by Todd (1986).

7 The literature is extensive. Weitzman (1984) provides a polished case on behalf of much wider share ownership and profit related pay and Russell (1987) provides a recent review of the main literature.

8 Bradley and Gelb (1983b) is characteristically thorough. Spear (1985) includes some more critical material. Wiener and Oakshott (1987) provides a very interesting update on recent developments and the group's success in weathering the economic storms of the 1970s and 1980s.

9 Most of the information was gathered in 1986. However, much of the Spanish material dates from 1987, and the UK cases include ones prepared in 1987 and 1988–9. In general, it has been easier to keep in touch with developments in France and West Germany (as well as the UK, of course) and some references to recent development in these countries are included in the discussion. The principal sources of information have been: published and unpublished accounts of WTOs and analyses of WTOs; original research, by visiting WTOs and talking to those involved; the first-hand experiences of those who worked on the original policy study from which this book has been developed; interviews with people who have been involved in supporting or funding WTOs in, e.g. local government, co-operative associations and agencies.

Chapter 2

1 This rough estimate is derived from the assortment of figures on the Italian co-operative movement provided in Earle (1986) and Gherardi (1987). The main problems are that not all registered co-operatives are active; not all active co-operatives are registered; how far the increase in the number of co-operatives is accounted for by WTOs is uncertain – as is the number of co-operatives that have ceased trading or merged with other ones.

2 See Vidal Martinez (1987) and Otero-Hidalgo (1987) for figures on the number and distribution of SALs and co-operatives, and the uncertainty associated with them. Both the writers refer mainly to Catalonia. For discussions of co-operatives and WTOs in Andalusia see Haubert (1986) and Boswall (1987).

3 See Laville and Mahiou (1987). The figures for France, provided by CG-SCOP, the movement's central organization, are much more reliable. However CG-SCOP distinguishes between WTO and 'conversions'. The latter are, in general, viable enterprises that are changed into co-operatives on the initiative of the owner (who may be retiring). About twenty of these conversions occurred each year (Job Ownership Ltd. 1986). In practice, though, a number of these 'viable' enterprises are marginal businesses with somewhat obsolete equipment that would not easily attract a private purchaser. Some cases of 'conversions', therefore, are almost certainly better understood as WTO in the terms of this study; and hence the figures in the text probably underestimate the incidence of WTO in France.

4 Spear (1987) listed between 70 and 80 known cases (from which the estimate of average size is derived). However, this now appears to underestimate the total quite significantly. Hobbs (1989) found that 11 per cent of the 571 cases on which the 1988 Survey of Worker Co-operatives is based, classified their origins as arising from a closure (though a few were not in the same line of business). However, a further 8 per cent arose from the conversion of existing businesses or training projects, some of which will certainly be WTOs in the terms of this study. Hence, it is likely that between 10 and 15 per cent of cases were WTOs. Taking account of additional information from local CDAs etc., the estimated total population of co-operatives in 1988 was 1497. Hence using the 10 per cent figure, and allowing that WTOs might be somewhat over-represented among respondents, perhaps 120 WTOs were surviving in 1988 – and so *at least* 150 WTOs have taken place. Using the 15 per cent figure and similar assumptions suggests that well over 250 WTOs may have taken place. Hence the estimate of 'around 200'. A key element in such estimates is the assumed failure rate among WTOs. The severe problems in estimating this are outlined in Chapter 6.

5 A fuller description of Lake is given in Cornforth (1989).

6 The interpretation in this and the next paragraph are influenced by the general model of 'complex adaptive systems' – see, for example, Buckley (1967).

7 The motivations and orientation of those involved in WTOs has been a vexed question in the literature. Bradley and Gelb (1980; 1983a) have gone to some length to discredit Westergaard's (1970) simplistic suggestions concerning the

'radicalizing' potential of 'cash-nexus breaks' (i.e. compulsory redundancy with the prospect of unemployment). They use evidence, mainly from the short and unhappy life of the Scottish Daily News to demonstrate that for the great majority of those involved such co-operatives represent a pragmatic response rather than radical initiative. There may well be a difference here between larger (defensive and financial) and smaller (participative) WTO, but in any event Bradley and Gelb's analysis has some shortcomings. In a rapidly deteriorating commercial situation it is hardly surprising that the workforce gave priority to their economic concerns. The model of workforce motivation that Bradley and Gelb construct from this says more about their training as economists than it does about the sources of human behaviour in novel, changing and uncertain situations. The distinction between 'radical' and 'pragmatic' motivations is itself simplistic and misleading as later chapters indicate. A desire for trade-union representation and influence is not necessarily 'radical' any more than a concern for structure, direction and competence is necessarily 'pragmatic'. This distinction (rather than, for example, one between 'radical' and 'managerial' orientations) rules out the possibility of being a pragmatic radical – which might not be a bad description of what many of those involved in WTO seem to become. (But this term, too, is a static oversimplification and begs many questions about the nature of the radicalism implied.) Workforce motivation in the context of a WTO is discussed further in Chapter 3.

8 It is surely no coincidence that the concept of 'firm-saving' WTOs emerged in Scandinavia – see Westenholz (1987).

Chapter 3

1 The idea of organizational learning, as elaborated by Argyris and Schon (1978) provides a useful perspective on the WTO process. As will become obvious it usually involves an accelerated process of organization-building or change that requires extensive single-loop and double-loop learning.

2 UK workers do not really have any rights to lose, in this respect.

3 In relation to management buy-outs from a receiver Wright and Coyne report the view that the 'price paid in such cases was closely related to which receiver happened to be dealing with the case and the number of other receiverships he was dealing with at the time' (Wright and Coyne 1985:23).

4 Quite apart from initial underfunding, as the market situation develops, a conflict may well arise between the principle of job preservation on which the enterprise has been based, and the commercial logic of asset reduction to finance the longer-term prospects. Even if the workforce gradually accept the commercial logic it may be a case of 'too little too late'.

5 This provides some support for the view that WTOs have an inherently radical potential. However, the extent to which such broadly social aspirations emerge, how far they are shared among the workforce, the nature of the aspirations, and

whether they are likely to be sustained, seem to vary considerably and are affected by a wide range of factors, some of which will emerge in later chapters. Nor, of course, can one assume that such industrial or organizational radicalism will lead to some kind of political radicalism.

6 The Mondragon co-operatives have also been able to reconcile solidarity and economic considerations by co-operation between co-operatives, and they have weathered the recession very successfully in consequence – see Wiener and Oakshott (1987) and Bradley and Gelb (1987). But see also Commisso (1979) which provides an important analysis of the oscillations between plan and market in Yugoslavia, and the forces that generate them.

7 Management buy-outs need help as well: 'Skilled negotiators can help prevent management being out-manouvered by receivers who are used to driving hard bargains or by bosses taking advantage of a superior hierarchical position' (Wright and Coyne 1985:25).

8 The sorts of issues that arise (involving conflicting social and economic priorities and assumptions) require 'double-loop learning' on the part of the workforce. According to Argyris and Schon (1978), the organizational climate needed for this to occur is one which is supportive, rather than defensive, in which confrontation and challenge are accepted, and in which the task is subject to joint, rather than unilateral, control. My impression is that the atmosphere in many smaller WTOs is quite often like this.

9 Interestingly, much recent management writing and research has questioned the value of clear, well-defined structures, suggesting instead that in time of rapid change much more fluid and 'untidy' organizations are more effective. See for example Peters (1989) and Nystrom and Starbuck (1981).

10 Stanton (1989) provides an important analysis of the development of collective working (albeit in social services). He suggests it is common for those involved to go through an 'oppositional phase' in which anything associated with hierarchy is rejected.

Chapter 4

1 Hence the interest currently being shown in European co-operative circles for the idea of a mutual guarantee scheme for personal loans taken out to provide capital for a new co-operative. In essence, co-operative movements would run insurance schemes to repay such loans for individuals in the event of them losing their jobs because the co-operative had failed (Thomas 1989).

2 Often, these funds are based on some combination of the co-operative movement's own resources and a contribution of public funds from national or local government. However, in recent years a number of new funds have emerged using finance that can be described as *general* 'sympathy capital' – for examples, the Ökobank in Germany; the CIGALS (Clubs d'Investissement pour la Gestion

Alternative) and La Garrigue in France; Mercury Provident and the ICOF share issue in the UK (Thomas 1989).

3 This can be a real problem for many newly formed worker co-operatives. In the UK small businesses usually start with the owner providing (very roughly) 85 per cent of the capital and the remainder coming from a bank in the form of an overdraft. Five years on, if the firm has been successful, these proportions will be much the same, but the owner's capital will have increased through retained earnings, and the bank's contribution will now be an arranged loan. By contrast, the members of start-up worker co-operatives usually provide (very roughly) 30 per cent of their initial capital; the remainder comes from special loan funds and is topped up by a commercial loan. As the co-operative matures these proportions are roughly reversed: about 70 per cent is the members' capital – arising from retained earnings, so called 'sweat equity' – and 30 per cent is in loans, though the 'soft' loans may have been paid back, to be replaced by further commercial borrowing (Jefferis 1988). So worker co-operatives often do have to pull themselves up by their own bootstraps (Cornforth *et al*. 1988), and in the early years the capital structure of a co-operative means that obtaining the finance needed to run the business costs the members dear. On the other hand, if and when a co-operative has built itself up through retained earnings, the capital structure may work to its advantage: since it is not having to meet the expectations of external shareholders, the cost of its capital is likely to be significantly lower than in a comparable private firm – thus the occasional complaints that mutual financial institutions (like building societies) have an unfair advantage.

4 Similar but less severe problems are experienced in many management buyouts. The management team may be reluctant to dilute its control and share the capital gain which is often the primary financial objective. See Wright and Coyne (1985).

Chapter 5

1 Neils Mygind (1986) provides a useful theoretical demonstration of the importance of this point for the economic performance of worker-owned enterprises. It has quite far-reaching implications – for example, how can the match best be maintained over time, given that the objectives of the workforce may tend to change?

2 Share company worker co-operatives have also been devised recently – in essence, one voting share is bought by each member; the remaining shares are non-voting shares. Given the scope for such arrangements it can certainly be argued that the distinction between company law and co-operative law is actually misleading. For a useful discussion of the incomprehension surrounding the term workers co-operative in the UK see Hansen (1986) who, while acknowledging that the small numbers of them makes them unfamiliar, says 'A fundamental cause in the UK, however, is the lack of clear definition of what in substance and in form is meant by the term.'

3 'Normal' equity shares held by non-members – carrying rights of control and a potentially unlimited return – would violate at least two of the six co-operative principles. However, a complete ban on any external shareholding under any circumstances is a severe restriction, and so most countries have versions of co-operative rules that allow for external members who contribute share capital, or for attenuated forms of equity, or for the use of limited amounts of equity that does not threaten the workforce's overall control. The point is that shares need not carry the full rights associated with 'normal' equity; for example, they may be non-voting shares, or fixed interest, preference shares. However, such manoeuvres do not fully resolve the problem. Indeed, if the rights of equity investors are so restricted that only those who would in any case be willing to lend money to the co-operative are prepared to buy the shares, then the only advantages is cosmetic (making what would otherwise be loans appear as equity).

4 The dominance of this form in the UK appears almost accidental. The distinctive ideas of common ownership were originally put forward by philanthropic (not to say paternalistic) Christian businessmen in the Society for Democratic Integration in Industry. Since they were primarily concerned with promoting the conversion of established business the problems this structure would cause for new enterprises seeking loan finance were ignored. In due course this organization became the Industrial Common Ownership Movement and during the 1970s, as the only body in the field, began to attract more widespread support and interest from both the 'alternative' movement and centre and left political groups interested in worker co-operatives or ownership. In 1976 a sympathetic MP was lucky in the parliamentary ballot for private members' bills; this resulted in the Industrial Common Ownership Act which provided a legal definition of common ownership and some finance to initiate a loan fund. These developments largely neglected the experience of the traditional UK co-operative movement in the area of producer co-operatives, let alone that of European movements. Currently, the philanthropists' common ownership principle is strongly supported by those on the left of the broader movement for worker co-operatives – in opposition to 'individualist' tendencies.

5 Flieger (1984) describes the difficulties caused by German co-operative law and associations – but he pleads for more use to be made of this legal structure. The gap between the traditional and the new co-operative movement may be seen from the following quotation. The President of the (traditional) National Association of Co-operative Banks publicly declared that he was unwilling to accept the 'Ökobank' (new co-op movement bank founded in 1988) as a member of his organizations, saying, 'the political elements of the Öko-Bank, such as collective working, co-determination and self-management, don't fit into the traditions of the co-operative banks' (quoted in *Weser-Kurier* 19.9.1986:3).

6 'Popular capitalism' refers to the idea of a 'share-owning democracy', where *individuals* own shares directly (rather than through pension funds, etc.) in a range of enterprises and receive a significant part of their income from them. It is

therefore quite different from 'worker capitalism', in which workers individually own the shares in the companies for which they work.

7 These (rather large) issues are explored a bit further in Chapter 8.

8 The restrictions and requirements that co-operative legal forms impose have been described as 'unhelpful Victorian baggage' (Job Ownership Ltd. 1986:7). Less provocatively, one can point to the fact that the differences between SALs and co-operatives are clearly far less than their protagonists pretend; and to the fact that in countries like the UK, where most worker co-operatives are tiny 'new-starts', the movement cannot offer WTOs much contact with other comparable enterprises.

Chapter 6

1 Particularly, it seems, in shoes and textiles – for example, Wajcman (1983), Bate and Carter (1986).

2 Figures are from CG-SCOP and were provided in an interview with one of their officials.

3 The second quotation in Box 1.2 also gives an example. Bradley and Gelb (1983a) provide numerous impressive examples from defensive and financial WTOs and suggest that reductions in unit labour costs of 35–50 per cent are common. Of course it is not only on the shop floor that WTOs bring out the best in people. Technical managers and office staff are often transformed into general managers in the heat of a WTO – as the cases of Duncans of Edinburgh (Box 3.4), Northwest Pre-cast (Box 4.1) and MOSTA (Box 6.4) illustrate. Hence, one general explanation for the success of WTOs is that they liberate firm-specific human capital (to use the delicate phrasing of economists).

4 More sophisticated versions of this criticism see the very structure of these industries as a means of control and more efficient capital accumulation – e.g. 'it would now seem to be in the interest of large companies to foster the growth of co-operatives' (Bates and Carter 1986:67). The argument is that by 'contracting out', large firms greatly simplify their own management problems and increase their strategic flexibility; at the same time they have the economic power to force down and keep down the prices paid to suppliers. Arguably, this 'labour process' argument (Braverman 1974) may have some application in particular sectors, but is unconvincing as a general explanation. One can equally well argue that the decline of Fordist mass production is creating many opportunities for latter-day 'craft producers', who can achieve considerable autonomy on the market by producing specialist quality products and services (Piore and Sabel 1984).

5 As an example of academic writing in this vein, see Keil (1987), who says of WTO: 'the desire to achieve a reasonable rate of return is going to force the rank-and-file to engage in economic self-exploitation, and it is going to force them to accept limitations on their ability to exercise democratic control over the enterprise'

178 RELUCTANT ENTREPRENEURS

(p. 229). If this is supposed to mean that the workforce in a WTO have essentially similar motivations to capitalists in other contexts (i.e. obtaining a 'reasonable' return on their investment), then that is an extraordinary empirical claim (for a typical attitude, see the remark quoted in the case of Equipos Industriales, in Box 5.2). But the real interest of the passage lies in its use of language. For a critique of the concept of 'self-exploitation' see Carter (1989 forthcoming).

6 The neglect of marketing seems to have been crucial in the failure of several of the new products devised by the Bitteswell Employment Alliance. Spear (1987) provides a brief account.

7 In this life cycle-model (Batstone 1982; 1983) there are three phases. In the beginning the co-operative is small, the motivation is great and a primitive (direct) democracy is used. In the second phase the co-operative has existed for some years. It is growing and some members have specialized in management functions. New employees are not becoming members (owners) and direct democracy is decreasing. In the third phase the members want to reinforce democracy and they develop a form of collective representative system besides the management system. (In the Danish case the regeneration did not develop a representative form but a direct one.)

Chapter 7

1 These and other quotations concerning the CGT's views are taken from statements by its leading officials appearing in its publication *Journees d'Etudes*, in1983.

2 For an analysis of the organizational articulation of the Italian co-operative movement, its willingness to become an economic group which democratically coordinates the strategies of the single associated forms, see: Zan (1980) and (1982) and Sapelli (1981). In English, Earle (1986) provides a descriptive account. Holstrom (1989) is also very relevant.

3 In 1987 an official of FESALC claimed that only 6 out of 450 federated SALs had closed since 1983 when FESALC was formed. This figure did not include re-SALs as closures – and it was admitted that some were in danger of closing. Despite these qualifications, and the possibility that more of the weaker SALs do not join the federation, these figures are quite impressive.

4 The best known and strongest support organization is Netzwerk Selbsthilfe (self-help network, a registered association) with some 32 regional branches. There are also some local associations of self-managed firms/co-ops, as well as first steps of co-operation on a larger scale in areas like purchasing, electronic accounting, distribution, advertising, etc. Part of the infrastructure is a monthly periodical, 'Contraste'. Moreover, some independent (mainly regionally operating) financing co-operatives (for crediting and credit securing) have been established; the first bank of the movement (Ökobank) was founded in 1988. Several attempts were made to obtain a quantitative estimate of the expansion of the new co-op scene. The figures differ quite a bit. Here is one version:

c.14,000 projects and co-operatives in the Federal Republic; c.4,000 of them are commercial and producer co-operatives employing some 24,000 people (not all of them fully paid); the other 10,000 projects (with about 80,000 people working there, many of them without, or with only very little, pay) belong to the socio-cultural sector (from Kück 1985).

5 The distinction between 'top-down' and 'bottom-up' approaches has been central in discussions about co-operative support and development in the UK. The latter is avidly espoused for its democratic values but is not always appropriate, let alone effectively carried out. See Paton and Emerson (1988) for a discussion.

6 This is essential if the advisors themselves are to be controlled, and also to reduce the problems of 'dependence' – see Paton and Emerson (1988).

7 The complete original text (in French) from which this case was derived is Marchat (1981).

8 These dilemmas arise in relation to many local employment initiatives. In general it is clear that support in the form of investments is more effective than a subsidy of day-to-day running costs and that such projects have to alternate between periods of experimentation and periods of evaluation (and renegotiation).

Chapter 8

1 But not indefinitely. Worker co-operatives in particular are still disadvantaged compared to other firms in so far as they have peculiar difficulties both in taking over other firms and in being taken over – the usual ways in which other economic units ensure their own continuity as part of larger, more diversified economic groupings. Bennett (1984) argues that this factor explains the decline in the number of producer co-operatives in the UK.

2 Wholefoods and certain alternative products have diffused partly in this way, and the same may well prove to be true as regards certain environmental services and products. One can also include new services provided on a local basis mixing monetary resources (both public and private) and non-monetary resources (including voluntary work) – see Eme and Laville (1988).

3 Coherent and sophisticated versions of this view are to be found in Jefferis (1988) and Mellor et al. (1988) – the latter rounding off their pessimistic prognosis with some vintage utopianism. Variants of this critique apply to most LEIs and to worker ownership and co-operatives in general.

4 Of course the left critique can also be challenged on more general grounds – e.g. what is the alternative? Whether or not one is still looking forward to the final crisis of capitalism, it seems fair to say that for the foreseeable future a more likely alternative to the fringe economy is not a socialist economy, but no economy at all – or perhaps, in some areas anyway, one based on drugs and crime.

5 How big is 'large'? This probably depends on existing experience and extent of support available. In France and the UK 100 employees may be approaching the limit; in Italy and Spain 250 may be a better guide. This does not mean that the

experience of WTOs is irrelevant to the large plant problem. It might be possible to gain many of the advantages of a WTO – in enlisting the skills and intelligence of the workforce, in cultivating an ethic of self-help and self-reliance, in providing a resource and organizational base for product and business development, in protecting the locality from complete and sudden closure – without the project becoming demoralized, or appearing as a failure because it was unable to achieve commercial viability, and unable to provide continuity of employment for all those involved in it. Despite its difficulties, the experience of the Bitteswell Employment Alliance – see Spear (1987) – is suggestive of the scope for work-force-based initiatives of this sort which, by being less individualistic and paternalistic, would seem to have considerable advantages over the usual employment advice services introduced in the context of large plant closures (limited to employment counselling, retraining guidance, business advice, etc.).

6 Although the scope of these principles is fairly limited, this does not mean the implementation of polices based on them would be straightforward in regions with little existing experience. A terrible mismatch exists between the logic of social learning (based on varied experimentation, the sharing of experience and gradual evolution) that is suited to developing innovative measures; and the logic of political strategy (based on plans, pressure for results, and control) under which such new measures are often demanded.

7 Expectancy theory provides grounds for some scepticism about these presumed benefits, especially in the larger firms within which employee shareholding is often promoted. The link between effort and reward is rather tenuous and uncertain. However, the suggested effects would seem much more likely to arise in small and medium-sized enterprises, especially where the extent of employee shareholdings is enough to give them some latent influence in management, and thereby to affect the climate, or culture of the organization. For an analysis of such a firm in these terms, see Paton (1978).

8 Scepticism and hostility to the idea of worker ownership/co-operatives is still quite common – vide the British TUC statement opposing the formation of co-operatives in the context of privatization, even as a last resort. Arguably this does little (if anything) to resist privatization, and passes up a unique opportunity of establishing, comparatively quickly, networks of worker co-operatives in specific sectors, backed by specialist support agencies. The arguments against such a strategy often echo those that were used 100 years ago against the leaders of some of the first Italian worker co-operatives – see Earle (1986).

9 A possible model in this context is provided by the provisions under Danish law that give tenants an option to buy a house that their landlord has arranged to sell to a third party: if within a specified period the tenants can raise the finance to match the third party's price, they are entitled to purchase it at that price.

10 See Fairclough (1987) for a detailed and useful (if at times rather shrill) 'exposé' of the Mondragon co-operatives in relation to the fiscal and other advantages provided to co-operatives under fascism. Jefferis (1988) provides a broader review of the issue also taking in France, Italy and (in the UK) the role of the retail co-

operatives in supporting the co-operative productive societies. Such support does appear, on the face of it, to have been quite helpful – but how important was it? For example, post-war Spanish protectionism certainly helps explain Spain's economic growth during that period; but does it really follow that therefore the success of the Mondragon co-operatives is attributable to their operating in a protected market – was there really no domestic competition?

11 The principles insist on a *limited* return (contra the unlimited return of normal shareholders). This does not mean the return must be either low or invariate. Likewise an external party providing funds can share control through a contractual agreement (as in Mondragon) without having a constitutional role in the direction of the co-operative. The charge that a rather more conventional approach to financing would be 'capitalist' is not helpful – it seems to imply that there would be no real difference between (i) a loan from and supervised by the co-operative movement's own institutions, with the return going to further strengthen the movement; and (ii) a loan from a body that did not share the co-operatives aspirations and was simply seeking to secure the best possible return on its investment.

12 A sharp critique of the idea that market forces determine management form is provided by Tomlinson (1981) who points out that private companies vary quite considerably in management practices and organizational structure.

13 Some of the larger Italian co-operatives (like CMC of Ravenna with more than 4,000 employees) have had to institute special programmes to try to revive themselves socially. The Mondragon co-operatives believe it important to limit the size of any individual co-operative.

14 The Catalan Federation of Worker Co-operatives (FCTAC) found it took several years before the clothing co-operatives in their region were willing to support a modest project to explore the scope for collaboration. The GLEB's efforts to promote collaboration among printing co-operatives in London was viewed with great hostility and suspicion by most of the 20 or so co-operatives who attended an initial meeting. In due course five or six or the larger ones did form the London Co-operative Printers Association. This has stayed in existence for several years and managed to arrange joint purchasing (on certain products and materials), and specialist training courses on co-operative and printing management. However, it has made no progress at all as regards the strategic co-ordination of their marketing and production.

15 Vienney (1982) explains the sectoral specialization of French worker co-operatives, and argues that they have a specific socio-economic role, on the basis of their advantages in sectors characterized by a particular combination of the level of professional or craft skills required and the level of capital intensity; and by comparatively complex production activity being associated with comparatively straightforward commercial activity. Quite how restricted such a role for worker co-operatives is in a knowledge-based economy is far from clear, however. Recent research based on case studies of small and medium sized enterprises in several European countries highlights how the professional model of organiza-

tion can be adapted to uncertain environments and changing markets, and how it seems to be re-emerging after a period dominated by the 'Taylorian' or 'Fordist' model. A more collective entrepreneurship undertaken by homogeneous teams of skilled or professional workers may well be an increasingly effective, and up to date form –and not simply a nostalgic throw-back to associations of craft producers (Laville 1989).

16 An incisive but sympathetic analysis of the tendency of social movements to fail to recognize movements for compromise (due to the social processes occurring within them) is provided in Mansbridge's (1986) account of the failure of the Equal Rights Amendment in the US. She suggests that, in effect, social movements have to choose whether they are going to be sects, or turn into institutions.

17 There have been earlier forms of collective entrepreneurship in most countries – the co-operative movement (including the building societies); and the municipal socialism of the 1920s and 30s in Britain. Arguably, under current conditions, enterprises whose character is shaped by substantial (or complete) worker ownership provide a much more appropriate and dynamic form.

References

Argyris, C. and Schon, D. (1978). *Organizational Learning: A Theory in Action Perspective*. Wokingham, Addison-Wesley.

Barnsley Metropolitan Borough Council (undated), *From Closure to Co-operation*. Barnsley Metropolitan Borough Council.

Bate, P. and Carter, N. (1986). 'The future for producers' co-operatives', *Industrial Relations Journal*, **17**(1), 57–70.

Batstone, E. (1982). 'France'. In F. Stephen (ed.), *The Performance of Labour Managed Firms*. London, Macmillan.

Batstone, E. (1983). 'Organization and orientation: a life cycle model of French co-operatives, *Economic and Industrial Democracy*, **4**(2), 139–61.

Bennett, J. (1984). *Producer Co-operatives: A Case for Market Protection*. Discussion paper 11, Centre for Research in Industrial Democracy and Participation, University of Glasgow.

Boswall, P. (1987). *Co-operatives of Associated Workers in Andalusia: Their Social and Historical Roots and the Current Situation*. Dissertation towards a BA degree. Norwich, University of East Anglia (mimeo).

Bradley, K. (1986). 'Employee ownership and economic decline in Western industrial democracies', *Journal of Management Studies*, **23**, 57–71.

Bradley, K. and Gelb, A. (1980). 'The radical potential of cash-nexus breaks', *British Journal of Sociology*, **XXX**(2), 118–20.

Bradley, K. and Gelb, A. (1983a). *Worker Capitalism: The New Industrial Relations*. London, Heinemann.

Bradley, K. and Gelb, A. (1983b). *Co-operation at Work: The Mondragon Experience*. London, Heinemann Educational Books.

Bradley, K. and Gelb, A. (1985). 'Employee buy-outs of troubled companies', *Harvard Business Review*, September–October, 121–30.

Bradley, K. and Gelb, A. (1987). 'Co-operative labour relations: Mondragon's response to recession', *British Journal of Industrial Relations*, **XXV**(1).

Braverman, H. (1974). *Labour and Monopoly Capital*. New York, Monthly Review Press.

Brusco, S. (1982). 'The Emilian Model: productive decentralization and social integration', *Cambridge Journal of Economics*, **6**, 167–84.

Buckley, W. (1967). *Sociology and Modern Systems Theory*. New York, Prentice-Hall.

Carter, A. (1990 forthcoming). 'Self-exploitation and workers' co-operatives', *Journal of Applied Philosophy*.

Cespe (1986). *Il Ruolo della Imprese Cooperative di Fronte al Mutamento Tecnological-industriale. Opportunita e Vincola Connessi ai Problemi Economico Finanziari e instituzionali*. Seminario di Studio, Bologna, April.

Clarke, T. (1979). 'The market constraints to self-management: the experience of a British workers' co-operative'. In H. C. Jain (ed.), *Workers' Participation: Success and Problems*, New York, Praeger.

Coates, K. (1976). *The New Worker Co-operatives*. Nottingham, Spokesman Books.

Commisso, E. H. (1979). *Workers' Control under Plan and Market: Implications of Yugoslavian Self-Management*. New Haven, Conn., Yale University Press.

Cornforth, C. (1982). 'Trade unions and producer co-operatives', *Economic and Industrial Democracy*, **3**, 17–30.

Cornforth, C. (1989). 'Lake School of English'. In A. Thomas and J. Thornley *Co-ops to the Rescue*. London, ICOM Co-publications.

Cornforth, C, et al. (1988). *Developing Successful Worker Co-operatives*. London, Sage Publications.

Demoustier, D. (1984). *Les Cooperatives de Production*. Paris, Editions la Découvertes.

Duhm, R. (1987) 'Worker takeovers in the Federal Republic of Germany'. In R. Paton (ed.), *Analysis of the Experiences of and Problems Encountered by Worker Takeovers of Companies in Difficulty or Bankrupt*. Report to the Commission of the European Communities, Study No. 85/4. III, 92–127.

Earle, J. (1986). *The Italian Co-operative Movement: A Portrait of the Lega Nazionale delle Co-operative e Mutue*. London, Allen & Unwin.

Eccles, T. (1981). *Under New Management*. London, Pan.

Eme, B. and Laville, J.-L. (1988). *Les Petits Bulots en Question*. Paris, Syros.

Fairclough, M. (1986). *The Political Economy of Produce Co-operatives: The Story of Triumph Motocycles (Meriden) Ltd*. PhD Thesis. University of Bristol.

Fairclough, M. (1987). *Mondragon in Context*. Research Report No. 1. Dept. of Sociology, University of Bristol.

Flieger, B. (ed.) (1984). *Produktivgenossenschaften oder her Hindernislauf zur Selbstverwaltung* (AG SPAK M 61). Munich, 3rd section, Grundungshilfen, 253 ff.

Gherardi, S. (1987). 'Worker takeovers: the Italian experience'. In R. Paton *Analysis of the Experiences of and Problems Encountered by Worker Takeovers of Companies in Difficulty or Bankrupt*. Report to the Commission of the European Communities, Study No. 85/4, V, 160–92.

Gherardi, S. (1988). 'Worker takeovers in Europe: a comparative cultural analysis'. Paper for the Conference of the European Consortium for Political Research. Trento Universiti Degli Studidi Trento, Dipartimento di Politica Sociale (mimeo).

Hansen, O. (1986). 'Workers' co-operatives in the UK: the legal obstacles'. In A. Holand et al. *Rechtliche, Stelerliche, Soziale und Administrative Hindemisse Fur Die Entwicklung, Ortlich Beschaftigungsinitiativen*, Luxembourg, Zentrum fur Europaische Rechtspolitik.

Haubert, M. (1986). *Producer Co-operatives and Regional Development in Andalusia: The Current Challenge*. Paper to the XI World Congress of Sociology, New Delhi.

Hobbs, P. (1989). *1988 Survey of Worker Co-operatives, Summary Report*. Milton Keynes, Open University Co-operatives Research Unit.

Hodgson, G. (1984). *The Democratic Economy*. Harmondsworth, Penguin Books.

Holand, A. *et al.* (1986). *Rechtliche, Steuerliche, Soziale und Administrative Hindernisse Fur Die Entwicklung Ortliche Beschaftigungsinitiativen*. Luxembourg, Zentrum fur Europaische Rechtspolitik (ZERP).

Holstrom, M. (1989). *Industrial Democracy in Italy: Workers Co-ops and the Self-Management Debate*. Aldershot, Gower.

Irecoop (ed.) (1985). *I Problemi delle Cooperative Industriali Nate de Aziende in Crisi*. Milan, Cens.

Jefferis, K. (1988). *The Performance of Worker Co-operatives in a Capitalist Economy: British Co-operatives 1975–1985*. PhD Thesis. Milton Keynes, The Open University.

Job Ownership Ltd. (1986). *A Neat Exit: The Transformation of French Family Businesses into Co-operatives*. London, Participation Research Ltd.

Jordan, J. (1986). 'A system of interdependent firms as a development strategy'. In S. Jansson and A. B. Hellmark (eds), *Labor-Owned Firms and Workers' Co-operatives*, Aldershot, Gower.

Keil, T.J. (1987).' "Democracy" in worker owned enterprises: the US experience'. In J. Child and P. Bate (eds), *Organization of Innovation: East-West Perspectives*. Berlin, de Gruyter.

Kück, M. (1985). *Neue Finanzierungsstrategien für Selbstverwaltete Betriebe*. Frankfurt and New York.

Laville, J.-L. (1989). *L'Evaluation des Practiques de Gestion Participative dans les PME et les cooperatives*. Recherche réalisée pour la Task-Force PME Commission des Communautés Européenes. Paris, CRIDA.

Laville, J.-L. and Mahiou, I. (1984). *Interactions Économiques et sociales dans les coopératives de production*. Recherche réalisée pour le Ministère de la recherche, Paris, CRIDA.

Laville, J.-L. and Mahiou, I. (1986). 'Les cooperatives dans la crise', *Autogestions*, **22**, 47–103.

Laville, J.-L. and Mahiou, I. (1987). 'Worker take overs: the French experience'. In R. Paton, *Analysis of the Experiences of and the Problems Encountered by Worker Takeovers of Companies in Difficulty or Bankrupt*. Report to the Commission of the European Communities, Study No 85/4. VI.

Mansbridge, J. (1986). *Why We Lost The ERA*. Chicago, University of Chicago Press.

Marchat, J. F. (1981). 'Le fait cooperatif et mutualiste. Actes du colloque'. *Trames*. Limoges.

Mellor, M. *et al.* (1988). *Worker Co-operatives in Theory and Practice*. Milton Keynes, Open University Press.

Miester, A. (1974). *La Participation dans les Association*. Paris, Editions Ouvrières.

Mygind, N. (1986). 'From the Illyrian firm to the reality of self-management'. S. Jansson and A. B. Hellmark (eds), *Labor-owned Firms and Workers' Co-operatives*. Aldershot, Gower.

Nystrom, P. C. and Starbuck. W. J. H. (eds) (1981). *Handbook of Organizational Design*. Oxford, Oxford University Press.

Oakshott, R. (1978). *The Case for Workers' Co-ops*. London, Routledge & Kegan Paul.

Otero-Hidalgo, C. (1987). 'Worker takeovers in Spain'. In R. Paton. *Analysis of the Experience of and Problems Encountered by Worker Takeovers of Companies in Difficulty or Bankrupt*. Report to the Commission of the European Communities, Study No. 85/4. VI, 194–207.

Paton, R. (1978). *Fairblow Dynamics*. Milton Keynes, Co-operative Research Unit, Open University.

Paton, R. and Emerson, T. (1988). 'Top down versus bottom up: goodbye to all that?', *Local Economy*, **3**(3), 159–68.

Paton, R. *et al.* (1987). *Analysis of the Experiences of and Problems Encountered by Worker Takeovers of Companies in Difficulty or Bankrupt*. Report to the Commission of the European Communities, Study No. 85/4.

Peters, T. (1989). *Thriving on Chaos: Handbook for a Management Revolution*. London, Macmillan.

Piore, M. J. and Sabel, C. F. (1984). *The Second Industrial Divide: Possiblities for Prosperity*. New York, Basic Books.

Rainnie, A. (1985). 'Small firms, big problems: the potted economy of small businesses', *Capital and Class*, **25**, 140–68.

Russell, R. (1985). *Sharing Ownership in the Workplace*. Albany, NY, State University of New York Press.

Russell, R. (1987). *Forms and Extent of Employee Participation in the Contemporary United States*. Paper for the Fifth International Conference on the Economics of Self-Management, Vienna.

Sapelli, G. (ed.) (1981). *Il Movimento Cooperativo in Italia*. Torino, Einaudi.

Slatter, S. (1984). *Corporate Recovery*. Harmondsworth, Penguin.

Spear, R. (1985). *Mondragon: Myth or Model?* Milton Keynes, Open University Co-operatives Research Unit.

Spear, R. (1987). 'Worker takeovers in Britain'. In R. Paton, *Analysis of the Experiences of and Problems Encountered by Worker Takeovers of Companies in Difficulty or Bankrupt*. Report to the Commission of the European Communities, Study No. 85/4. VII, 209–33.

Stanton, A. (1989). *Invitation to Self-Management*. Middlesex, Dab Hand Press.

Stern, R. N. and Hammer, T. H. (1978). 'Buying your job: factors affecting the success or failure of employee acquisition attempts', *Human Relations*, **31**(12), 1101–17.

Thomas, A. (1989). *Methods of Financing Co-operatives*. Report to the SME Task Force of the European Commission (publication pending).

Thomas, A. and Thornley, J. (1989). *Co-ops to the Rescue!* London, ICOM Co-publications.

Thornley, J. (1981). *Workers' Co-operatives: Jobs and Dreams*. London, Heinemann.

Todd, G. (1986). 'Job creation in the UK: a national survey of local models'. OECD/*The Economist*.

Tomlinson, J. (1981). 'British politics and co-operatives', *Capital and Class*, **12**, 58–65.

Tomlinson, J. (1982). *The Unequal Struggle*. London, Methuen.

Tynan, E. and Thomas, A. (1984). *KME: Working in a Large Co-operative*. Milton Keynes, Co-operatives Research Unit, Open University.

Vidal Martinez, I. (1987). *Crisis Económica y Transformaciones en el Mercado de Trabajo: el Asociacionismo de Trabajo en Cataluña*. Barcelona, Diputació de Barcelona.

Vienney, C. (1982). *Socio-économie des organisations coopératives* (2 vols). Paris, CIEM.

Wajcman, J. (1983). *Women in Control: Dilemmas of a Workers' Co-operative*. Milton Keynes, Open University Press.

Wales TUC (1981). *Cooperation and Job Creation in Wales: A Feasibility Study*. Cardiff, Wales TUC.

Webster, J. (1984). 'Experience in a workers co-operative', *Industrial Participation*, summer.

Weitzman, M. L. (1984). *The Share Economy*. Cambridge, Mass., Harvard University Press.

Westenholz, A. (1987). 'Worker takeovers in Denmark'. In R. Paton, *Analysis of the Experiences of and Problems Encountered by Worker Takeovers of Companies in Difficulty or Bankrupt*. Report to the Commission of the European Communities, Study No. 85/4, II, 69–91.

Westergaard, J. (1970). 'The rediscovery of the cash nexus'. In R. Miliband and J. Saville (eds), *The Socialist Register*, London, Merlin.

Wiener, H. with Oakshott, R. (1987). *Worker Owners: Mondragon Revisited*. London, Anglo-German Foundation.

Williamson, O. E. (1975). *Markets and Hierarchies*. New York, Free Press and Collier Macmillan.

Woodworth, W. *et al*. (1985). *Industrial Democracy: Strategies for Community Revitalization*. Beverly Hills, Sage Publications.

Wright, M. and Coyne, J. (1985). *Management Buyouts*. London, Croom Helm.

Zan, S. (1980). 'Il movimento cooperativo come organizazione complessa', *Studi Organizzativi*. **1**.

Zan, S. (1982). *La Cooperazione in Italia*. Bari, De Donato.

Index

Workers' takeover is referred to as WTO throughout. Numbers in italics refer to figures and tables.